Research Directions in Database Security

Teresa F. Lunt
Editor

Research Directions in Database Security

With 16 Illustrations

Springer-Verlag
New York Berlin Heidelberg London Paris
Tokyo Hong Kong Barcelona Budapest

Teresa F. Lunt
Program Manager Secure Systems
SRI International
333 Ravenswood Avenue
Menlo Park, CA 94025 USA

Library of Congress Cataloging-in-Publication Data
Research directions in database security / Teresa F. Lunt, editor
p. cm.
Discussions of topics presented at a workshop held at the Vallombrosa Conference and Retreat Center, Menlo Park, Calif., May 24-26, 1988, sponsored by the US Air Force, Rome Air Development Center.
Includes bibliographical references and index.
ISBN 0-387-97736-8. -- ISBN 3-540-97736-8
1. Data base security--Congresses. I. Lunt, Teresa F. II. Rome Air Development Center.
QA76.9.D314R47 1992
005.8--dc 2091-36226

Printed on acid-free paper.

Production managed by Karen Phillips; manufacturing supervised by Robert Paella.
Photocomposed pages prepared from the editor's LaTeX file.
Printed and bound by Edwards Brothers, Inc., Ann Arbor, MI.
Printed in the United States of America.

9 8 7 6 5 4 3 2 1

ISBN 0-387-97736-8 Springer-Verlag New York Berlin Heidelberg
ISBN 3-540-97736-8 Springer-Verlag Berlin Heidelberg New York

Contents

	Contributors	**xiii**
1	**Workshop Summary**	**1**
	TERESA F. LUNT	
	1.1 Introduction	1
	1.2 Labels	1
	1.3 Aggregation	2
	1.4 Discretionary Security	3
	1.5 The Homework Problem	4
	1.6 Classification Semantics	4
	1.7 Assurance	5
	1.7.1 Balanced Assurance	5
	1.7.2 TCB Subsetting	6
	1.7.3 Layered TCB	6
	1.8 New Approaches	7
	1.9 Classifying Metadata	8
	1.10 Conclusions	9
	1.11 References	10
2	**SeaView**	**13**
	TERESA F. LUNT	
	2.1 Introduction	13
	2.2 Multilevel Security	15
	2.3 Multilevel Relations	17
	2.3.1 The Extended Relational Integrity Rules	18
	2.3.2 Polyinstantiation	19
	2.3.3 Constraints	20
	2.4 Discretionary Security	21
	2.5 Multilevel SQL	21
	2.5.1 The Access Class Data Type	22
	2.5.2 Dealing with Polyinstantiation	24
	2.5.3 Creating Multilevel Relations	24
	2.6 The SeaView Verification	27

2.7 The SeaView Design 27
2.8 Data Design Considerations 29
2.9 Conclusions 29
2.10 References 30

3 A1 Secure DBMS Architecture **33**
THOMAS H. HINKE, CRISTI GARVEY, AND AMY WU
3.1 Introduction 33
3.2 The A1 Secure DBMS Modes of Operation 34
3.3 The A1 Secure DBMS Security Policy Overview 35
3.4 A1 Secure DBMS Architecture 36
3.5 Why is ASD Needed? 38
3.6 For Further Information 39
3.7 References 39

4 An Investigation of Secure Distributed DBMS Architectures **41**
JAMES P. O'CONNOR, JAMES W. GRAY III, CATHERINE MCCOLLUM, AND LOUAANNA NOTARGIACOMO
4.1 Introduction 41
4.1.1 Background 41
4.1.2 Requirements 42
4.2 Concept of Operation 43
4.2.1 Users 43
4.3 Security Policy Overview 44
4.3.1 Discretionary Access Control 45
4.3.2 Mandatory Access Control 45
4.4 Architecture Definition 46
4.4.1 Abstract Model 47
4.4.2 Architectural Parameters 47
4.4.3 Family of Architecture Generation 49
4.5 Discretionary Access Control Enforcement 57
4.6 Summary and Conclusions 59
4.7 References 61

5 LOCK Data Views **63**
PAUL STACHOUR
5.1 Introduction 63
5.1.1 Problem Statement 63
5.1.2 Security Policy Overview 64
5.2 LOCK Security Policy Overview 64
5.2.1 DBMS Policy Extension Needs 67
5.2.2 DBMS Policy Extensions 67
5.3 Pipelines 69
5.3.1 The Response Pipeline Design 69

5.3.2 LOCK Pipeline Organization . . . 74
5.3.3 Response Pipeline Organization . . . 75
5.3.4 Pipeline Implications . . . 78
5.4 Conclusions . . . 79
5.5 References . . . 79

6 Sybase Secure SQL Server **81**
HELENA WINKLER
6.1 Introduction . . . 81
6.2 Terms and Definitions . . . 81
6.3 Objectives . . . 82
6.4 B2 Design Philosophy . . . 83
6.4.1 Database Server On A Network . . . 84
6.4.2 B2 Sybase Secure SQL Server . . . 84
6.5 Flow of Control . . . 84
6.5.1 Login . . . 85
6.5.2 Parsing and Compilation . . . 85
6.5.3 Description of Procedures . . . 86
6.5.4 Execution of Procedures . . . 86
6.6 Trusted Operations . . . 87
6.6.1 SSO Trusted Interface . . . 87
6.6.2 User - Trusted Interface . . . 88
6.7 Auditing . . . 88
6.8 Conclusions . . . 89

7 An Evolution of Views **91**
DOROTHY E. DENNING
7.1 Introduction . . . 91
7.2 References . . . 94

8 Discussion: Pros and Cons of the Various Approaches **97**
DOROTHY E. DENNING AND WILLIAM R. SHOCKLEY
8.1 Introduction . . . 97
8.2 Inference Problem . . . 97
8.3 Aggregation Problem . . . 98
8.3.1 Problem Instances . . . 99
8.3.2 Two Approaches . . . 100
8.4 Retrospective . . . 101
8.5 References . . . 102

9 The Homework Problem **105**
RAE K. BURNS

10 Report on the Homework Problem **109**
RAE K. BURNS
10.1 Introduction 109
10.2 The Example Database 110
10.3 Summary 122

11 Classifying and Downgrading: Is a Human Needed in the Loop? **125**
GARY W. SMITH
11.1 Introduction 125
11.1.1 Underlying Concepts 126
11.1.2 Classifying Outputs 126
11.1.3 Semantic Level Approach 126
11.1.4 Classifying and Downgrading 127
11.2 The Issue 127
11.3 The Answer 127
11.4 Structured Data 128
11.5 Security Semantics of an Application 129
11.6 Types of Security Semantics 130
11.7 Textual Data 131
11.8 Summary 132
11.9 References 133

12 Session Report: The Semantics of Data Classification **135**
GARY W. SMITH
12.1 Introduction 135
12.2 References 140

13 Inference and Aggregation **143**
MATTHEW MORGENSTERN, TOM HINKE, AND BHAVANI THURAISINGHAM
13.1 Introduction 143
13.2 Database Inference 144
13.2.1 The Problem 144
13.2.2 A Solution Approach 144
13.3 The Inference Problem 147
13.4 Analysis of Logical Inference Problems 148
13.4.1 When Classifying a Rule is Worse than Useless . . . 148
13.4.2 Sphere of Influence Analysis 149
13.4.3 Network of Constraints 151
13.4.4 Questions 151
13.5 General Discussion 152
13.6 References 158

14 Dynamic Classification and Automatic Sanitization **161**
MARVIN SCHAEFER
14.1 Introduction 161
14.2 Sanitization 163
14.3 Initial Overclassification 163
14.4 Initial Underclassification 164
14.5 Discovered Misclassification 166
14.6 Automatic Classification 166
14.7 References 166

15 Presentation and Discussion on Balanced Assurance **167**
WILLIAM R. SHOCKLEY
15.1 Introduction 167
15.2 References 170

16 Some Results from the Entity/Relationship Multilevel Secure DBMS Project **173**
GEORGE E. GAJNAK
16.1 Project Goals and Assumptions 173
16.2 A Multilevel Entity/Relationship Model 174
16.2.1 Data Model Semantics 175
16.2.2 Multilevel Security Characteristics 180
16.3 Results of Research 181
16.3.1 The Underlying Abstraction 182
16.4 Conclusions 189
16.5 References 190

17 Designing a Trusted Application Using an Object-Oriented Data Model **191**
CATHERINE MEADOWS AND CARL LANDWEHR
17.1 Introduction 191
17.2 The Object-Oriented Data Model 192
17.3 The SMMS as an Object-Oriented Database 194
17.4 Conclusion and Future Directions 197
17.5 References 197

18 Foundations of Multilevel Databases **199**
BHAVANI THURAISINGHAM
18.1 Introduction 199
18.2 Definitional Preliminaries 201
18.3 Model Theoretic Approach 202
18.3.1 Query Evaluation 205
18.3.2 Database Updates 206
18.4 Proof Theoretic Approach 207
18.4.1 Query Evaluation 209

18.4.2 Database Updates 209
18.5 Environments and Fixed Points 210
18.5.1 Environments 211
18.5.2 Mappings 211
18.5.3 Fixed Points 212
18.5.4 Least Environment 213
18.5.5 Declarative and Procedural Semantics 213
18.6 Environments and Inference 214
18.7 Handling Negative and Indefinite Information 215
18.7.1 Closed-World Assumption 216
18.7.2 Negation by Failure 218
18.8 Formal Semantics of Time 219
18.9 Other Related Topics 220
18.9.1 Theory of Relational Databases 221
18.9.2 Consistency and Completeness of Security Constraints 221
18.9.3 Assigning Security Levels to Data 222
18.10 Conclusion 222
18.11 References 223

19 An Application Perspective on DBMS Security Policies 227
RAE K. BURNS
19.1 Introduction 227
19.2 Problems with Automatic Polyinstantiation 227
19.2.1 Polyinstantiation and Entity Integrity 228
19.2.2 Polyinstantiation and Referential Integrity 228
19.2.3 Polyinstantiation verses Application Consistency . . 230
19.2.4 Problems with Simplistic Mandatory Policies 230
19.3 Problems with View-Based Controls and Constraints 231
19.4 Requirement for Transaction Authorizations 232
19.5 Summary 232
19.6 References 233

20 New Approaches to Database Security: Report on Discussion 235
CATHERINE MEADOWS
20.1 Introduction 235
20.2 Report on Discussion 236
20.2.1 Open Problems in Computer Security 236
20.2.2 Old Problems for Operating Systems but New Problems for Database Systems 237
20.2.3 Database-Specific Problems 239
20.2.4 Challenge Posed by Advances in Database Technology 240
20.3 Conclusion 241
20.4 References 242

21 Metadata and View Classification **243**
LouAnna Notargiacomo
21.1 Introduction 243
21.2 Justification for Metadata Protection 243
21.3 Metadata Classification Approaches 244
21.3.1 Internal Schema 245
21.3.2 Conceptual Schema 245
21.3.3 External Schema 245
21.4 Metadata Protection Schemes 246
21.5 User Access to Metadata 246
21.6 Affect of User Session Level on Data Classification 247

22 Database Security Research at NCSC **249**
John R. Campbell
22.1 Introduction 249
22.2 Sponsored Research Projects 249
22.3 The Future 251
22.4 Discussion Topics 252

23 Position Paper on DBMS Security **253**
Joseph Giordano
23.1 Introduction 253
23.2 Conclusions 255

Index **257**

Contributors

Rae K. Burns
The MITRE Corporation
Burlington Road
Bedford, Massachusetts 01738

John R. Campbell
National Computer Security Center
9800 Savage Road
Fort Meade, Maryland 20755-6000

Dorothy E. Denning
Georgetown University
225 Reiss Science Building
Washington, DC 20057

George E. Gajnak
DEC
151 Taylor Street TAY1
Littleton, Massachusetts 01460

Cristi Garvey
TRW Defense Systems Group
One Space Park
Redondo Beach, California 90278

Joseph Giordano
Rome Laboratory
Griffiss Air Force Base
Rome, New York 13441-5700

James W. Gray III
Naval Research Laboratory
Washington, DC 20375

Thomas H. Hinke
Computer Science Department
University of Alabama in Huntsville
Computer Science Building
Huntsville, Alabama 35899

Carl Landwehr
Office of Research and Development
Center for Secure Information Technology
Naval Research Laboratory
Washington, DC 20375-5000

Teresa F. Lunt
SRI International, Computer Science Laboratory
333 Ravenswood Avenue
Menlo Park, California 94025

Catherine McCollum
Unisys
8201 Greensboro Drive, Ste 1000
McLean, Virginia 22101

Catherine Meadows
Office of Research and Development
Center for Secure Information Technology
Naval Research Laboratory
Washington, DC 20375-5000

Matthew Morgenstern
Xerox Advanced Information Technology
4 Cambridge Center
Cambridge, Massachusetts 02142

LouAnna Notargiacomo
The MITRE Corporation
7525 Colshire Drive
McLean, Virginia 22102-3481

James P. O'Connor
Software Productivity Consortium
Rock Hill Road
Herndon, Virginia 22070

Marvin Schaefer
Trusted Information Systems, Inc.
3060 Washington Road
Route 97
Glenwood, Maryland 21738

William R. Shockley
DEC
TP West
800 West El Camino Real
Mountain View, California 94040

LTC Gary W. Smith
IBM College
DOD Computer Institute
Washington Navy Yard, Bldg. 175
Washington, DC 20374

Paul Stachour
Secure Computing Technology Center
1210 County Road E. West, Ste 1000
Arden Hills, Minnesota 55112-3739

Bhavani Thuraisingham
The MITRE Corporation
MS-Z53 1
7525 Colshire Drive
McLean, Virginia 22102

Helena Winkler
Sybase Inc.
6475 Christie Avenue
Emeryville, California 94608

Amy Wu
TRW Defense Systems Group
One Space Park
Redondo Beach, California 90278

1

Workshop Summary

Teresa F. Lunt[1]

1.1 Introduction

On May 24-26, 1988, about 25 researchers working on multilevel security for database systems met at Vallombrosa Conference and Retreat Center in Menlo Park, California. The workshop was organized and led by Teresa Lunt of SRI International and was sponsored by the U.S. Air Force, Rome Air Development Center (RADC). The workshop's focus was on multilevel security for database systems. It was the first extended technical interchange among those participating in the following projects, most of which were inspired by the 1982 Air Force Summer Study [AFSS83]: SRI's and Gemini Computer's SeaView A1 multilevel relational database system [LSS+88]; TRW's A1 Secure Prototype DBMS [Gar88]; the Unisys B3 secure database system project; Honeywell's LOCK Data Views (LDV) project [DOST88]; MITRE's Kernelized Trusted DBMS project; the Naval Research Laboratory's Secure Military Message System [LHM84]; AOG Systems' secure entity-relationship (E/R) project [CI88]; MITRE's Integrity Lock project [Gra84]; and the Hinke-Schaefer secure database project [HS75].

The workshop began with short presentations on the research projects currently under way, and most of the rest of the sessions were devoted to discussions of the advantages and disadvantages of the various approaches to multilevel database security that have been tried, difficult issues that have resisted solution, and new approaches to multilevel database security. Below we review some of the discussions on these topics.

1.2 Labels

The group debated the issue of trusted versus advisory labels for data. Some projects (e.g., SeaView) return an advisory label with the data because, according to the star property, the data returned to a user are classified at the subject class; moreover, any internal labels on the individual data

[1]SRI International, Computer Science Laboratory

elements have been handled by untrusted (relative to mandatory security) code, so they cannot be guaranteed to be correct for the stored data. Some projects (e.g., TRW's A1 prototype) do not return any labels with the data, on the theory that advisory labels could be harmful if they cannot be guaranteed to be correct. Other projects (e.g., the Unisys project) return a trusted label, with the mandatory TCB extending out to the user's screen.

The participants expressed diverse opinions about these approaches. Some said the lack of labels could be confusing if data are polyinstantiated. Others believed trusted labels are essential for trusted multilevel applications, and yet others doubted that users would make any use of trusted labels, whether returned directly by the database system or through a trusted application, because trusted applications are too complex and difficult to build.

1.3 Aggregation

The aggregation problem arises when a set of items of information, all of which are classified at some level, become classified at a higher level when combined. The group debated the approaches taken in LDV and SeaView. The LDV approach is to store all the data forming the aggregate at the low level, detect when the aggregate has been retrieved, and mark up (or withhold) the result. In the SeaView approach, all (or some) of the items forming the aggregate are stored at the aggregate-high level, and subsets can be retrieved at the lower level only through sanitization. Some participants agreed that storing all the aggregate data at a level lower than the aggregate level may not be safe. In addition, one attendee noted that withholding data from one file when a related file has been accessed (as in LDV) can create an unnecessary denial-of-service problem.

Another issue between LDV and SeaView is that many of the so-called aggregation problems that LDV is designed to detect can be readily solved through appropriate data design. When the intent is to hide sensitive relationships between data items that individually are not sensitive, the data can be stored at a low level and the sensitive relationships can be stored at a high level. The data are thus available to low subjects while the sensitive relationships are automatically protected by the underlying mandatory security mechanisms, without relying on complicated trusted software to detect violations. With adequate database design tools (such as the inference control tool proposed by Matthew Morgenstern [Mor88]), a proposed database design can be analyzed for such problems and restructured to eliminate or minimize the problems.

1.4 Discretionary Security

Dorothy Denning raised the question of whether a database could be partitioned by discretionary permissions as well as by classification. If so, stored data (i.e., storage objects) could be appropriately marked with their access control lists, and the discretionary authorizations for relations and views would be derived from those of the underlying storage objects. This offers the possibility of achieving greater assurance for discretionary security than if discretionary security attributes are associated with views because of the complex mechanism involved in view evaluation. Views do not partition a database because they may overlap, and views defined using conditional clauses may map to changing subsets of the database as the data are modified. Helena Winkler of Sybase explained that Sybase's secure database product associates access control attributes not with views but rather with the base relations, which are mapped directly to storage objects. Sybase believes that although access to the program implementing the view could be controlled, because the view compiler is untrusted no assurance exists that the compiled view maps to the same set of data that is described in the view definition.

Some participants believed that partitioning the database with discretionary security attributes would mean that a repartitioning would be required when authorizations were granted and revoked. Others pointed out, however, that no repartitioning or modifying access control lists is necessary if users are moved in and out of groups.

Lunt raised some other discretionary security issues for A1 and B3 database systems that stem from the requirements in the Trusted Computer System Evaluation Criteria [Cen85b] for support for group authorizations and specific denial of authorizations. Because the set of users and groups authorized for an object is independent of the set denied authorization, apparent conflicts between the two sets may exist, raising the questions: What does denial of authorization mean, and how do we reconcile the authorizations granted to users individually and as members of groups?

Denial of authorization can be used merely as a convenience in forming access control lists. For example, granting group G authorization and denying user U in G authorization can make the object in question available to everyone in G except U. With this interpretation, if user U is denied authorization by one user but is later granted authorization by another, then U becomes authorized. A stronger interpretation of denial is that denials take precedence over authorizations: One user's denial operation could not be negated by another's later grant operation.

In some applications, a user may belong to more than one group. In assigning privileges to subjects acting on behalf of a user, one must decide whether the subject should operate with the union of the user's individual privileges and the privileges of all the groups the user belongs to, whether the subject should operate with the privileges of only one group at a time, or whether some other policy should be adopted. These questions should be examined further [Lun88a].

1.5 The Homework Problem

Experience with applying MITRE's Integrity Lock secure database system to a particular secure database application motivated Rae Burns to devise a homework problem, which she posed to the group. The group broke up into three teams to work on it. They worked late into the evening and on the following morning animatedly discussed the homework problem, as the team leaders presented their approaches to the problem. Many of those attending considered the homework problem the single most valuable part of the workshop.

1.6 Classification Semantics

Gary Smith led a discussion on the semantics of data classification. Smith believes that information should be classified at a level that reflects its contents, not its derivation. He introduced three dimensions to security semantics: content (e.g., flights to Iran can be classified because of the value 'Iran'), description (e.g., the fact that flights to Iran are classified may itself be classified), and existence (e.g., the existence of a flight to Iran may be classified, or the existence of classified flights may be classified). For data, he enumerated the following security semantics: data values classified by themselves (e.g., self-describing data or implicit associations), data values classified in association with an attribute name, multiple attribute associations, functional dependencies, temporal associations, and quantity aggregations.

The group also discussed automatic classification of text. Smith graded the following tasks from easy to hard: keyword search, classifying simple references, classifying disambiguated text, classifying text in limited domains, and classifying free-form text. Some argued that systems such as *Classi*, an automated text classification system proposed by Lunt and Berson [LB87], should be pursued because humans are not as consistent as machines that classify text and because systems like *Classi* could address the undersupply of qualified human experts. Others cautioned that such consistency may lead to a false sense of security if the inconsistency of the humans can be attributed to rules that were not captured by the expert system. They warned of the risk that the expert system may be used outside its domain of expertise, in which case the system should recognize this and answer, "I don't know." Untrusted subjects in the expert system classifier could tamper with the classification rules. In addition, many ways of signaling through text (e.g., modulating the space width) would be extremely difficult to detect by automatic classifiers or downgraders. Although some participants believed it might be reasonable to assume that *Classi* would not operate in a hostile environment, these issues underscore the need to investigate how to achieve a high degree of assurance for AI systems, such as *Classi*, that are used to assign access classes to text or data. In the absense of high assurance, a human may still be needed in the loop, but, as the group noted, putting a human in the loop is not an answer either.

1.7 Assurance

1.7.1 BALANCED ASSURANCE

Balanced assurance has been proposed in SeaView (and earlier by Roger Schell and others in formulating the Trusted Network Interpretation [Cen87]) as a means of achieving A1 (or B3 or B2) assurance for the system as a whole by applying all the A1 (or B3 or B2) assurance techniques to the portion of the system enforcing mandatory security and less stringent assurance measures (comparable to Class C2) to those portions of the TCB enforcing the less critical security properties, such as database consistency and discretionary access control [LDS+88,Lun88]. According to Schell, the idea of applying balanced assurance to database systems stems from a question raised by Dorothy Denning at the NCSC's Invitational Workshop on Database Security in June 1986 [NCS86]. Her contention was that although views are not appropriate as objects for mandatory security, views could provide an extremely flexible mechanism for discretionary security, especially for content- and context-dependent controls. At that time, she felt strongly that the use of views for discretionary security in IBM's System R [A+79] pointed to the direction that database systems would take in the future and that requiring A1 assurance for discretionary security mechanisms would rule out view-based discretionary controls because of their complexity.

The argument for balanced assurance is as follows. A system X meets the assurance requirements for Class C2 and operates in system-high mode at class c. Suppose system X is connected across a single-level connection at class c with system Y, an A1 system whose range of classes includes c. In the resultant system, we have A1 assurance that only information whose class is dominated by c can flow to system X. Because system X's C2 assurance was good enough to enforce its (nonmandatory) security policies before the connection was made, no further threat is countered by applying additional assurance techniques, such as formal analysis, to the C2 system. Thus, the overall system (comprising the A1 and C2 components) should meet the assurance requirements for Class A1. If we consider a Class A1 multilevel database system to be a collection of several single-level "virtual machines" (one for each class), each enforcing discretionary and consistency policies, each having C2 assurance, and each executing on an underlying A1 mandatory security kernel, the balanced assurance argument would be that the overall system is A1. The C2 portions of the system are constrained by the underlying mandatory security kernel and thus can introduce no compromise to mandatory security.

The discussion of balanced assurance, led by Bill Shockley, was animated. Although some believed that users will not want systems that are "A1 here and C2 there," Shockley emhasized that balanced assurance does not mean just "slapping a C2 on an A1." Rather, the overall system should be well engineered. Just what system engineering requirements should be adhered to still needs to be defined.

1.7.2 TCB Subsetting

The balanced assurance argument goes hand in hand with the *TCB subsetting* argument [SS87]. TCB subsetting is a term introduced by Bill Shockley, drawing on earlier work by Marvin Schaefer and Roger Schell on extensible TCBs [SS84], to mean structuring a TCB in layers, with each layer enforcing its own policies and with each layer constrained by the policies enforced by the lower layers. If a previously evaluated TCB is used for the lowest layer, as in SeaView's use of GEMSOS, TCB subsetting allows the addition of a new layer to form an extended TCB without disturbing the basis for the evaluation of the original TCB. With this layered approach, a mandatory security kernel as the lowest layer enforces mandatory security for the entire system without the need to verify the entire extended TCB for mandatory security.

Several workshop participants argued that TCB subsetting is the way of the future. The TCB subsetting approach allows third-party vendors to build independent products to extend a system's TCB to enforce additional non-mandatory policy without having to verify mandatory security. TCB subsetting also allows one to build a system that enforces different discretionary policies in different domains, with the underlying kernel providing domain isolation. For example, a mandatory security kernel could support three different domains—one for a file system, one for a database system, and one for a mail system—with each domain enforcing its own discretionary security policy. Thus, an underlying global discretionary policy need not be enforced by the operating system.

1.7.3 Layered TCB

The Unisys project designed a layered TCB (composed of a system TCB plus component TCBs). Honeywell's LDV also has a layered TCB, with the LOCK TCB underneath, plus an additional LDV TCB on top, designed to facilitate proving properties about the LDV TCB. SeaView has a layered TCB, with the GEMSOS TCB underneath and a lesser-assurance TCB enforcing database consistency properties and discretionary access controls on views and multilevel relations on top. Some participants were concerned about enforcing the nonbypassability of the database system. LDV uses the LOCK type-enforcement mechanism and "trusted pipelines" for this; SeaView uses the GEMSOS ring mechanism. Other participants pointed out that a Biba integrity category could also be used. Another alternative is a dedicated database machine. Several noted that discretionary access controls in the underlying TCB could not guarantee that the database system could not be bypassed.

1.8 New Approaches

The group discussed several new approaches to multilevel database systems. George Gajnak described a security model for entity-relationship systems and engendered a lively discussion contrasting his work with the SeaView model. Gajnak introduced what he called the *determinacy principle*, which requires that references be nonambiguous. He used an example to demonstrate the principal advantage of his secure E-R model over a relational model, namely, that in the relational model, one cannot avoid referential ambiguity when data is polyinstantiated. The problem is due to a fundamental weakness of the relational model. Because the relational model matches on value rather than establishing specific references for specific entities, when new data are added, new possibly inappropriate relationships are automatically formed. In Gajnak's secure E-R model, even though entities may be polyinstantiated, no referential ambiguity exists because a reference is not a relationship but applies to a particular tuple or value in the entity—that is, an explicit link to particular data is required. Thus, unlike the relational model, when a new entity is added in the E-R model, the old references do not apply to it. In the relational model, the higher the access class, the greater the ambiguity.

Another of the new approaches was presented by Bhavani Thuraisingham. In her talk, "Foundations of Multilevel Databases," she advocated applying formal logic to develop a theoretical foundation for multilevel databases. Cathy Meadows discussed multilevel security for an object-oriented data model and sketched how NRL's Secure Military Message System might be modeled as an object-oriented system.

Rae Burns presented what she calls a practical database security policy, that calls for certain features to be built into multilevel database systems to accommodate the requirements of the applications that will be built on top of them. These features include an interface for trusted applications that would provide trusted labels for elements and/or tuples (depending on the classification granularity), transaction authorization controls (as in the Clark-Wilson model), automatic classification and sanitization, automatic enforcement of classification of related data based on foreign keys (that is, the data that the foreign key refers to are constrained to be at least as high as the foreign key itself), no polyinstantiation, and enforcement of entity and referential integrity *inside* the DBMS kernel (that is, ordinary entity and referential integrity, not multilevel versions of them). For example, she feels that if a low user tries to insert a tuple when a high tuple with the same key already exists, he or she should be told that the data cannot be accepted. Although some of these requirements (namely, the automatic classification of related data, the prohibition of polyinstantiation, and the enforcement of ordinary entity integrity) may be in conflict with multilevel security and lead to potentially high-bandwidth covert channels, Burns said she would rather live with the covert channels than inflict polyinstantiation on the applications with which she is familiar.

On the whole, the group had many reservations about her requirements. First, automatic initial classification of data must be distinguished from automatic reclassification: Automatically reclassifying related data can create high-bandwidth covert channels. Also, the advantage of polyinstantiation is that low subjects need no access whatsoever to high data; thus, rejecting a low subject's request based on the existence of high data is not even an option. Moreover, the existence of multilevel secure database systems may change the way world does its business. Instead of mimicking the current way of doing business in the external environment and translating the paper world's low-bandwidth information flow channels into high-bandwidth covert channels, we should be building secure systems and requiring the external environment to adjust to achieve secure operation. In other words, today's research projects should create possibilities for the future rather than build around today's limitations.

1.9 Classifying Metadata

The group discussed how to classify metadata and views. The group examined whether a query is a labeled object and whether the data in a query, especially strings entered by the user, have classifications. The group agreed that a query is a labeled object classified at the subject class and that a user operating in a range of levels should be able to specify the level of the query. Then the level of the tuples returned should dominate the level of the query object. The group also agreed that a view definition is a labeled object with a classification at least as great as any relation or view it refers to, as in SeaView, and possibly also dominating the level of any strings it contains or the level of the subject that created the definition. A classified view definition is like a classified program: In order for a subject to execute the query defining the view, its access class must dominate the class of the view definition. The group also debated whether the level of the view definition or of the strings in the view definition should contribute to the level of the result of any query using the view. In the Unisys system, the level of the view definition is a lower bound for the result of any query against the view. In addition, in the Unisys system, if a user specifies a level $L1$ for a tuple to be inserted through a view V whose definition has access class $L2 > L1$, the operation is denied because there is information flow from the view definition to the data inserted through the view. Consequently, SECRET tuples cannot be inserted through a TOP-SECRET view, for example.

Asked who should be permitted to browse the descriptions of relations and views in the database, the group agreed that if a user is not cleared for a relation or view, he or she should not be able to read the description for the relation or view (the *description* is the names and types of attributes, as opposed to a view *definition*, which is the query defining the view). The group also believed that if a user does not have discretionary authorization for a relation or view, the user should not be able to read the description (because it would violate least privilege). A separate 'browse' or 'list' access mode, as in SeaView, can be used to allow users to be independently authorized to list the descriptions of relations and views they are cleared to see in a database.

The group agreed that metadata (such as integrity constraints and classification constraints) are classified at least as high as the relation(s) to which they refer.

1.10 Conclusions

The state of the art in multilevel database security has advanced considerably since the Air Force Summer Study, and the past few years have in fact made the findings of that study obsolete. Projects such as SeaView, originally inspired by the Summer Study, have demonstrated that many of the directions suggested by that study are unworkable. This is not bad news, however, because today's research projects have made possible the introduction of high-assurance multilevel database products in the near future. Moreover, the new research directions suggested at this workshop open up exciting new possibilities for the future.

Acknowledgements: We are grateful for partial funding for this workshop from the U.S. Air Force, Rome Air Development Center (RADC), under contract F30602-85-C-0243. In acknowledgment of RADC's continued commitment to developing the theory and technology for multilevel database systems over the past fifteen years, the workshop attendees unanimously moved to name this workshop the RADC Database Security Workshop. The group gave a round of applause to Joe Giordano of RADC (who was unable to attend the workshop) for his part in creating today's research program in multilevel database security.

1.11 References

[A+79] M.M. Astrahan et al. System R: A relational database management system. *Computer*, 12(5), 1979.

[AFSS83] Committee on Multilevel Data Management Security Air Force Summer Study. Multilevel data management security. *Technical report*, Air Force Studies Board, National Research Council, National Academy Press, 1983. For Official Use Only.

[Cen85] National Computer Security Center. Department of defense trusted computer system evaluation criteria. *Technical Report DOD 5200.28-STD*, Department of Defense, December 1985.

[Cen87] National Computer Security Center. National computer security center trusted network interpretation. *Technical Report NCSC-TG-005*, Version 1, Department of Defense, July 1987.

[CI88] AOG Systems Corporation and Gemini Systems Inc. Multilevel secure entity-relationship DBMS. *Draft*, AOG Systems Corporation, May 19 1988.

[DOST88] P.A. Dwyer, E. Onuegbe, P. Stachour, and B.M. Thuraisingham. Secure distributed data views—implementation specification for a dbms. Interim report a005, Honeywell Systems Research Center and Corporate Systems Development Division, May 1988.

[Gar88] C. Garvey. ASD views. In *Proceedings of the 1988 IEEE Symposium on Security and Privacy*, April 1988.

[Gra84] R.D. Graubart. The integrity-lock approach to secure database management. In *Proceedings of the 1984 IEEE Symposium on Security and Privacy*, 1984.

[HS75] T.H. Hinke and M. Schaefer. Secure data management system. Technical Report RADC-TR-75-266, System Development Corporation, November 1975.

[LB87] T.F. Lunt and T.A Berson. An expert system to classify and sanitize text. In *Proceedings of the Third Aerospace Computer Security Conference*, December 1987.

[LDS+88] T.F. Lunt, D.E. Denning, R.R. Schell, M. Heckman, and W.R. Shockley. Element-level classification with A1 assurance. *Computers and Security*, February 1988.

[LHM84] C.E. Landwehr, C.L. Heitmeyer, and J. McLean. A security model for military message systems. *ACM Transactions on Computer Systems*, 2(3), August 1984.

[LSS+88] T.F. Lunt, R.R. Schell, W.R. Shockley, M. Heckman, and D. Warren. A near-term design for the SeaView multilevel database system. In *Proceedings of the 1988 IEEE Symposium on Security and Privacy*, April 1988.

[Lun88a] T.F. Lunt. Access control policies for database systems. In *Proceedings of the 2nd IFIP WG11.3 Workshop on Database Security*, October 1988.

[Lun88b] T.F. Lunt. Multilevel database systems: Meeting class A1. In *Proceedings of the 2nd IFIP WG11.3 Workshop on Database Security*, October 1988.

[Mor88] M. Morgenstern. Controlling logical inference in multilevel database systems. In *Proceedings of the 1988 IEEE Symposium on Security and Privacy*, April 1988.

[NCS86] NCSC, editor. *Proceedings of the National Computer Security Center Invitational Workshop on Database Security.* Baltimore, Maryland, June 1986.

[SS84] M. Schaefer and R.R. Schell. Toward an understanding of extensible architectures for evaluated trusted computer system products. In *Proceedings of the 1984 IEEE Symposium on Security and Privacy*, April 1984.

[SS87] W.R. Shockley and R.R. Schell. TCB subsetting for incremental evaluation. In *Proceedings of the Third AIAA Conference on Computer Security*, December 1987.

2

SeaView

Teresa F. Lunt[1]

ABSTRACT SeaView is a multilevel secure database system targeted for Class A1. SeaView provides for individual data elements to be labeled with their classifications. SeaView has defined a query language called MSQL, for multilevel SQL, that allows data to be manipulated and controlled based on their classifications. The MSQL operations have been specified in a formal language and have been partially verified, using an automated theorem prover, to correspond to the SeaView security model. SeaView's design makes use of existing security kernel and database technology so as to be quickly implementable.

2.1 Introduction

Many civilian, defense, and commercial applications require a multilevel database system that supports data of different access classes (security markings). Military information systems typically handle data with a variety of classifications, but until recently the security technology did not exist to allow users to obtain data they are cleared for from systems that also contain data clarified higer than their clearance. The SeaView project has produced a design for a multilevel secure database system that addresses this problem [LSS+88a]. SeaView is designed to meet the criteria for Class A1 of the DoD evaluation criteria for trusted computer systems [Cen85b].

SeaView was a three-year project that produced many new results. The SeaView security policy defines what security means for a database system [LDN+88]. Our multilevel relational data model extends the standard relational model to explicitly support classification labels for elements and tuples [DLS+87]. Our formal security model [LDS+89] includes security properties that define a secure state, and transition properties that further restrict allowable state transitions. SeaView has provided the first interpretation of database integrity in the context of multilevel security, by requiring that database integrity hold with respect to the subset of the database visible at any security level. This approach allows database integrity to be achieved without introducing inference channels [LDN+88].

[1]Computer Science Laboratory, SRI International

We introduced the notion of polyinstantiation, which prevents low users from inferring the existence of high data objects [LDN+88,DLS+87]. Our model includes rules for determining the appropriate label for derived data [DLS+87], and also includes a rule-based approach to labeling incoming data, to free the user from the burden of remembering or looking up classification rules [LDN+88]. The project has made important contributions in the area of inference and aggregation control [Den86a,Lun89]. We have completed a demonstration system to illustrate certain key concepts. We also developed implementation specifications.

Our design approach provides element-level labeling with A1 assurance for mandatory security. SeaView constructs multilevel relations as views over stored single-level relations [DLS+87,LDS+88]. The single-level relations are stored in segments managed by an underlying mandatory security kernel. Thus, individually labeled data elements do not have to be stored in individually labeled storage objects, as was supposed prior to SeaView [LDS+88].

This approach allows multilevel insert, delete, and update operations to be decomposed into corresponding single-level operations on the single-level base relations, and lends itself to a design that uses a commercially available relational database management system for the single-level relations. The decomposition is intended to be transparent to the user, who would consider the multilevel relations to be the actual base relations of the database system. Thus the SeaView model extends the application-independent integrity rules of the relational model, namely, entity integrity and referential integrity [LDN+88], to multilevel relations; it allows application-dependent integrity rules to be defined on multilevel relations; and it ensures that updates of multilevel relations are well defined. In addition, the SeaView model constrains multilevel relations by a third application-independent integrity rule, polyinstantiation integrity, which specifies consistency for polyinstantiated tuples and elements [DLS+87,LDS+89].

SeaView has also begun to define a standard implementation-independent multilevel query language we call MSQL (Multilevel Structured Query Language (SQL) for defining and manipulating multilevel relations [LSS+88b]. The SeaView project has produced a formal specification of its security rules and of the MSQL operations [LW89], using the specification language of SRI's Enhanced Hierarchical Development Methodology (EHDM) system [CLR+88,CJL+86a,CJL+86b]. Using EHDM, we have formally verified that two of the MSQL operations are compliant with the security rules [WL89a]. We plan to complete the formal verification of the remaining MSQL operations [WL89b].

In ongoing research we plan to develop multilevel concurrency control and recovery algorithms that can be implemented using single-level subjects [Lun89b]. Other extensions include a rule based classifier to label incoming data with security classifications [Lun89b] and an inference control tool that would detect potential inference problems by analyzing the schema for a multilevel database [Mor88,Mor87]. (The inference problem is when a collection of data at one classification allows one to infer information of a higher classification [Lun89].) We are also extending the SeaView ideas to object-oriented database systems, to knowledge-based systems, and to distributed database systems [BL87,LB87,Lun89b].

2.2 Multilevel Security

The concern for multilevel security arises when a computer system contains information with a variety of classifications and has some users who are not cleared for the highest classification of data contained in the system. The classification of the information to be protected reflects the potential damage that could result from unauthorized disclosure of the information. The clearance assigned to a user reflects the user's trustworthiness not to disclose sensitive information to individuals not cleared to see it (and thus not so trusted).

A security classification consists of a hierarchical sensitivity level (such as TOP-SECRET, SECRET, CONFIDENTIAL, and UNCLASSIFIED) and a set of nonhierarchical categories. In order for a user to be granted access to classified information, the user must be cleared for the hierarchical sensitivity level as well as for each of the categories in the information's security classification. For example, information might be classified TOP-SECRET SPOOK OUTER-SPACE. In order for a user to obtain access to this information, the user would have to be cleared for TOP-SECRET as well as for the categories SPOOK and OUTER-SPACE. The sensitivity levels are hierarchical because they are linearly ordered; TOP-SECRET is greater than SECRET, which is greater than CONFIDENTIAL, which in turn is greater than UNCLASSIFIED. Thus, for example, persons cleared for TOP-SECRET information may also have access to SECRET information. The categories are nonhierarchical because they do not have such a linear ordering. However, the set of security classifications (<sensitivity level, category set> pairs) is partially ordered and forms what is known as a lattice[Den82]. By a partial ordering we mean that given any two security classifications, either one is "greater" than or equal to the other, or the two are said to be be noncomparable. For example, TOP-SECRET is greater than SECRET, but TOP-SECRET SPOOK and TOP-SECRET OUTER-SPACE are noncomparable, because neither is "greater" than the other: a TOP-SECRET SPOOK user cannot obtain access to TOP-SECRET OUTER-SPACE information, and vice-versa.

We call the partial ordering relation on the lattice of security classifications the *dominance* relation. We say that one security classification A dominates another security classification B if the sensitivity level of A is greater or equal to the sensitivity level of B and if the security categories of A include all those of B. For example, TOP-SECRET SPOOK OUTER-SPACE dominates TOP-SECRET OUTER-SPACE.

In most of the computer security literature, security classifications and clearances are referred to as "security levels," although what is meant by "security level" is both a sensitivity level and a category set. Here we use the term "access class" to refer to clearances and classifications.

The DoD policies restricting access to classified information to cleared personnel are called *mandatory security policies.* In addition to mandatory security, additional access controls may be imposed; these additional controls enforce what is called *discretionary security.* The access controls commonly found in most database systems are examples of discretionary access controls.

Mandatory security requires that classified data be protected not only from direct access by unauthorized users, but also from disclosure through indirect means, such as covert signaling channels and inference. Covert channels were not designed to be used for information flow but can nevertheless be exploited by malicious software to signal high data to low users.[2] For example, a high process (i.e., a program instance having a high clearance because it is acting on behalf of a high user) may use read and write locks observable to a low process over time to encode high information (e.g., locked = 1, unlocked = 0). Inference occurs when a low user can infer high information based on observable system behavior. For example, a low user attempting to access a high object can infer something depending upon whether the system responds with "object not found" or "permission denied." Thus, mandatory security requires that no information can flow from high access classes to low.

The "trust" in trusted computer systems rests on the ability to provide convincing arguments or proofs that the security mechanisms work as advertised and cannot be disabled or subverted. In building multilevel database systems, providing such assurance is especially challenging because large, complex mechanisms may be involved in policy enforcement. To satisfy mandatory security, we assign security levels to processes, or subjects, derived from the clearance of the user on whose behalf the subject is operating. Traditional practice is to segregate the security-relevant functions into a security kernel or reference monitor. The reference monitor mediates each reference to an object by any subject, allowing or denying the access based on a comparison of the access classes associated with the subject and with the object. The reference monitor must be tamperproof; it must be invoked for every reference; and it must be small enough to be verified to be correct and secure with respect to the policy it enforces. A high degree of assurance must be provided not only that the mandatory security mechanisms control access to sensitive information, but also that they enforce confinement, or secure information flow. The reference monitor forms

[2]We are using the terms "high" and "low" to refer to any two security classifications when the second does not dominate the first in the lattice.

the core of the trusted computing base (TCB), which contains all security-critical code. The DoD Trusted Computing System Evaluation Criteria include requirements for "minimizing the complexity of the TCB, and excluding from the TCB modules that are not protection-critical" [Cen85b], so that the reference monitor is "small enough to be verifiable" [Cen85b]. Without such a requirement, the high degree of assurance required would not be feasible.

In pursuit of Class A1 assurance [Cen85b], in SeaView we have adopted a design approach that reuses and builds on previously built and verified trusted systems [LSS+88a,Lun88]. SeaView builds a database system on top of a reference monitor for mandatory security, so that the mechanisms responsible for enforcing multilevel security are segregated in the reference monitor, which is small enough to be verified.

In SeaView, every database function is carried out by a single-level subject. The use of only single-level subjects for routine database operations provides the greatest degree of security possible and considerably reduces the risk of disclosure of sensitive data. Thus, a database system subject, when operating on behalf of a user, cannot gain access to any data whose classification is not dominated by the user's clearance.

This approach means that there must be at least one database server instance for each active security level: a security level is considered to be active if there is a subject active at that level. Thus, the database system must be able to support multiple database server instances that share the same logical database.

2.3 Multilevel Relations

The SeaView model supports classification at the granularity of individual atomic facts through element-level classification. In addition, the model assigns a classification to each tuple, to represent the access class of the information in (or encoded in) the tuple. For tuples in multilevel relations, the tuple class is the least upper bound of the element classes. For tuples in views defined over multilevel relations, the tuple class represents the least upper bound of the tuple classes for all tuples used to derive the tuple.

Subjects with different access classes may retrieve data from the same multilevel relation, but will see different instances of the relation. Thus, in any given state, each relation has potentially different instances at different access classes. A subject's access class is an upper bound on the classes of all tuples and elements in the instance at that class. For example, Figures 2.1 and 2.2 show SECRET and TOP-SECRET instances of the same relation.

Multilevel relations have a degree and an associated access class. The access class represents the class of the relation name. The access class of a relation name must be dominated by the access class of any data that can be stored in the relation. Each multilevel relation is associated with

employee	$C1$	job	$C2$	salary	$C3$	T
burns	S	sales	S	100,000	S	S
smith	S	student	S	45,000	TS	TS
shockley	TS	spy	TS	250,000	TS	TS

FIGURE 2.1. TOP-SECRET instance.

employee	$C1$	job	$C2$	salary	$C3$	T
burns	S	sales	S	100,000	S	S
smith	S	student	S	null	S	S

FIGURE 2.2. SECRET instance.

some database name, which has an access class representing the class of the database name. The access class of a relation name must dominate the access class of the name of the database to which it belongs.

2.3.1 The Extended Relational Integrity Rules

In the relational data model, consistency is defined, in part, by the two basic integrity rules of the relational model: entity integrity and referential integrity. The SeaView model includes these rules along with an additional rule, polyinstantiation integrity, which governs polyinstantiation [DLS+87, LDN+88]. All three rules must apply at each access class; that is, every instance of a multilevel relation must satisfy the rules.

Entity integrity states that no tuple in a relation can have null values for any of the primary key attributes. If this constraint is to be satisfied with respect to the data visible at each access class, then in any given tuple, all the elements forming the primary key must all have the same access class. Otherwise, a subject whose access class is lower than that of the highest key element would see null values for some of the elements forming the key. In addition, the access class for the primary key must be dominated by the access classes of all other elements in the tuple. If the primary key class were not dominated by the class of some element in the tuple, then that element could not be uniquely selected by a subject operating at that element's access class. We call these extensions *multilevel entity integrity.*

Referential integrity states that every secondary key must reference a tuple that exists in some other relation where the key is primary. In a multilevel database, this means that a secondary key element cannot reference a tuple with a higher or noncomparable access class because the referenced tuple would appear to be nonexistent at the access class of the reference. *Multilevel referential integrity* requires that if a foreign key is visible at a given access class, then a tuple containing the referenced primary key must also be visible at that access class, and that the class of the foreign key element must equal the class of the referenced primary key.

2.3.2 POLYINSTANTIATION

Unlike the standard relational model which prohibits multiple tuples with the same primary key, in the SeaView model a multilevel relation can have multiple tuples with the same primary key data value(s), but different access classes for either the key value(s) or for other data elements in the tuples. These tuples are referred to as *polyinstantiated data* [LDN+88, DLS+87]. Polyinstantiation refers to the simultaneous existence of multiple data objects with the same name, where the multiple instantiations are distinguished by their access classes. Polyinstantiated tuples are identified by a primary key and associated key class, so that the same multilevel relation may contain several tuple instances for a primary key value corresponding to different access classes. Polyinstantiated elements are identified by a primary key, key class, and element class in addition to the attribute name, so that there may be multiple elements for an attribute that have different access classes, but are associated with the same (primary key, key class) pair.

A polyinstantiated tuple arises whenever a subject inserts a tuple that has the same primary key value as an existing but invisible (more highly classified) tuple. The effect of the operation is to add a second tuple to the relation, whose primary key is distinguishable from the first by its access class. Although the polyinstantiation is invisible to this subject, subjects at the higher access class can see both tuples. To illustrate, if a SECRET subject adds a tuple with primary key "shockley" to the SECRET relation shown in Figure 2.2, then the outcome, as seen from a TOP-SECRET subject, is as shown in Figure 2.3.

employee	$C1$	job	$C2$	salary	$C3$	T
burns	S	sales	S	100,000	S	S
smith	S	student	S	45,000	TS	TS
shockley	TS	spy	TS	250,000	TS	TS
shockley	S	engineer	S	75,000	S	S

FIGURE 2.3. A polyinstantiated tuple.

In Figure 2.3, the fact that employee Shockley is an engineer and earns \$75,000 could be a cover story for the fact that Shockley is a spy earning \$250,000.

A polyinstantiated element arises whenever a subject updates what appears to be a null element in a tuple, but which actually hides data with a higher access class. In this case, the update has the effect of creating a polyinstantiated element for the tuple. We model polyinstantiated elements as separate tuples. To illustrate, if our SECRET subject now replaces the perceived null value for the salary attribute for the tuple with primary key "smith" (see Figure 2.2) with the value "15,000," the outcome, as seen by a TOP-SECRET subject, is as shown in Figure 2.4. Note, however, that the SECRET subject does not see two "smith" tuples—the SECRET subject's view of the relation is as shown in Figure 2.5.

employee	$C1$	job	$C2$	salary	$C3$	T
burns	S	sales	S	100,000	S	S
smith	S	student	S	45,000	TS	TS
smith	S	student	S	15,000	S	S
shockley	TS	spy	TS	250,000	TS	TS
shockley	S	engineer	S	75,000	S	S

FIGURE 2.4. A polyinstantiated element.

employee	$C1$	job	$C2$	salary	$C3$	T
burns	S	sales	S	100,000	S	S
smith	S	student	S	15,000	S	S
shockley	S	engineer	S	75,000	S	S

FIGURE 2.5. View of polyinstantiated element to a SECRET subject.

In Figure 2.4, the fact that employee Smith earns $15,000 could be a cover story for the fact that he is really earning $45,000.

Polyinstantiation integrity specifies that there must never be two tuples with the same primary key unless they represent polyinstantiated tuples or elements and controls the effects of polyinstantiation.

2.3.3 Constraints

Application-dependent constraints govern the values and classes that can be assigned to data entered into a multilevel relation. When an element is inserted or updated in a relation R, the value of the element must satisfy the value constraints associated with the corresponding attribute of R. In addition, the access class of the element must satisfy the classification constraints associated with the corresponding attribute of R, and this class must dominate the class of the relation name.

Application-dependent value constraints correspond to user-specifiable integrity rules to restrict the values that data elements may take. The constraints may specify the allowable set of values for an element, or the relationship between data elements. Application-dependent classification constraints are analogous to value constraints but govern the allowable access classes that the data may take. The access class of a value constraint or a classification constraint must dominate the access class of the name of the relation to which it applies. In addition, the set of classification constraints is required to be consistent and complete.

2.4 Discretionary Security

The model allows users to specify which users and groups are authorized for specific modes of access to particular databases, relations, and views, as well as which users and groups are explicitly denied authorization for particular databases, relations, and views. No user may obtain access to a database object unless that user has been granted discretionary authorization to the information and is not explicitly denied authorization to the information.

A user may be authorized for access mode m to a view defined on one or more multilevel relations without being authorized for mode m to the underlying multilevel relation(s). However, for a user to obtain access to a view, the user must be authorized for the reference mode on all referenced multilevel relations. This allows for the use of views to control discretionary access to subsets of a relation. The reference mode also allows for control over the use and propagation of views. Because a view may exclude certain attributes of the underlying multilevel relations and/or certain tuples by using a "where" clause, or may present only derived data such as a statistical computation on the data, views provide a flexible means for specifying discretionary access controls, including value-dependent, time-dependent, context-dependent, and history-dependent controls.

2.5 Multilevel SQL

SeaView presents users with the abstraction of multilevel relations with element-level classification. So that users can define and manipulate multilevel relations, we have begun designing a multilevel query language called MSQL. MSQL, an extension of ANSI standard SQL, is meant to be upward compatible with SQL; that is, SQL programs and queries should also run on systems implementing MSQL. This section describes a subset of MSQL, focusing on the constructs most critical in enabling users to handle multilevel data.

Each MSQL statement must be executable by a single-level subject. This means that each statement can involve writing data at only a single access class (and reading data at the subject class and below).

The primary enhancements for MSQL are the inclusion of an access class data type, provision for primary key, and the provision of access class domains for attributes. Each of these enhancements is described below.

2.5.1 The Access Class Data Type

So that users can select data based on its access class, MSQL includes a data type *access class* as well as the lattice operators (such as *dominates*, *least upper bound*) on that type. Access classes have both secrecy components and integrity components, which may each include a level and category set. For example, the access class `TS A,B critical` has secrecy class `TS A,B` and integrity class `critical`. MSQL provides the following capabilities.

- Display access class values
- Display secrecy components of access classes
- Display integrity components of access classes
- Display secrecy levels of access classes
- Display integrity levels of access classes
- Display secrecy categories of access classes
- Display integrity categories of access classes
- Perform comparator operators on access classes
    - *dominates* (`dom`)
    - *is dominated by* (`is-dom`)
    - *equals* (=)
    - *is non-comparable to* (`non-comp`)
    - *strictly dominates* (`str-dom`)
    - *is strictly dominated by* (`is-str-dom`)
- Perform comparator operators on secrecy and integrity levels
    - *is greater than* (>)
    - *is less than* (<)
    - *equals* (=)
    - *is greater than or equal to* (>=)
    - *is less than or equal to* (<=)
- Perform lattice operations on access classes
    - *least upper bound* (`lub`)
    - *greatest lower bound* (`glb`)
- Perform membership checks for ranges or sets of access classes
- Use access class functions in MSQL commands
- Use access class values in MSQL clauses
- Use the built-in constants `sys-high` and `sys-low`.

Access classes are omitted by default when data are displayed. Access classes can be displayed when data are displayed by using the `showclass` option. Access classes for particular attributes can be specified in the format `flt.class`.

The secrecy and integrity components of an access class can be displayed by using the **sec** and **int** functions; their argument is an access class and they return a secrecy class, for example, `sec(flt.class)` and `int(flt.class)`.

The secrecy and integrity levels of an access class can be displayed by using the **sec-level** and **int-level** functions; their argument is an access class and they return a secrecy level, for example, `sec-level(flt.class)` and `int-level(flt.class)`.

The secrecy and integrity categories of an access class can be displayed by using the **sec-cats** and **int-cats** functions; their argument is an access class and they return a set of secrecy or integrity categories, for example, `sec-cats(flt.class)` and `int-cats(flt.class)`.

The tuple class can be selected by using the keyword **tuple-class**.

Operations on Access Classes

The following expressions illustrate the use of the comparator operators for access classes:

- `employee.class dom'S A,b'`
- `employee.class str-dom 'C'`
- `employee.class is-dom 'TS NATO'`
- `employee.class = sys-high`
- `employee.class is-str-dom 'TS'`
- `employee.class non-comp job-title.class`

These comparator operators can also be used for secrecy and integrity classes, as follows:

- `sec(employee.class) is-str-dom sec(job-title.class)`

The following expressions illustrate the use of the comparator operators for secrecy and integrity levels:

- `sec-level(employee.class) > 'S'`
- `int-level(employee.class) <= 'critical'`

Set operators can be used for secrecy and integrity categories as illustrated in the following expression:

```
NATO in sec-cats(job-title.class)
```

The least upper bound (**lub**) and greatest lower bound (**glb**) operators can be performed on sets of access classes, as follows:

```
lub (select employee.class from employees)
```

One can check whether an access class belongs to a given range as illustrated by the following expression:

```
employee.class in
                   (select dept.class from departments)
```

2.5.2 Dealing with Polyinstantiation

To allow users to deal with polyinstantiated data, MSQL provides the functions **highest-class**, **highest-tuple**, **most-recent**, and **most-recent-tuple**. Using these built-in functions, one can select the tuple with the highest access class for a potentially polyinstantiated element, and one can select the highest access class for all elements.

Similarly, one can select the tuple with the highest tuple class from among a set of polyinstantiated tuples, one can select the tuple with the most recently updated or inserted value for a potentially polyinstantiated element, one can select the most recent values for all elements, and one can select the most recently updated or inserted tuple from among a set of polyinstantiated tuples.

2.5.3 Creating Multilevel Relations

MSQL includes a **create relation** command that allows a user to define a multilevel relation.

Keys

Using the **create relation** command, a user can designate an attribute or set of attributes as a primary key of a multilevel relation. If no primary key is designated, all attributes will be assumed to be part of the primary key. The **create relation** command specifies the name of the relation, the name of each attribute, the type of data (domain) to be stored in each attribute, and other optional information, such as which attributes form the primary key and which attributes are designated as foreign keys to other relations.

The following example shows how primary and foreign keys are designated in the MSQL **create relation** command.

```
create relation projects
(projno number primary-key,
projname char(10),
deptno number foreign-key departments
startdate date,
enddate date,
budget number(8,2))
```

The relation name and schema information are classified with the access class of the subject.

If a foreign key is designated in the **create relation** command, MSQL will not accept the command unless the multilevel relation with the indicated primary key exists. For example, MSQL will not accept the above *create relation* statement unless the multilevel relation DEPARTMENTS exists and has primary key DEPTNO.

Attribute Ranges

When no classification domain is specified for an attribute, the default domain contains the single level that is the access class of the relation name.

Classification domains can be specified for attributes as follows.

```
create relation projects
(projno number [U:S] primary-key,
projname char(10) [U:S],
budget number(8,2) [U:TS A,B] )
```

This MSQL command allows values for the attributes PROJNO and PROJNAME to have access classes ranging from UNCLASSIFIED through SECRET, and allows values for the attribute BUDGET to have access classes ranging from UNCLASSIFIED through TOP SECRET A,B. The lower bounds of all the attribute ranges must dominate the access class of the subject creating the relation. Thus, in the above example, the relation must be created by an UNCLASSIFIED subject.

Note that if the lower and upper bounds of an attribute's range are the same, then the attribute is single-level. Single-level attributes cannot have polyinstantiated elements.

Attribute Groups

If there is more than one attribute forming the primary key, then these must have the same access class range. Attributes having the same access class range are specified by designating attribute groups of uniformly classified attributes. An attribute group is uniformly classified if, within any tuple, all the attributes have the same classification. The following example illustrates how uniformly classified attribute groups are designated.

```
create relation flights
(group (flightno number, flightdate date)
        [U:S] primary-key,
dest char(10) [U:TS] )
```

This MSQL command creates a uniformly classified attribute group consisting of the two primary key attributes FLIGHTNO and FLIGHTDATE.

Grouping attributes reduces the amount of polyinstantiation that can occur. For example, if all the attributes of a multilevel relation belong to a single uniformly classified attribute group, then there can be no polyinstantiated elements, although there can be polyinstantiated tuples (because then all tuples are single-level). If, in addition, the classification range for the attribute group contains only a single access class, then no polyinstantiation can occur because the relation is single-level.

Attribute Class Types

Rather than specifying ranges for the access class attributes, MSQL also allows the classification domain for an attribute to be specified as an enumerated set. The following example illustrates this.

```
create relation projects
(projno number [S] primary-key,
projname char(10) [S],
budget number(8,2) [TS A; TS B; TS C] )
```

This MSQL command requires values for the attributes PROJNO and PROJNAME to have access class SECRET, and allows values for the attribute BUDGET to have access classes in the set $\{$ TOP SECRET A, TOP SECRET B, TOP SECRET C $\}$.

Constraints

Integrity constraints define the valid states of the database by constraining the values in the multilevel relations. Integrity constraints are checked at the end of each MSQL insert, update, and delete operation, or before the execution of a commit statement. An integrity constraint may relate to the content of individual tuples of a relation, to the entire contents of a relation, or to a state existing between a number of relations.

Integrity constraints can be defined as follows.

```
create integrity-constraint CONSTRAINT-NAME
on RELATION-NAME as (EXPRESSION)
```

Classification constraints are similar to integrity constraints but govern the allowable access classes for the data. The following examples illustrate classification constraints.

```
create class-constraint FLIGHT-RULES
on FLIGHTS as
    FLIGHT#.class = SECRET,
    DEPART-TIME.class = SECRET,
    DEST.class =
        (if FLIGHTS.DEST = 'nicaragua' then TOP-SECRET
            else SECRET )
```

```
create class-constraint CARGO-RULES
on PASSENGERS as
    ALL.class = FLIGHTS.FLIGHT#.CLASS
        where PASSENGERS.FLIGHT# =
            FLIGHTS.FLIGHT#
```

2.6 The SeaView Verification

Our formal top-level specification (FTLS) for SeaView [LW89] includes a formalization of the SeaView security model, consisting of a set of objects (tuples, relations, views, databases), a set of functions on those objects, and a set of axioms and properties that define the security of the system. The FTLS also specifies the functionality of the SeaView MSQL interface and provides definitions of the MSQL operations.

The SeaView formal specifications were designed to provide a foundation for a subsequent design and implementation of MSQL. Thus, it is important that the operations as specified satisfy the security properties of the SeaView security model. We have formally verified that two of the database operations specified in the SeaView FTLS obey all SeaView security properties. The benefit we obtained from this exercise was enormous [WL89a]. During the process of performing the proofs, we found numerous areas in which our initial specification of SeaView operations was faulty, errors in the statement of SeaView security properties, and missing security properties that were needed in the model. We expect the completion of the SeaView verification to lead to more such discoveries.

The verification attempts to show that each operation specified in the SeaView FTLS (1) results in a secure state if it starts in a secure state, and (2) results in a secure state transition. This establishes that the design of the MSQL operations obeys the security properties of the model, which defines security for SeaView.

2.7 The SeaView Design

The SeaView system uses available technology to the extent possible. We use the commercially available GEMSOS TCB. GEMSOS enforces the mandatory security policy using a label-based mechanism. A label comparison is performed whenever a subject attempts to bring a storage object into its address space. A subject is prevented from accessing storage objects not in the subject's current address space by hardware controls. GEMSOS also provides user identification and authentication, maintenance of tables containing user clearances and human-readable labels, and a human interface for a security administrator.

SeaView implements multilevel relations as views over single-level stored relations, while presenting the user with the abstraction of multilevel "base" relations. The single-level relations are transparent. This is accomplished through a formula, or relational expression, which decomposes user-defined multilevel relations to store the data in single-level relations. The formula is used to "recover" or compute a multilevel relation from the single-level ones when the user poses a query.

The single-level relations are in turn stored in GEMSOS objects of the corresponding access class. Thus, SeaView's design is a layered one: at the base is a traditional security kernel. Residing on this is a standard database engine, the *DBMS (Database Management System) Nucleus*, that manages the single-level stored relations. Above this is a layer of software that presents the user with the abstraction of multilevel relations—we call this layer the *MSQL Preprocessor*.

The DBMS Nucleus manages the SeaView single-level decomposed relations. For the DBMS Nucleus we are using portions of the ORACLE database management system. SeaView requires one database server process per active security level. With this processing model, multiple database servers can share the same logical database, which is essential if processing is to be done by single-level subjects. Other system models of a single server process would not work in a multilevel environment. The multiple database servers must operate with separate single-level buffer areas.

SeaView has shown that global integrity cannot be enforced without introducing high-bandwidth signaling channels [DLS+87,LDN+88,SD86, Den86b]. This is not a result peculiar to the SeaView design, but is a fundamental principle that arises whenever both integrity and secrecy properties are to be enforced for the same data. This has implications for concurrency control, serializability, and recovery [LDG89]. Thus, SeaView requires concurrency controls that allow high users to read low data without setting locks which would introduce a potential high-bandwidth signaling channel. And separate recovery logs are needed, one at each active security level. Special utilities are required for performing recovery using the separate logs. With this approach, recovery may be performed one level at a time using single-level subjects.

The MSQL Preprocessor translates programs with embedded MSQL statements into equivalent programs containing embedded SQL statements for execution against the single-level decomposed relations. As tuples are inserted into a multilevel relation, the MSQL preprocessor creates the single-level base relations as needed to contain the data. Thus, when a multilevel relation is created, MSQL does not statically create a base relation in advance for every class in the allowable range; instead, MSQL dynamically creates base relations only as they are needed for the actual classes for which data exists.

MSQL uses a naming convention for the single-level base relations that comprise a multilevel relation [LSS+88a]. When a multilevel relation is accessed by a low user, the MSQL preprocessor translates the request into the corresponding queries on the associated underlying low base relations. When the relation is accessed by a high user, the MSQL preprocessor translates the request into the corresponding queries on the associated underlying low and high base relations.

All access to data must be mediated through the MSQL preprocessor. Thus, the data abstraction available to users is that of multilevel relations, and the underlying single-level base relations are transparent. The MSQL preprocessor enforces multilevel entity integrity and multilevel referential integrity. SeaView's decomposition and recovery formulas automatically enforce polyinstantiation integrity [LSS+88a].

We note that SeaView does not require that the MSQL processor and DBMS nucleus be separate layers requiring a translation of MSQL into SQL. We anticipate that longer-term implementations will provide support for MSQL operations directly. Our near-term design includes the layers as a minimum effort solution that is quickly implementable.

2.8 Data Design Considerations

When a multilevel relation is defined, an allowable access class domain is specified for each data attribute or attribute group. If all attribute groups of a multilevel relation R are single-level (i.e., their domains all contain a single class), then polyinstantiation does not arise in R and no unions are used to recover R. If furthermore all the single-level attribute groups are the same class, then the decomposition of R yields a single base relation, so that there is no overhead in instantiating R.

Uniformly classified attributes form attribute groups in a multilevel relation schema; for example, latitude and longitude would probably be uniformly classified. If all attributes form a single group, the relation is in effect classified at the tuple level, and no joins are needed to instantiate the multilevel relation.

Specifying narrow classification ranges for attributes can potentially improve performance of the recovery algorithm by reducing the number of unions needed. Grouping uniformly classified attributes whenever possible reduces the number of base relations needed in the decomposition and the number of joins needed in the recovery. Both narrowing the classification ranges and grouping the attributes also reduce the effects of polyinstantiation. MSQL allows users to specify these data design decisions.

2.9 Conclusions

SeaView was a pioneering project that greatly advanced the state of the art in database security. SeaView's design uses existing security kernel technology to enforce mandatory security rigidly with the most secure approach possible—no "trust" is needed for routine database operations. SeaView's layered design brings highly assured database technology into the grasp of database sytem vendors.

Acknowledgments

This work was supported by the U.S. Air Force, Rome Air Development Center, under contract F30602-85-C-0243.

2.10 References

[BL87] T. A Berson and T. F. Lunt. Multilevel security for knowledge-based systems. In *Proceedings of the 1987 IEEE Symposium on Security and Privacy*, April 1987.

[Cen85] National Computer Security Center. Department of defense trusted computer system evaluation criteria. *Technical Report DOD 5200.28-STD*, Department of Defense, December 1985.

[CJL+86a] J. S. Crow, S. T. Jefferson, R. Lee, P. M. Melliar-Smith, J. M. Rushby, R. L. Schwartz, R. E. Shostak, and F. W. von Henke. SRI specification and verification system version 3.1 - user's guide. *Technical report*, Computer Science Laboratory, SRI International, Menlo Park, California, October 1986.

[CJL+86b] J. S. Crow, S. T. Jefferson, R. Lee, P. M. Melliar-Smith, J. M. Rushby, R. L. Schwartz, R. E. Shostak, and F. W. von Henke. SRI specification and verification system version 3.0 - preliminary definition of the revised special specification language. *Technical report*, Computer Science Laboratory, SRI International, Menlo Park, California, May 1986.

[CLR+88] J. S. Crow, R. Lee, J. M. Rushby, F. W. von Henke, and R. A. Whitehurst. EHDM verification environment: An overview. In *Proceedings of the 11th National Computer Security Conference*, October 1988.

[Den82] D. E. Denning. *Cryptography and Data Security.* Addison-Wesley, Reading, Massachusetts, 1982.

[Den86a] D. E. Denning. The inference problem in multilevel database systems. In *Proceedings of the National Computer Security Center Invitational Workshop on Database Management Security*, June 1986.

[Den86b] D. E. Denning. Secure databases and safety: Some unexpected conflicts. In *Proceedings of the Safety and Security Symposium*, Centre for Software Reliability, October 1986.

[DLS+87] D. E. Denning, T. F. Lunt, R. R. Schell, M. Heckman, and W. R. Shockley. A multilevel relational data model. In *Proceedings of the 1987 IEEE Symposium on Security and Privacy*, April 1987.

[LB87] T. F. Lunt and T. A. Berson. Security considerations for knowledge-based systems. In *Proceedings of the Third Expert Systems in Government Conference*, October 1987.

[LDG89] T. F. Lunt, A. Downing, and I. Greenberg. Issues in distributed database security. In *Proceedings of the 5th Aerospace Computer Security Conference*, December 1989.

[LDN+88] T. F. Lunt, D. E. Denning, P. G. Neumann, R. R. Schell, M. Heckman, and W. R. Shockley. Final report Vol. 1: Security policy and policy interpretation for a class A1 multilevel secure relational database system. *Technical report*, Computer Science Laboratory, SRI International, Menlo Park, California, 1988.

[LDS+88] T. F. Lunt, D. E. Denning, R. R. Schell, M. Heckman, and W. R. Shockley. Element-level classification with A1 assurance. *Computers and Security*, February 1988.

[LDS+89] T. F. Lunt, D. E. Denning, R. R. Schell, M. Heckman, and W. R. Shockley. Final report Vol. 2: The SeaView formal security policy model. *Technical report*, Computer Science Laboratory, SRI International, Menlo Park, California, 1989.

[LSS+88a] T. F. Lunt, R. R. Schell, W. R. Shockley, M. Heckman, and D. Warren. A near-term design for the SeaView multilevel database system. In *Proceedings of the 1988 IEEE Symposium on Security and Privacy*, April 1988.

[LSS+88b] T. F. Lunt, R. R. Schell, W. R. Shockley, M. Heckman, and D. Warren. Toward a multilevel relational data language. In *Proceedings of the Fourth Aerospace Computer Security Applications Conference*, December 1988.

[Lun88] T. F. Lunt. Multilevel database systems: Meeting class A1. In *Proceedings of the 2nd IFIP WG11.3 Workshop on Database Security*, October 1988.

[Lun89a] T. F. Lunt. Aggregation and inference: Facts and fallacies. In *Proceedings of the 1989 IEEE Symposium on Research in Security and Privacy*, May 1989.

[Lun89b] T. F. Lunt. Final report Vol. 4: Secure distributed data views: Identification of deficiencies and directions for future research. *Technical report*, Computer Science Laboratory, SRI International, Menlo Park, California, 1989.

[LW89] T. F. Lunt and R. A. Whitehurst. Final report Vol. 3a: The seaview formal top level specifications. *Technical report*, Computer Science Laboratory, SRI International, Menlo Park, California, 1989.

[Mor87] M. Morgenstern. Security and inference in multilevel database and knowledge-base systems. In *Proceedings of the ACM International Conference on Management of Data (SIGMOD-87)*, May 1987.

[Mor88] M. Morgenstern. Controlling logical inference in multilevel database systems. In *Proceedings of the 1988 IEEE Symposium on Security and Privacy*, April 1988.

[SD86] R. R. Schell and D. E. Denning. Integrity in trusted database systems. In *Proceedings of the 9th National Computer Security Conference*, 1986.

[WL89a] R. Alan Whitehurst and T. F. Lunt. Final report Vol. 3b: The SeaView formal verification: Proofs. *Technical report*, Computer Science Laboratory, SRI International, Menlo Park, California, 1989.

[WL89b] R. Alan Whitehurst and T. F. Lunt. The SeaView verification. In *Proceedings of the Second Workshop on the Foundations of Computer Security*, June 1989.

3

A1 Secure DBMS Architecture

Thomas H. Hinke,[1] Cristi Garvey,[2] and Amy Wu[2]

3.1 Introduction

TRW's A1 Secure Database Management System is a multilevel secure relational database management system (DBMS) that is currently being developed under the Advanced Secure DBMS (ASD) IR&D (Internal Research and Development) project by the Defense Systems Group of TRW. This paper will describe the security architecture of the A1 Secure DBMS.

The objective of the ASD project is ultimately to achieve a high performance secure DBMS that will be successfully evaluated as meeting the A1 standards as defined by the yet to be released Trusted DBMS Interpretation (TDI) of DoD 5200.28-STD (the "Orange Book") [Cen85b].

The A1 Secure DBMS project is reusing much of the code from an earlier DBMS project that was unique in that its basic architecture mirrored the classical security kernel and the multiply instantiated untrusted DBMS server design. In this paper, this initial DBMS is called Version 0.

The A1 Secure DBMS is being written to the greatest extent possible in Ada[3]. This is consistent with the fact that Version 0 was written in Ada.

The A1 Secure DBMS is not currently a product. It is a prototype development of researchers who are attempting to do research and advanced development on secure DBMS technology appropriate to the A1 level of evaluation by the National Computer Security Center (NCSC). While initial development of the A1 Secure DBMS is taking place prior to the availability of the Trusted Database Interpretation, it is anticipated that the DBMS A1 criteria would closely follow the existing operating system A1 criteria.

The A1 Secure DBMS will ultimately be hosted on an A1 secure operating system under development by TRW. However, since Version 0 runs on UNIX[4] on the Sun Workstation, the initial development of the A1 Secure

---

[1] University of Alabama at Huntsville

[2] TRW Defense Systems Group.

[3] Ada is a registered trademark of the U.S. Government, Ada Joint Program Office.

[4] Trade Mark of AT&T.

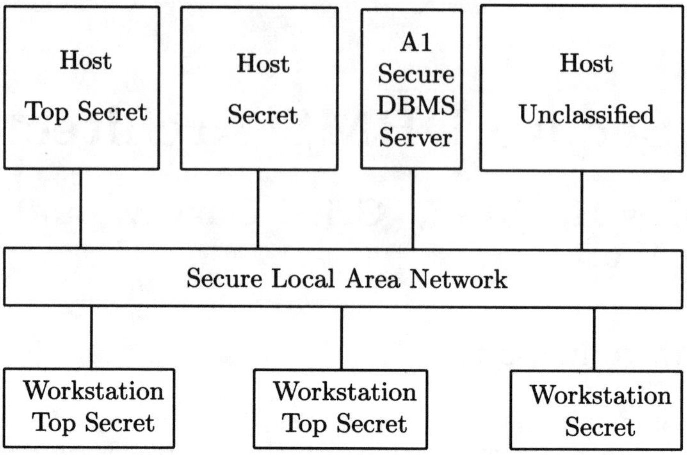

FIGURE 3.1. Local area network mode.

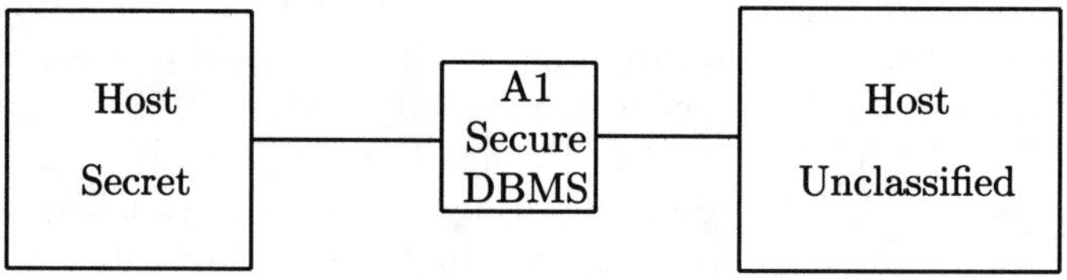

FIGURE 3.2. Back-end mode.

DBMS is also under UNIX on the Sun Workstations. When the A1 secure operating system becomes available, the A1 Secure DBMS will be ported to it.

The remainder of this paper will consider three aspects of the A1 Secure DBMS design.

Section 2 will present the operating modes in which the A1 Secure DBMS can be operated. Section 3 will present an overview of the A1 Secure DBMS security policy. Section 4 will discuss the architecture of the A1 Secure DBMS.

3.2 The A1 Secure DBMS Modes of Operation

The A1 Secure DBMS can be operated in three different modes illustrated by Figures 3.1, 3.2, and 3.3.

Under the first mode of operation, the A1 Secure DBMS functions as a

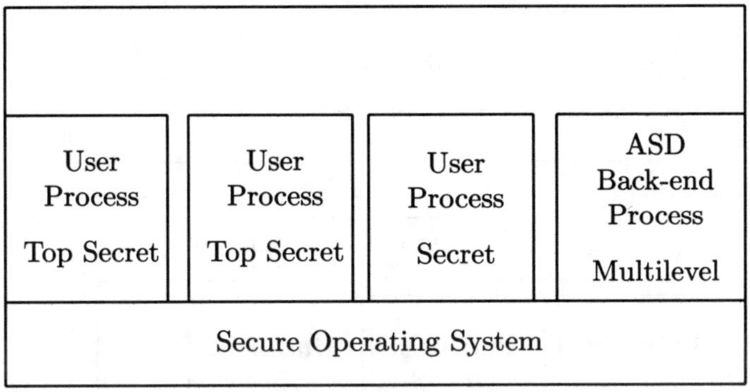

FIGURE 3.3. Stand-alone mode.

DBMS server on a local area network. Under the second mode of operation, the A1 Secure DBMS can serve as a back-end DBMS for various single level or multilevel host computers. Under the final mode of operation, the A1 Secure DBMS can serve as a host resident DBMS within a multilevel host running an A1 secure operating system.

3.3 The A1 Secure DBMS Security Policy Overview

The mandatory "object" of protection in the A1 Secure DBMS is the tuple of a table[5]. The mandatory security policy enforced satisfies the Bell and LaPadula security policy model [BL76].

Tuples inherit their discretionary access from the tables in which they are located. Discretionary access is specified for tables in terms of permissions for access and denials of access. Permissions and denials may be specified with respect to user's, groups, or public. The permissions are select, insert, delete and update. Under the current design, the most specific discretionary access specification takes precedence over a less specific specification and a denial (at a given specificity) takes precedence over a permission. A user is more specific than a group which is more specific than public.

The A1 Secure DBMS also enforces the Biba [Bib77] integrity model which states that a subject may read a tuple if and only if the integrity level of the tuple dominates the integrity level of the subject. A subject

[5]See [Wil88,Gar88] for an approach in which the view is the object of protection. While the work reported on in these two papers was funded under the same research project as the A1 Secure DBMS, it was not targeted for inclusion in the A1 Secure DBMS.

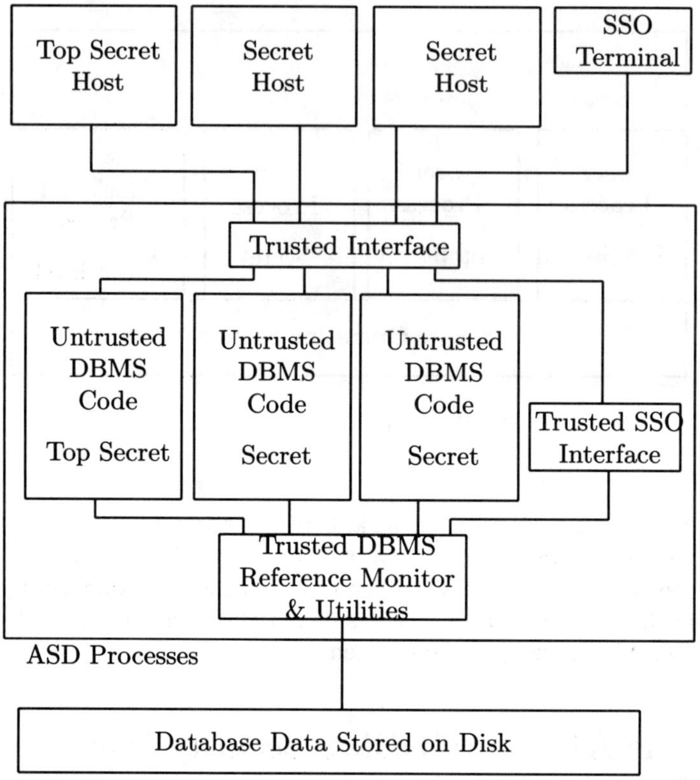

FIGURE 3.4. Top level A1 Secure DBMS architecture.

may write a tuple if and only if the integrity level of the subject dominates the integrity level of the tuple.

3.4 A1 Secure DBMS Architecture

The ASD system code is divided into two groups; trusted code and untrusted code.

Trusted code is that code whose incorrect operation could lead to disclosure of classified data in violation of the security policy. Untrusted code is that code whose incorrect operation could not possibly lead to disclosure of data in violation of the security policy.

The architecture of the ASD system has been designed to satisfy the most stringent security standards. These are the A1 standards defined by the Department of Defense Trusted Computer System Evaluation Criteria

[DoD 5200.28-STD], also known as the "Orange Book", as interpreted for database management systems.

The trusted code within ASD becomes part of what is called the "Trusted Computing Base." At the A1 level, the security correctness of this code is assured through mathematical proofs, using formal specification and verification technology. For ASD, TRW has selected the Gypsy Verification Environment Methodology developed at the University of Texas. Gypsy is one of the formal verification methodologies that have been approved for secure system use by the National Computer Security Center.

Within ASD, the untrusted code is replicated by security level into separate, untrusted processes. The ASD trusted computing base ensures that each untrusted process can send and receive data only at the security level of the process.

Each untrusted process supports a single ASD user. The security level of the user's untrusted process is the same as the user's session. If the user is accessing ASD while operating on a multilevel secure operating system, then the level of the ASD process is the same as the level of the user's process on the multilevel operating system. If the user is accessing ASD from a single security level host or workstation, then the security level of the ASD process is the same as the security level of the user's workstation or host.

Figure 3.4 illustrates the A1 Secure DBMS architecture. The A1 secure operating system provides the following services to the DBMS:

1. Separation of processes, both trusted from untrusted and untrusted from each other
2. Secure communications services between untrusted processes and the DBMS kernel via message processing calls to the secure OS
3. Protection of the file holding the database data, such that only the DBMS kernel can have direct access to it
4. User authentication
5. Trusted path.

The file containing the database data is protected by the mandatory access policy of the secure operating system. The database file is labeled at DBMS high, the same level at which the DBMS kernel runs. The secure operating system also enforces discretionary access control on the DBMS data file. The DBMS data file can only be accessd by the special user "DBMS." In addition, the DBMS file is assigned a special integrity compartment, to prevent any process other than the trusted DBMS kernel from modifying the data in the file, including the security labels of the rows.

In operation, a query is formulated in the host (or application process if the A1 Secure DBMS is used in stand-alone mode) and sent to the A1 Secure DBMS server. The trusted interface ensures that the request is serviced by the appropriately classified untrusted DBMS code. This code processes the request and sends requests to trusted DBMS Reference Monitor code to actually retrieve the data. Various trusted utilities are present in the system to create and maintain the A1 Secure DBMS database.

Under the A1 Secure DBMS design, multiple instantiations of the untrusted DBMS code run, each at the same level as the host application process that it is supporting. The untrusted DBMS code is considered as an untrusted process. This process is only given that data permitted according to the A1 Secure DBMS security policy. Hence, the untrusted DBMS code plays no role in mandatory security enforcement. It is only given access to data which it dominates in security level. It can only write objects at the same level as the process in which it is currently executing. The security levels of newly created tuples are equal to the security level of the untrusted DBMS process that requested the tuple creation.

Since the A1 Secure DBMS will operate under the control of a secure operating system, some security functions that are normally associated with a secure system are not part of the A1 Secure DBMS, but are provided by the secure operating system. Identification and authentication is a primary example.

3.5 Why is ASD Needed?

The ASD system is designed to mediate access to data securely at multiple levels (including compartments) by users possessing different security clearances. Because of this capability, users need only be cleared to the level of data to which they require access. They no longer need to be automatically cleared to system high, the security level of the most classified data on the system. This reduces both the cost and lead time of providing users with necessary clearances.

ASD can also permit the interconnection of trusted and untrusted systems. Data to be shared between systems can be placed on ASD with the assurance that it will only be output to systems under the conditions of mandatory and discretionary security policy satisfaction.

In many of today's systems, all of the data may be within, for example, a Top Secret DBMS. Such data would normally include a large amount of Unclassified and Secret data. But to gain access to any of the data, a user would be required to have a Top Secret clearance. This is expensive and subjects the Top Secret data to more potential for compromise. If all users no longer require system high clearances, then this reduces the number of users who can have access to system high data.

A second justification for a secure DBMS is that it permits a single copy of user data to be shared by users or applications at different security levels. No longer is it necessary to have a Top Secret copy for Top Secret applications and an unclassified copy for unclassified applications. With ASD, a Top Secret and an unclassified application can securely share the same copy of data. This improves data integrity since no longer is it necessary to ensure that two copies of the same data are always identical.

In its network server mode of operation, ASD is a security system that meets todays distributed processing needs. Computing is moving closer to the user in the form of low cost, high performance workstations. Under this mode of operation, a principal security concern is the secure storage and retrieval of data to/from a DBMS server on the network. ASD provides a secure means to support the data needs of workstations (and hosts) on a network. ASD also provides the vehicle by which data can be shared among workstations, even if those workstations are processing data at different security levels.

Under this mode of operation, no trusted workstation is required. The network provides for the secure movement of data between workstation and ASD server, and ASD ensures that a workstation receives only that level of data authorized by the level of the workstation. ASD also ensures that no workstation can write data down in security level in violation of the ⋆-property (star property).

Of course, as multilevel workstations become available, ASD will also be able to support their need for the multilevel processing of data.

The data sharing capability provided by ASD means that data need not be replicated by security level, and as previously discussed, users need not be cleared automatically to system high.

3.6 For Further Information

Additional information about this system can be found in other ASD papers [HGJ+88,GJW88,Jen88].

This work also spawned research efforts into inference and aggregation [Hin88,Hin88a] and secure views [Gar88,Wil88].

3.7 References

[Bib77] K.J. Biba. Integrity considerations for secure computer systems. *Technical Report ESD-TR-76-372*, USAF Electronic Systems Division, Bedford, Massachusetts, April 1977.

[BL76] D.E. Bell and L.J. LaPadula. Secure computer systems: Unified exposition and Multics interpretation. *Technical Report ESD-TR-75-306*, The MITRE Corporation, Bedford, Massachusetts, March 1976.

[Cen85] National Computer Security Center. Department of defense trusted computer system evaluation criteria. *Technical Report DOD 5200.28-STD*, Department of Defense, December 1985.

[Gar88] C. Garvey. ASD views. In *Proceedings of the 1988 IEEE Symposium on Security and Privacy*, April 1988.

[GJW88] C. Garvey, N. Jenson, and J. Wilson. The advanced secure DBMS: Making secure DBMSs usable. In *Proceedings of the IFIP Working Group 11.3 Workshop on Database Security*, October 1988.

[HGJ+88] T.H. Hinke, C. Garvey, N. Jensen, J. Wilson, and A. Wu. A1 secure DBMS design. In *Proceedings of the 11th National Computer Security Conference - Appendix*, October 1988.

[Hin88a] T.H. Hinke. Database inference engine design approach. In *Proceedings of the IFIP Working Group 11.3 Workshop on Database Security*, October 1988.

[Hin88b] T.H. Hinke. Inference aggregation detection in database management systems. In *Proceedings of the 1988 IEEE Symposium on Security and Privacy*, April 1988.

[Jen88] N. Jensen. System security officer functions in the A1 secure DBMS. In *Proceedings of the IFIP Working Group 11.3 Workshop on Database Security*, October 1988.

[Wil88] J. Wilson. Views as the security objects in a multilevel secure relational database management system. In *Proceedings of the 1988 IEEE Symposium on Security and Privacy*, April 1988.

4

An Investigation of Secure Distributed DBMS Architectures

James P. O'Connor,[1] James W. Gray III,[2] Catherine McCollum,[3] and LouAnna Notargiacomo[3]

4.1 Introduction

The objective of this paper is to describe an architecture for a multilevel secure distributed database management system (SD-DBMS). This work was part of a project, funded by Rome Air Development Center (RADC), to design a multilevel secure (MLS) database management system (DBMS) capable of processing information at a minimum of three classification levels and/or categories. The SD-DBMS was designed in accordance with the Trusted Computer System Evaluation Criteria (TCSEC) requirements for a Class B3 trusted computer system [Cen85b].

4.1.1 Background

In the summer of 1982, the U.S. Air Force sponsored a study on "Multilevel Data Management Security" at Woods Hole, Massachusetts [AFSS83]. The participants in this study were divided into three study groups, of which Group 1 investigated near-term approaches to multilevel data management. Among the approaches recommended by this group were two distributed DBMS architectures. Each of these architectures consisted of a single trusted front-end component connected to two physically separated DBMSs. The DBMSs were used to store and process two security levels of data, high and low. It was recognized that by employing physically separated untrusted DBMSs these architectures could provide a high level of security and performance in the near-term without requiring extensive research and development costs.

[1]Unisys Defense systems
[2]Naval Research Laboratory
[3]MITRE Corporation

In the first architecture, called case E, one DBMS is used to store high data and the other to store low data. All user queries are sent to the trusted front-end which controls their execution. Queries that access only low data (submitted by both high and low users) are directed to the low DBMS; queries that access only high data (submitted by high users only) are directed to the high DBMS. Queries that access both high and low data (submitted by high users only) are decomposed by the front-end into one or more subqueries that access only a single level of data, which are then directed to the appropriate DBMS. These queries are executed on the DBMSs and the results are returned to the front-end where they are integrated and returned to the requesting user. It is the responsibility of the front-end to assure that a low user does not gain access to the high data, and that high data are not stored in the low DBMS. The front-end provides both high and low users with the abstraction of an integrated multilevel DBMS.

In the second architecture, called case I, one DBMS stores low data, and the other stores high data and a copy of the low data. As in the previous architecture, user queries are sent to the trusted front-end which controls their execution. Queries submitted by low users are directed to the DBMS containing the low data only, and queries submitted by high users are directed to the DBMS containing both high and low data. The results of these queries are returned to the trusted front-end and then to the requesting user. It should be noted that this architecture is not truly multilevel, but rather, the high user is provided with a system high security mode.

4.1.2 Requirements

The requirements that must be fulfilled by the SD-DBMS were used as a guide in the development of potential architectures and made it possible to evaluate which architectures best fulfilled the requirements. These requirements are:

- The architecture must be based on the physical distribution approach developed during the Woods Hole Summer Study on "Multilevel Data Management Security" [AFSS83].
- The data model supported by the system must be the relational model [Cod70].
- The system must support a minimum of three hierarchical and/or non-hierarchical security levels.
- The system must be extendible to four hierarchical or non-hierarchical security levels.

- The system must meet the TCSEC requirements for a Class B3 trusted computer system [Cen85b].
- The design for the system must be implementable in the near term (one to three years).
- The system must be capable of processing queries that reference data at different security levels.
- The system must support the return of reliable tuple level labels to the user.
- The system must support concurrent retrievals and updates from users operating at different security levels.

4.2 Concept of Operation

The SD-DBMS was designed as a general-purpose multilevel relational DBMS that can be used in a variety of applications. The architecture of the SD-DBMS uses physical distribution as the basis for mandatory access control (MAC), as recommended at Woods Hole. While the system has a distributed architecture, it is not intended to be a distributed DBMS from the user or application point of view. Data distribution is used for the enforcement of MAC and is internal to the system.

It is assumed that the SD-DBMS will be used in an MLS local area network (LAN) based operational environment. In such an environment, the SD-DBMS would be configured as a multilevel database server connected to the MLS LAN. In this configuration, multiple independent user hosts, connected to the MLS LAN, would be permitted to access the SD-DBMS. The MLS LAN and user hosts would be independently maintained by their own administrative users and could host other applications as well. The SD-DBMS would rely on the MLS LAN to support access by single-level and multilevel user hosts operating at different security levels.

4.2.1 Users

The SD-DBMS will have both administrative users and end users. The administrative users include a System Security Officer (SSO), one or more Database Administrators (DBAs), a System Auditor, and a System Operator.

The SSO is responsible for controlling and monitoring access to the entire system. It is the responsibility of the SSO to create user accounts, assign roles (e.g., end user, DBA), and audit system level events. To perform this task, the SSO must be cleared to the system high level.

A DBA may create new multilevel databases that he would then own and administer. The DBA defines multilevel relations and views, authorizes end user access to the database, and authorizes access to the data contained in the database. The DBA is also responsible for auditing database accesses. In order to perform these duties, the DBA must be cleared to at least the database high level.

The System Auditor is an administrative user whose sole responsibility is to oversee the actions of the SSO by reviewing the audit trail of SSO actions. The entire system is supported by a System Operator who is responsible for backups and routine operation of the system.

SD-DBMS end users will have the capability of retrieving and updating data contained in multilevel databases managed by the system. Each end user will be assigned a security level by the SSO that reflects the level of the user's clearance. It is expected that end users will interact with the system via an interactive user interface or application program.

4.3 Security Policy Overview

The SD-DBMS is being designed to support a set of at least three *access classes.* An access class consists of two components: a hierarchical level (e.g., TOP SECRET), and a set of non-hierarchical categories (e.g., NATO, NOFORN, NUCLEAR). The set of access classes is partially ordered by a relation called *dominates.* If C_1 and C_2 are access classes, C_1 is said to dominate C_2 if and only if the hierarchical classification of C_1 is greater than or equal to that of C_2, and the categories in C_2 are a subset of those in C_1. C_1 is said to *strictly dominate* C_2 if and only if C_1 dominates but is not equal to C_2. Many of the discussions and examples in this report will use the terms *high* and *low* to refer to any two access classes where the first strictly dominates the second.

Subjects are the active entities in the system. A subject at the system level is a process or collection of processes operating on behalf of a user. Each subject is assigned an ordered pair of access classes <*min, max*> that define the subject's *range.* If a subject's range consists of a single access class it is a *single-level subject*; otherwise, it is a *multilevel subject.*

Data are stored in the SD-DBMS in the form of *relations.* Given a collection of sets $D_1, D_2, ..., D_n$ (not necessarily distinct), R is a *relation* on these n sets if it is a set of ordered n-tuples $< d_1, d_2, ..., d_n >$ such that d_1 belongs to D_1, d_2 belongs to D_2, . . . , and d_n belongs to D_n. The sets $D_1, D_2, ..., D_n$ are the *domains* of R. The value n is the *degree* of R [Dat86]. Each relation is assigned an ordered pair of access classes <*min, max*> that define the relation's *range.* Relations that are physically stored are called *base relations.* The tuples contained in base relations are called *base tuples.*

4.3.1 Discretionary Access Control

The SD-DBMS uses *access views* as a mechanism to enforce discretionary access control (DAC). An access view is a virtual relation derived from base relations. Views are a powerful mechanism for DAC because they provide a way to define arbitrary subsets of the database. Since views can be defined using a high level language, such as SQL [Dat86], they can support a semantically rich set of discretionary access controls including content- and context-dependent protection.

Subjects are not permitted to directly access base relations. All access to base relations must go through access views. An access view consists of three parts: an *access view schema*, *access view data*, and an *access view definition*. The access view schema describes the structure of the access view. This information includes the name of the access view, its attributes and their data types, and any restrictions on the access view (e.g., DISTINCT). The access view schema does not change over time (except when modified by the DBA). The access view data are the set of tuples obtainable through the access view. These tuples have no existence on their own; but rather, are derived from tuples in base relations. Access view data can change over time as changes are made to the underlying base relations. The access view definition is a named query statement that defines the mapping between the access view schema and the schemata of the base relations on which it is defined. This mapping is expressed as a relational expression in terms of base relations.

Each access view has an attached access control list (ACL) that specifies the users or groups that are permitted to, or restricted from, access to the database through the access view and the operations they are permitted to, or restricted from, performing on it. The permitted operations are a subset of the legal data manipulation language (DML) commands (i.e., SELECT, UPDATE, INSERT, DELETE). In addition, end users may be permitted SELECT access to the access view schema by specifying SCHEMA permission on the access view. End users are not permitted access to any other descriptive (Data Dictionary) data.

4.3.2 Mandatory Access Control

The foundation for mandatory security in the SD-DBMS is the association of access classes with the individual tuples in base relations. These are the lowest level objects in the system. Subjects can access these tuples through operations on access views defined on base relations. Subjects are permitted to read tuples having an access class dominated by the maximum of their range. Subjects are permitted to write tuples having an access class that falls within their range.

When a relational operator is applied to one or more access views, the result is a *derived relation*. The tuples in derived relations are called *derived tuples.* In order to enforce MAC, derived tuples must be labeled correctly. One possible approach is to label derived tuples at the least upper bound of the access classes of the tuples that entered into their derivation. For example, when a tuple is selected or projected, its access class is unchanged; when two tuples are joined, the resulting tuple is labeled at the least upper bound of the access classes of the original tuples. This is the approach taken in the SeaView effort [LDS+89]. However, as pointed out in Appendix A of [LDS+89], these labels do not accurately reflect the access classes of parameters embedded in queries, or the access classes of data upon which the decision to evaluate a particular query might have been conditioned. Furthermore, these labels ignore the access classes of parameters embedded in the access views themselves. This makes these labels unsafe for MAC. To avoid this problem, the SD-DBMS considers both queries and access views as labeled objects. Tuples in derived relations are labeled at the least upper bound of the access classes of the tuples that entered into their derivation, the access class of the access views through which they were accessed, and the access class of the query. This approach permits the labels associated with derived tuples to be safely used for MAC enforcement.

Since queries and access views are labeled objects, there must be a way to determine the security class of these objects. If a query is submitted by a single-level subject, its access class is set to be the access class of the subject. This has the effect that, for all untrusted subjects, results are returned at the access class of the subject. If a query is submitted by a multilevel subject, the subject must supply the SD-DBMS with the access class of the query. This access class is restricted to fall within the subject's range. The correctness of labels supplied by multilevel subjects can be verified through an information flow analysis of the application program [Den82].

The access class for an access view is specified by the DBA at the time of creation. The label on an access view is set to be the least upper bound of the lower bounds of all base relations on which the view is defined, and the level of the view definition statement. The classification of a view definition statement is equal to the least upper bound of the classification of all embedded parameters.

4.4 Architecture Definition

The SD-DBMS architecture definition was a four step process. First, an abstract model of a secure distributed DBMS was defined that would serve as the foundation of a family of architectures. Second, various architectural parameters were identified that could be varied to produce different architectures when applied to the abstract model. Third, all possible combinations of parameters were applied to the abstract model to generate a wide range of architectures. Finally, the most promising architectures were selected for further exploration. This process not only served as a framework to investigate different SD-DBMS architectures, but also provided assurance that important architectures were not overlooked.

4.4.1 Abstract Model

An abstract model of a secure distributed DBMS architecture was defined by generalizing the two Woods Hole architectures discussed above. This abstract model, shown in Figure 4.1, consists of back-ends, a Data Manager, user programs, and the interconnection component. The back-ends are used to store and process portions of the multilevel database. There is one back-end per access class supported by the system. The Data Manager is a central component that performs the reference monitor functions of the SD-DBMS. Certain configurations may require that the Data Manager perform other functions, including query decomposition, execution control, and various DBMS operations. User programs are user interfaces or application programs permitted to issue queries against the multilevel database. User programs can be single-level (i.e., untrusted) or multilevel (i.e., trusted). Each of these components is isolated in its own domain. The only connections permitted between components are those provided by the interconnection component.

Multilevel relations are stored by horizontally partitioning them into single-level fragments which are then stored under the appropriate back-ends. When a user creates a multilevel relation, a set of single-level fragments is created in which to store the relation. This is done using the following algorithm.

> **Algorithm**: Given a multilevel relation $R(A_1, A_2, ..., A_n)$, with a range CL, for each security class $c > CL$, create a fragment $R_c(A_1, A_2, ..., A_n)$ on the back-end with security class c.

For example, a multilevel relation R with a range high, low would be mapped into two fragments, R_{high} and R_{low}. The fragment R_{high} would be created on the high back-end and used to store the high tuples in R, and the fragment R_{low} would be created on the low back-end and used to store the low tuples in R.

4.4.2 Architectural Parameters

Architectural parameters were identified that could be varied to produce different architectures from the abstract model. The parameters considered were:

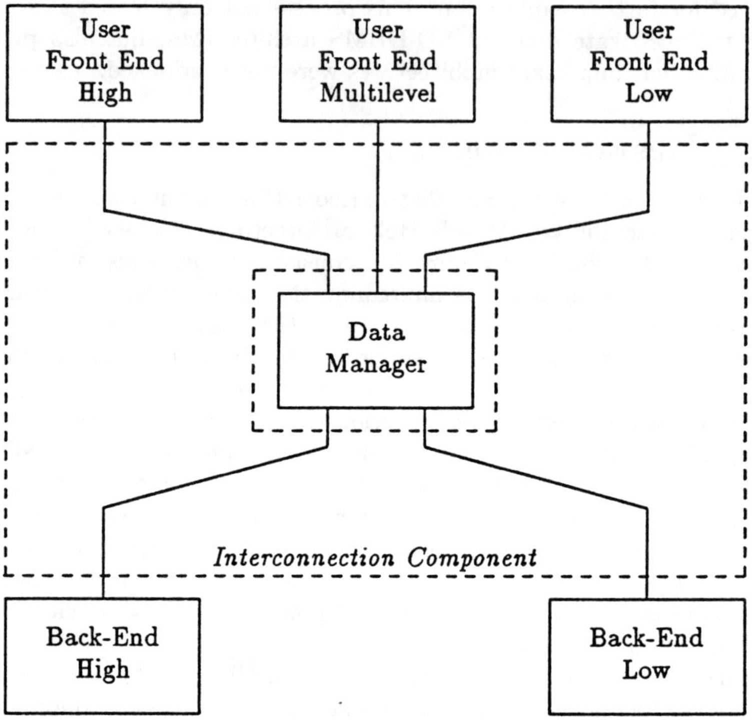

FIGURE 4.1. SD-DBMS abstract model.

- Security mode of the back ends,
- Data labeling strategy,
- Data replication strategy, and
- Query processing strategy.

The first parameter, security mode of the back-ends, can be either single-level or system high. In single-level mode, each back-end is assigned a single access class and is only permitted to store and process data at that access class. A consequence of this mode of operation is that all operations on multilevel data (e.g., multilevel joins) must be performed on the Data Manager. In system high mode, each back-end is assigned a single access class and is permitted to process data dominated by that access class. In this mode, low data can be replicated or copied to the high back-end for use in multilevel operations.

The second parameter, data labeling strategy, determines whether or not data stored in the back-ends are explicitly labeled. In the explicitly labeled case, tuples in the back-ends are stored with attached access class labels. Since the back-ends are untrusted, an important consideration is how to maintain the integrity of the label and its binding to a tuple. One effective method of doing this is to compute a cryptographic checksum over the label and data and store the checksum as part of the tuple or in a separate shadow database [Uni87]. In the second case, tuples stored in the back-ends are unlabeled and the access class associated with a particular tuple is taken to be the access class of the back-end from which it was retrieved.

The third parameter, data replication strategy, determines whether or not data are replicated. Replication can be beneficial for both security and performance reasons. Three replication strategies are considered: full, partial, and no replication. Under full replication, all low fragments are replicated on the high back-end. Under partial replication, low fragments are selectively replicated on the high back-end. Finally, under the unreplicated option, back-ends maintain only a single level of data.

The last parameter, query processing strategy, is concerned with where and how relational operations are performed. Three general query processing schemes were considered: user level, central, and distributed. Under the user level processing scheme, relational operations are performed on the back-end having the same access class as the maximum of the range of the requesting user program. Under the central processing scheme, relational operations are performed on the Data Manager. Finally, under the distributed query processing scheme, relational operations are performed in a distributed manner across multiple back-ends.

4.4.3 Family of Architecture Generation

A family of architectures was generated by taking the Cartesian product of the four parameter sets, resulting in a set of 4-tuples, each of which represents a candidate architecture. There were two problems with this approach. First, the obvious combinatorial explosion resulted in a large number of architectures. Second, since the variables are not independent, a large number of the candidate architectures were meaningless. However, once the unsound architectures were eliminated, seven viable architectures remained. This set of seven architectures was further narrowed by eliminating those with inappropriate replication strategies (e.g., single-level back-ends and data replication). This resulted in a family consisting of three architectures called Architectures A, B, and C. These three architectures are described based on how they enforce MAC. DAC is not covered in this section because it is enforced in the same way for all three architectures. A description of DAC enforcement in the selected architecture is presented in Section 4.

Architecture A

In Architecture A, the back-ends are system high, tuples are labeled, low data are fully replicated on the high back-ends, and queries are executed on the back-end having the same access class as the maximum of the range of the user program that submitted the query. This architecture is essentially Woods Hole case I with labeled tuples.

In this architecture, both high and low data are stored in the high back-end. In order to return multilevel results, the tuples in the high back-end must be labeled with their access class. The integrity of the labels and their binding to the tuples are protected with a cryptographic checksum computed over both the tuple and label (see [Uni87]). One result of computing the checksum over the entire tuple is that projections must be performed by the Data Manager. The reason for this is that, if projections were done in the back-end, the Data Manager would not have the necessary data to recompute the checksum to validate the label.

Retrieval requests submitted by user programs are directed to the back-end with the same access class as the maximum of the range of the requesting user program. The way in which a particular retrieval request is processed depends on whether or not the requesting user program is multilevel. If the requesting user program is single-level, the query is executed completely on the appropriate back-end, the labels and checksums are projected off, and the results are returned to the Data Manager. The Data Manager labels these results at the access class of the back-end on which they were executed (which is also the maximum of the range of the requesting user program) and mediates their return to the requesting user program.

If the user program is multilevel, then it is desirable to return multilevel results. This is done by removing projections from the query and executing the modified query on the appropriate back-end. The results of this query are returned to the Data Manager. Since the back-ends are untrusted these results must be tentatively labeled at the access class of the back-end. The Data Manager must then validate the checksum(s) on each tuple. Note that each tuple in the result may contain multiple checksums because it may consist of multiple labeled tuples concatenated together as the result of a join or a Cartesian product operation. If a checksum is invalid, the tuple is discarded. However, if the checksums are valid, the Data Manager projects off the checksums, labels, and any other unwanted attributes, and labels the tuple at the access class that is the least upper bound of the access classes of the data in the tuple, the access class of the retrieval request, and the access classes of all access views specified in the retrieval request. The Data Manager then mediates the return of the labeled tuples to the requesting user program.

User programs are permitted to update data that fall within their range. Updates are performed based on a primary copy scheme. Under this scheme, the low (original) copy is designated as the primary copy and all replicated copies are designated as secondary copies. All updates by user programs are directed to the primary copy. This approach is safe for high users because only high users that are multilevel are permitted to update low data; therefore, the update does not constitute a write down. Once an update is successfully performed on the primary copy, the Data Manager propagates it to all secondary copies. The concurrency control mechanisms on the low DBMS prevent conflicting user updates to the primary copy. This approach avoids the problem of synchronizing updates to multiple copies of replicated data.

Individual tuples cannot be directly updated by the back-ends since this would invalidate its checksum. Instead, updates must be done internally by the Data Manager. This is done by retrieving the tuples into the Data Manager, validating their checksums, updating them, recomputing their checksums, deleting the old tuples from the back-end, and then reinserting the updated tuples.

This architecture is vulnerable to many of the threats associated with the integrity-lock architectures [Den84,Gra84,Uni87]. Specifically, this architecture is vulnerable to Trojan horse code in a high back-end encoding high data in a low response. Since a Trojan horse in the high back-end has access to all the data in the database, it can leak high data to an unauthorized user by encoding them in low data. This threat is not as great as in the integrity-lock approach because data from the high back-end are only returned to high users. However, if these data are incorrectly labeled at the low level, a high user is free to distribute them to low users. This threat can be reduced by hiding the sensitivity labels from the Trojan horse by encrypting them or by storing them in a shadow database apart from the data. This technique does not, however, prevent a Trojan horse from deducing the sensitivity of the data by other means, such as access patterns or dependency constraints known to exist in the database.

Architecture B

In Architecture B, back-ends are single-level, tuples are unlabeled, there is no data replication, and queries are processed mostly in the Data Manager. This architecture is similar to Woods Hole case E.

The basic query processing strategy for this architecture is to decompose queries into a series of single-level subqueries (i.e., queries on fragments at a single access class) that can be independently executed on the back-ends. Since many queries (viz., multilevel join, product, union, difference, and intersection) cannot be completely decomposed into single-level queries, these operations must be implemented on the Data Manager. Since these operations produce multilevel results, and the tuples in these results must be correctly labeled, the implementation of these operations must be trusted. Furthermore, since projection (a decomposable operation) cannot always be performed prior to multilevel operations, it must also be implemented on the Data Manager, and since it operates on multilevel data, it too must be trusted.

Retrieval requests are processed by decomposing them into a series of single-level subqueries that can be executed on the back-ends, followed by a series of multilevel subqueries that must be performed on the Data Manager. The single-level operations are first executed on the back-ends. The results of these operations are returned to the Data Manager where they are labeled at the level of the back-end from which they came. Next, the multilevel operations are executed on these results. The results of these operations are labeled at the least upper bound of the access classes of the data used in their derivation, the access classes of the access views referenced in the query, and the access class of the query. The Data Manager then mediates the return of these results to the requesting user.

User programs are permitted to update data stored in back-ends having an access class that falls within their range. Unlike the previous architecture, the tuples in this architecture do not have labels or checksums, therefore updates can be processed directly by the appropriate back-ends. Furthermore, since there is no replication, this architecture does not require an update propagation mechanism.

A problem with this architecture is that a selection query sent from an untrusted high user program to a low back-end can be used as a covert storage channel. The concern is that a Trojan horse in a high user program could encode high data in a query to be sent to the low back-end. A cooperating Trojan horse in the low back-end could then extract the high data from the query and release it to a low user. The most devastating form of this attack is when data are encoded in the qualification portion of a selection query. The following example, borrowed from Hinke [HSD86], illustrates this problem. Suppose the following query is submitted from an untrusted high user program:

```
SELECT NAME, ADDRESS, SALARY
FROM EMPLOYEE
WHERE ADDRESS = '504 Pershing Square'
```

If this query is directed to the low back-end, the Data Manager cannot determine whether it is a legitimate query asking for employees at a particular address, or whether it has been sent by a Trojan horse in the untrusted user program, with the intent of leaking the high fact that 504 Pershing missiles are to be deployed.

There are two ways in which this problem can be addressed. The first approach is to defer selections and perform them on the Data Manager. There is no risk involved with performing the selections on the Data Manager because the (potentially high) qualification data are never sent to the low back-end and therefore cannot be leaked to a low user. There are two performance problems with this approach. First, performing selections in the Data Manager requires that entire relations must be transferred from the back-end to the Data Manager. This can be a costly operation if relations are large. Second, performing selections in the Data Manager forces them to be delayed until later in the execution process. This can also be costly because a common technique of optimizing relational queries is performing selections and projections before joins in order to reduce the size of the relations to be joined.

The second approach, called the Trusted Select approach, addresses these problems by allowing the selections to be done early in the query execution process, and with a minimal amount of data transfer. In the Trusted Select process the relation to be selected is projected on its primary key and any attributes referenced in the selection clause, and the resulting relation is sent to the Data Manager. This is the minimum amount of data needed to determine which tuples qualify for the selection. The selection is then performed on the Data Manager, and the primary keys of the qualifying tuples are returned to the low back-end. The low back-end semijoins this result with the original relation to produce the result. This strategy is illustrated in the following example.

Suppose the query given above is entered by an untrusted high user program. In decomposing the query, the Data Manager would recognize that that the query contains (potentially high) qualification data and that the Trusted Select strategy should be used. First, the Data Manager would send the following query to the low back-end:

```
CREATE TEMP T1 AS
SELECT SSN, ADDRESS
FROM EMPLOYEE
```

The back-end would execute this query and store the result in the temporary relation T1. T1 contains the minimum amount of information the Data Manager needs to perform the select (i.e., the primary key, SSN, and the selection attribute, ADDRESS). The Data Manager retrieves T1 and executes the following query on it:

```
CREATE TEMP T2 AS
SELECT SSN
FROM T1
WHERE ADDRESS = '504 Pershing Square'
```

The result of this query is the unary relation T2 which contains the list of SSNs of employees living at 504 Pershing Square. The Data Manager then sends T2 to the low back-end and instructs it to execute the following query:

```
SELECT NAME, ADDRESS, SALARY
FROM EMPLOYEE, T2
WHERE EMPLOYEE.SSN = T2.SSN
```

The result of this semijoin is identical to the one that would have been obtained if the selection were done directly by the low back-end. The advantage of this approach is that the reductive effect of selection was obtained on the back-ends without sending the (potentially high) qualification data down in access class.

Although the Trusted Select processing strategy avoids sending qualification data to the low back-end, it does not completely eliminate the covert channel. It may still be possible for a Trojan horse in the low back-end to draw inferences (partial or complete) about the qualification data from the primary keys returned by the Data Manager; however, the bandwidth of this channel is small, and it would require a much more sophisticated Trojan horse to draw correct inferences.

It should be noted that the vulnerability is not limited to selection queries, since other types of queries (e.g., projections, joins, etc.) can potentially be used as a covert storage channel when sent down in access class (e.g., by modulating the attribute and relation names in the query). The Data Manager can control the bandwidth of this channel by:

- limiting the number of relations and attributes allowed in queries,
- limiting the number of relations and attributes allowed in any particular user's view of the database,
- rejecting queries that are not syntactically and semantically valid, and
- metering the flow of queries to the back-ends.

These steps have the effect of limiting the Trojan horse to an alphabet of legal queries, and controlling the speed at which it can use them to signal high data.

Architecture C

In Architecture C, back-ends are system high, tuples are unlabeled, data are partially replicated, and queries are decomposed into subqueries on single-level fragments that are executed on the back-ends.

The query processing strategy for this architecture is based on a property of the relational algebra that any query on a multilevel relation can be decomposed into a set of queries on single-level fragments, where each query in the set produces a single-level result. This is illustrated in the following examples.

Example 1: The selection query

SELECT $\star$ FROM R where $x > 10$

is decomposed into two queries:

SELECT $\star$ FROM R_{low} WHERE $x > 10$, and
SELECT $\star$ FROM R_{high} WHERE $x > 10$,

each of which yields a single-level result. The union of the results from these two subqueries forms the result of the original query.

Example 2: The join query

SELECT $\star$ FROM R, S WHERE $R.x = S.x$

is decomposed into four subqueries:

SELECT $\star$ FROM R_{low}, S_{low} WHERE $R_{low}.x = S_{low}.x$,
SELECT $\star$ FROM R_{low}, S_{high} WHERE $R_{low}.x = S_{high}.x$,
SELECT $\star$ FROM R_{high}, S_{low} WHERE $R_{high}.x = S_{low}.x$, and
SELECT $\star$ FROM R_{high}, S_{high} WHERE $R_{high}.x = S_{high}.x$

each of which yields a single-level result. The union of the results from these four subqueries forms the result of the original query.

As discussed in the SD-DBMS security policy [Uning], the access class of each of these results is the least upper bound of the access classes of the fragments that entered into their derivation, the access class of the access views referenced in the query, and the access class of the query. Since these individual subqueries produce only single-level results they can be implemented in untrusted code. These single-level results can be unioned together to form the (multilevel) result of the original query. Only the union that does the final assembly needs to be trusted.

The above query processing strategy is used in Architecture C as follows. User programs send queries to the Data Manager. The Data Manager decomposes each query into a sequence of subqueries that operate on single-level fragments. Once a query is decomposed into subqueries, each of the subqueries is executed on the back-end having the same access class as its result. Since queries executed on the high back-end may require access to low data, this architecture supports the transmission of data from the low to the high back-end. To assure that no data flow in the opposite direction, all such transfers are constrained to go through the Data Manager. Once the execution of the subqueries is complete, the Data Manager retrieves the results and labels them at the access class of the back-end from which they were retrieved. These results are unioned together and the Data Manager mediates their return to the user. This query processing strategy is discussed in detail in [OI88].

The query processing performance of this architecture is likely to suffer because of the need to transfer low fragments to the high back-end in order to process queries. In order to lessen or eliminate this performance penalty, some or all of the low fragments can be replicated on the high back-end. This strategy is referred to as partial replication. A low fragment replicated on the high back-end can be used in high queries instead of fetching a new copy from the low back-end each time it is needed. Partial replication is considered to be a viable alternative because it is expected that certain low fragments will be needed on the high back-end more frequently than others. Another motivation for selecting partial replication over the fully replicated and the unreplicated options is that both of these options are special cases of partial replication. The decision of which fragments to replicate could be based on statistics collected by the SD-DBMS. If a particular low fragment is frequently needed on the high back-end, then the overhead of replicating it is justified. However, if a particular low fragment is infrequently (or never) needed on the high back-end, then replication is not justified, and the fragment should be transferred to the high back-end on an as-needed basis. Thus, the partial replication approach provides a method of tuning the physical database structure.

User programs are permitted to update data that fall within their range. Since this architecture permits data to be replicated, it must support an update propagation mechanism. This is done using the same primary copy strategy used in Architecture A, with the exception that all low data are not necessarily replicated. Furthermore, since there are no labels or checksums on tuples in this architecture, these updates can be done directly by the back-ends.

Although Architecture C allows low data to be replicated on the high back-end, it does not suffer the vulnerability associated with architecture A (i.e., that high data can be encoded in low tuples returned from the high back-end). This is because the low data replicated in the high back-end are only used in computing high results, and all data leaving the high back-end are labeled high. Furthermore, Architecture C does not suffer from the query write-down vulnerability of Architecture B. This is because queries are never executed on a back-end that is strictly dominated by the access class of the query. For example, the query discussed in the previous section would not be a problem in this architecture. Since the query was entered by an untrusted high user program, the access class associated with the query would be high, and therefore the query would be executed on the high back-end and the results would be returned as high. However, if the high user program were trusted, it could reliably communicate to the Data Manager the level of the query as low, and the query could be sent to the low back-end to return low results.

It should be noted that a covert channel may still exist. The execution of queries that access unreplicated low data on the high back-end requires that data be copied from the low to the high back-end. These copy requests can be used as a covert channel, albeit one of substantially lower bandwidth than the channel associated with queries. This channel can be eliminated by fully replicating the low data on the high back-end, thereby eliminating the need to copy data. This approach eliminates the covert channel at the cost of increasing storage overhead and the overhead of propagating updates. Another approach would be to use partial or no replication, and simply audit the channel and prevent it from exceeding some predetermined threshold (e.g., by metering the flow of copy requests within the Data Manager).

A careful trade-off analysis was performed, based on the following set of criteria: security vulnerability, TCB size, read:write performance, write: read performance, cost to code, and hardware cost [OGJWG88]. As a result of this analysis, Architecture C was selected.

4.5 Discretionary Access Control Enforcement

When a distributed architecture was recommended at Woods Hole, the primary motivation was that it would provide a basis for the enforcement of mandatory security. DAC was explicitly removed from the applications of interest to Group 1 because it was felt that DAC could be satisfied by physical controls external to the computer system [AFSS83]. This section describes how discretionary access controls can be implemented in the SD-DBMS and discusses the problems introduced by the use of untrusted DBMSs to store and process data.

The SD-DBMS uses access views as a mechanism to enforce DAC. User programs submit queries to the Data Manager in terms of access views. The Data Manager checks the access control list for each access view referenced in the query to verify that the user is permitted to perform the operations specified in the query. If the user is authorized, the Data Manager transforms the query according to the view definitions to form a new (modified) query on the underlying global relations [SW74,Sto75]. The modified query is then executed on the back-ends. This process is illustrated by the following example.

Suppose there is a global relation:

EMPLOYEES(SSN,NAME,ADDRESS,POSITION,SALARY),

with the following access view defined on it:

DEFINE VIEW STAFF AS SELECT ⋆
FROM EMPLOYEES
WHERE SALARY > 20000.

If user 'joe' submits the following query to the Data Manager:

SELECT NAME, ADDRESS
FROM STAFF
WHERE POSITION = 'clerk',

the Data Manager would first check that STAFF is a legal access view and whether 'joe' has SELECT permission on the view. If 'joe' has SELECT privilege for STAFF, the Data Manager would transform the query according to the definition of STAFF to form a new (modified) query on the global EMPLOYEES relation:

SELECT NAME, ADDRESS
FROM EMPLOYEES
WHERE POSITION = 'clerk'
AND SALARY > 20000.

This query would then be executed on one or more back-ends.

Although one of the proposed advantages of a distributed architecture was that the back-ends could be untrusted, in fact, the back-ends play an important role in DAC enforcement. The root of the problem is that DAC involves controlling access to named objects, and therefore, its proper enforcement requires a positive binding between an object name and its contents. In the SD-DBMS, the objects for DAC are access views, which are derived objects. The problem that arises is that the system relies on the back-ends to perform the access view derivation, and if this derivation is done incorrectly, it could result in data being returned that are outside of the user's view. A possible solution to this problem is not to have DAC on views at all; however, the back-ends would still have to be involved in DAC enforcement even if DAC was implemented at the underlying relation level. This is because the back-ends would still have to maintain the binding between relation names and tuples. For example, suppose a user requests access to tuples in a relation R. The Data Manager would check to see that the user is authorized to access R, and if the user was authorized, the Data Manager would forward the request to the appropriate back-end. If the back-end returned tuples from another relation S for which the user was not authorized, the Data Manager would have no way of knowing that they were not the requested tuples, and would then return them to the user. This problem occurs because the Data Manager depends on the back-end to return the data that were requested.

A partial solution to this problem is to have the Data Manager add a unique relation identifier to each tuple as it is inserted into the database.

The integrity of the identifier could be protected by computing a cryptographic checksum [Den84,Gra84] over both the tuple and identifier. The idea of storing a logical entity name with data in the database as a means of protection was first proposed in [DP79]. The Data Manager could then enforce discretionary security by examining the relation identifier of each tuple and releasing the tuple only if the user is authorized to access that particular relation. Using this technique, the binding between tuples and relation names is maintained by the Data Manager and not the back-ends; therefore, the back-ends do not have to be included in the TCB.

Unfortunately, the above technique only provides a partial solution, since the back-ends have access to all the data, and can leak unauthorized data to the user by simply encoding them in data for which the user is authorized. Cryptographic sealing would also degrade performance due to checksum computation/validation; increase data transfer because projections would have to be done in the Data Manager; increase storage overhead for relation identifiers and checksums; and increase the size and complexity of the TCB since it would compute and validate checksums, perform key management, and perform projections. This technique will not be used in the SD-DBMS because it is too costly for a partially effective solution.

One possible method of attaining additional assurance in the correct operation of the back-ends is to use only certified DBMSs as back-ends. It is questionable how much additional assurance can be obtained by using certified DBMSs because it is not expected that the certification requirements for DBMSs will include correct operation, and this is the desired property. However, the operational and life-cycle assurance requirements should provide a modest amount of additional assurance.

4.6 Summary and Conclusions

It was recognized at Woods Hole that the physical separation provided by a distributed architecture could be the basis for mandatory access control in a multilevel DBMS. In this report, a family of architectures based on this idea was presented and described and the most promising architecture was selected for implementation.

The primary goal in the design of the SD-DBMS family of architectures was to develop an architecture that supported the return of reliable tuple level labels to the user. The problem turned out to be as much of a policy challenge as an architectural one. As discussed in Appendix A of [LDS+89], in order for tuple level labels to be reliable indicators of the sensitivity of a retrieved tuple, they must accurately reflect the access classes of any parameters embedded in the query (or access view), and the access classes of any data upon which the decision to submit the query might have been conditioned. This was accomplished in the SD-DBMS policy by treating queries and access views as labeled objects [Uning]. The levels of these objects are then considered when labeling data (derived or otherwise) retrieved from the database. This allowed the labels on tuples to reflect not only the access classes of the data contained (or encoded) within them, but also the parameters in queries or access views used in their derivation, and flows in application programs that requested the access.

In the development of the family of architectures, a number of obstacles had to be overcome:

1. If untrusted high programs are permitted to send queries directly to the low back-end, a Trojan horse in the high program can encode high data in the query and send it to the low back-end. These data could be stored by the low back-end and subsequently released to a low user.

2. If the back-ends are only permitted to store and process a single-level of data, all DBMS operations that involve more than a single level of data (e.g., multilevel joins) must be performed on the Data Manager. Since these operations may produce a multilevel result, they must be trusted.

3. If the high back-end produces low tuples (e.g., as the result of a multilevel join) there is no assurance that these tuples are labeled correctly.

4. If low data are permitted to be replicated on the high back-end, independent updates of the different versions of the data can result in an inconsistent database. Furthermore, mechanisms to synchronize updates to replicated data can introduce covert channels.

5. Using untrusted back-ends to store and process data limits the level of assurance that can be attained for DAC. The reason for this is that the correct enforcement of DAC requires that the binding between an object name and its contents is correctly maintained. In architectures that use untrusted back-ends, it is the back-ends that maintain this binding.

The architectures presented in this report addressed these five problems with differing degrees of success. The architecture selected as a result of the trade-off analysis successfully overcame four out of five of these obstacles.

Obstacles 1, 2, and 3 are primarily concerned with the enforcement of mandatory security and were overcome by the selected architecture as a result of its query processing strategy. Obstacle 1 is overcome because each query is assigned a label that reflects its classification, and the query processing strategy never sends a query to a back-end dominated by the query's access class. Obstacle 2 is overcome because all queries are decomposed into subqueries that can be executed on the back-ends. The only DBMS operation that needs to be implemented in the Data Manager is union. Obstacle

3 is overcome because queries on multilevel relations are decomposed into subqueries that produce single-level results. These subqueries are executed on the back-end with the appropriate level, and the results are labeled at the level of the back-end.

The fourth obstacle presented both a security and an integrity problem. This obstacle was overcome by adopting a primary copy based update strategy. Directing all updates to the low copy of replicated data allows the SD-DBMS to use the concurrency control mechanisms of the low DBMS to prevent conflicting updates. Having the Data Manager propagate updates avoids the covert channels that would arise if the low back-end were to propagate the update.

The selected architecture does not fully address Obstacle 5. The partial solution of tagging tuples with a relation identifier and cryptosealing the result was discarded because it is too costly for a partially effective solution. One possibility that remains under consideration is to use only certified DBMSs as back-ends. The additional assurance provided by these back-ends will depend on the security and integrity requirements mandated by the TDI.

In conclusion, the selected SD-DBMS architecture can be used as the basis for an MLS DBMS that provides reliable tuple level labels with a very high level of assurance. This architecture does, however, have serious limitations in the area of DAC assurance. Although certain measures can be taken to increase the DAC assurance associated with this architecture, its ultimate certifiability will depend on the discretionary assurance requirements mandated by the TDI.

4.7 References

[AFSS83] Committee on Multilevel Data Management Security Air Force Summer Study. Multilevel data management security. *Technical report*, Air Force Studies Board, National Research Council, National Academy Press, 1983. For Official Use Only.

[Cen85] National Computer Security Center. Department of defense trusted computer system evaluation criteria. *Technical Report DOD 5200.28-STD*, Department of Defense, December 1985.

[Cod70] E.F. Codd. A relational model for large shared data banks. *Communications of the ACM*, 13(6), June 1970.

[Dat86] C. J. Date. *An Introduction to Database Systems*, Volume I. Addison-Wesley, Reading, Massachusetts, 4th edition, 1986.

[Den82] D.E. Denning. *Cryptography and Data Security.* Addison-Wesley, Reading, Massachusetts, 1982.

[Den84] D.E. Denning. Cryptographic checksums for multilevel data security. In *Proceedings of the 1984 IEEE Symposium on Security and Privacy*, 1984.

[DP79] Deborah Downs and Gerald J. Popek. Data base management systems security and INGRES. In *Proceedings of Fifth International Conference on Very Large Data Bases*, October 1979.

[Gra84] R.D. Graubart. The integrity-lock approach to secure database management. In *Proceedings of the 1984 IEEE Symposium on Security and Privacy*, 1984.

[HSD86] T.H. Hinke, J.O. Solomon, and J.P. Dempsey. Design considerations for secure database management systems. *Technical Report TM-7526/100/01*, January 13 1986.

[LDS+89] T.F. Lunt, D.E. Denning, R.R. Schell, M. Heckman, and W.R. Shockley. Final report Vol. 2: The SeaView formal security policy model. *Technical report*, Computer Science Laboratory, SRI International, Menlo Park, California, 1989.

[OGJWG88] J.P. O'Connor, J.W. Gray, C. Jensen, and D.T. Westby-Gibson. Secure distributed database management system (SD-DBMS), Volume i: Architecture definition, tradeoff analysis. *Technical report*, Unisys System Development Group, August 1988.

[OI88] James P. O'Connor and James W. Gray III. A distributed architecture for multilevel database security. In *Proceedings of the 11th National Computer Security Conference*, October 1988.

[Sto75] Michael Stonebraker. Implementation of integrity constraints and views by query modification. In *Proceedings of the ACM SIGMOD International Conference on Management of Data*, May 1975.

[SW74] M. Stonebraker and E. Wong. Access control in a relational data base management system by query modification. In *Proceedings of the 1974 ACM Annual Conference*, 1974.

[Uni87] Unisys. Secure distributed database management system: State-of-the-art survey. *Technical Report TM-WD-8905/017/00*, November 9 1987.

[Uning] Unisys. Secure distributed database management system (sd-dbms): Security policy. *Technical Report TM-WD-8905/020/00*, Pending.

5

LOCK Data Views

Paul Stachour[1]

5.1 Introduction

This paper describes the design of a Multilevel Secure Relational Database Management System (MLS/RDBMS), LOCK Data Views (LDV), being designed to run on SCTC's LOgical Coprocessor Kernel (LOCK) Trusted Computing Base (TCB) [Hon87a]. This chapter presents the statement of the problem addressed by the design, an overview of the security policy enforced by the system, and an outline of the report.

This work was performed under contract F30602-86-C-0003 from Rome Air Development Center.

5.1.1 Problem Statement

Within the Department of Defense (DoD), the number of computerized databases containing classified or otherwise sensitive data is increasing rapidly. Access to these databases must be restricted and controlled to limit the unauthorized disclosure, or malicious modification, of data contained in them. Present DBMSs do not provide adequate mechanisms to support such control. Penetration studies have clearly shown that the mechanisms provided even by "security enhanced" database systems can be bypassed, often due to fundamental flaws in the systems which host the DBMS. This has led to a reliance on a number of techniques for isolating sensitive database information. These include physical protection, "system high" operation, and use of manual techniques for data sharing. These actions are very costly and detrimental to operational utility and flexibility.

TCBs, such as SCTC's LOCK, have been designed to provide control over access to data by means of abstract entities and operations which reflect an operating system orientation. The LOCK security policy consists of a discretionary security policy and a mandatory security policy. The discretionary security policy enforces the need to know structures, while the mandatory security policy provides a multilevel control policy. The multilevel control policy is a non-interference policy which addresses both access to data and the flow of information in the system.

[1]Honeywell Inc.

A DBMS presents a more difficult security problem than that dealt with by current TCBs with their operating system orientation. This results from the ability of the DBMS to preserve or even enhance the information value of the data it contains. This is possible because it captures information in addition to the raw data values themselves through the incorporation of knowledge about the types of data and relationships among the data elements. A DBMS also allows for the creation of new data and relationships through the application of complex functions to the data. Because of these capabilities, one is forced to consider a number of factors beyond those normally addressed when dealing with operating system security. These include the impact of data context, aggregation, and inference potential.

SCTC's LDV system addresses the above problems by allowing individuals possessing a range of clearances to create, share, and manipulate databases containing information spanning multiple sensitivity levels. In LDV the relational query language, Structured Query Language (SQL), is enhanced with constructs for formulating security assertions. These security assertions serve to imply sensitivity labels for all atomic values, contexts, and aggregations in a database. The labelled data are partitioned across security levels, assigned to containers with dominating security markings or levels, and may only flow upward in level unless authorized otherwise.

5.1.2 Security Policy Overview

To meet the DoD security policy requirement, as stated in DoD Directives 5200.28 [oD77], 5200.28-M [oD79],and 5200.1-R [oD84], LDV must itself define a security policy that it enforces. The LDV security policy [Hon87c] builds on the concepts of the LOCK security policy and extends them in a consistent and integrated fashion. The underlying LOCK security policy both constrains the actions of the DBMS and provides a foundation for the DBMS security policy. The latter provides extensions to the basic LOCK policy which respond to limitations pertaining to database security concerns. The next subsection presents an overview of the basic LOCK security policy, followed by an overview of the DBMS policy extensions.

5.2 LOCK Security Policy Overview

The LOCK TCB satisfies the security requirements defined for the A1 level in the Trusted Computer Security Evaluation Criteria [Cen85b]. These include requirements regarding mandatory and discretionary access control, object reuse, and maintenance, integrity, and export of sensitivity labels for objects, subjects, and devices. In addition, it supports the ancillary A1 requirements for accountability, audit, and assurance. The interested reader is referred to the Criteria [Cen85b] for a discussion of these requirements.

The LOCK security policy at the highest level of abstraction states that:

"Data is labeled with a level and flows upward in level unless authorized to do otherwise."

This captures the DoD notion of security, which focuses on the confinement and protection of information (data in a context) from compromise. Note that the simple-security and $\star$- properties which form the basis of discussion of most security policies can be derived from the LOCK security policy.

The policy statement is interpreted in terms of a series of increasingly detailed specifications of the security-relevant mechanisms for the system. This provides the basis for the enforcement of the security policy within LOCK. Supporting mechanisms, such as user authentication and accountability, provide assurance that the security mechanisms act in a manner consistent with the security policy.

The mechanisms which implement the LOCK security policy are defined in terms of abstract entities and operations. There are three principal entities in the LOCK security policy: subjects, objects, and the Effective Access Matrix (EAM). Subjects are the active, process-like, entities in the system and objects are passive, file-like, entities. The EAM defines the permissible flows of information within the system. The EAM is computed based on the security relevant attributes associated with subjects and objects. The LOCK policy describes these attributes and the allowed accesses based on the notion of potential interferences between subjects.

The security attributes associated with subjects include:

- Clearance Level (subject_level(S))
- User on whose behalf it is executing (subject_user(S))
- Domain in which it is executing (subject_domain(S)).

Objects have a set of corresponding security attributes which include:

- Classification Level (object_level(O))
- Access Control List (ACL(O))
- Type (object_type(O)).

The term "Level" (subject_level(S)) or object_level(O)) represents a sensitivity level that captures both the hierarchical classification levels and non-hierarchical categories which form a part of DoD security policy. Within LOCK it is assumed that the sensitivity levels form a partially ordered set (POSET). Level L_1 is said to dominate L_2 if $L_1 \geq L_2$ in the POSET. The term "User" refers to the human on whose behalf a subject is executing. The ACL(O) is a list of allowable access modes to an object, on a per user basis, which are maintained for all objects in the LOCK system. The subject Domain (subject_domain(S)) and the object Type (object_type(O)) are introduced to support the Type Enforcement Mechanism, as described in the LDV security policy [Hon87c]. The relationships between domains and types, in terms of allowable access modes, is captured in a Domain

Definition Table (DDT). The DDT is a matrix which is indexed by domain and type, and has as entries those modes for which access is allowed to objects of the given type by subjects in the given domain.

The LOCK security policy consists of a mandatory security policy and a discretionary security policy. The mandatory security policy is based on controlling the potential interferences among subjects. It consists of a mandatory access control policy and a type enforcement policy.

The mandatory access control policy restricts the accesses of a subject to an object based on the sensitivity levels of the subject and object. A subject is a process executing on behalf of a user, and an object is an area of storage, program variable, file, I/O device, or anything else that can hold information. The system enforces the Simple Security Condition (Property) and the $\star$-Property "for accesses between all subjects external to the TCB and all objects directly or indirectly accessible by these subjects". The Simple Security Property states that a subject can read from an object only if its sensitivity label dominates the sensitivity level of the object:

$$\mathrm{READ}(S,O) \Rightarrow \mathrm{dominates}(\mathrm{subject\_level}(S), \mathrm{object\_level}(O)).$$

The *-Property states that a subject can write into an object only if its sensitivity level is dominated by the sensitivity level of the object:

$$\mathrm{WRITE}(S,O) \Rightarrow \mathrm{dominates}(\mathrm{object\_level}(O), \mathrm{subject\_level}(S)).$$

The type enforcement policy deals with aspects of security policy that are inherently non-hierarchical in nature. For example, payroll and medical records found in a database should probably not both be accessible by the same people. The type enforcement policy restricts the flow of information between subjects in different Domains to objects of designated Types. It can be stated as:

$$\mathrm{READ}(S,O) \Rightarrow \mathrm{DDT}(\mathrm{subject\_domain}(S), \mathrm{object\_type}(O)).\mathrm{read}$$
$$\mathrm{WRITE}(S,O) \Rightarrow \mathrm{DDT}(\mathrm{subject\_domain}(S), \mathrm{object\_type}(O)).\mathrm{write}.$$

That is, subject S has read (or write) access to object O if and only if read (or write) is true for the DDT element indexed by S's Domain and O's Type.

The discretionary security policy allows users to specify and control sharing of objects. A subject's access to an object is restricted based on the ACL and the user on whose behalf it is executing. In the LOCK abstract model [Hon87b], an object's ACL is associated with a column of the Discretionary Overlay Matrix (DOM). The discretionary policy is:

$$\mathrm{READ}(S,O) \Rightarrow \mathrm{DOM}(\mathrm{subject\_user}(S),O).\mathrm{read}$$
$$\mathrm{WRITE}(S,O) \Rightarrow \mathrm{DOM}(\mathrm{subject\_user}(S),O).\mathrm{write}.$$

That is, subject S has read (or write) access to object O if and only if the subject's user is on the object's ACL with read (or write) access.

In addition to the mandatory and discretionary security policies, LOCK provides labeling, integrity, authentication, and accountability mechanisms. These are described in our specifications [Hon87a].

5.2.1 DBMS Policy Extension Needs

The LOCK security policy is incomplete in dealing with DBMS security because of its operating system orientation. The most significant contributor to complexity within the DBMS environment is the information carrying potential of the database structure. The DBMS preserves or even enhances the information content of the database by incorporating knowledge of the types of data and relationships among the data. The data manipulation capabilities of the DBMS also allow the creation of new data and relationships through the application of complex functions to the stored data.

Our approach to providing a complete and tractable DBMS security policy extends the basic LOCK security policy through the incorporation of an explicit classification policy. The classification policy must address those factors which are crucial to a correct determination of the sensitivity level of data within the DBMS context. In particular, the policy considers:

- Name-dependent classification: rules that refer to data items by name. This provides classification at the granularity of relations and attributes.
- Content-dependent classification: rules that refer to the content of data item occurrences. This provides classification at the granularity of tuples and elements.
- Context-dependent classification: rules that refer to combinations of data items. This can be used to reflect sensitivity of specific fields when accessed together.
- Inference control: determination of data sensitivity based on the potential inferences that can be made based on a sequence of access requests.

5.2.2 DBMS Policy Extensions

The additional concern for a DBMS in a Multi-Level Secure environment beyond that of LOCK is the proper labeling of information. To provide for that concern, two extensions to the Policy of the TCB are required. One extension summarizes the actions that happen when a database is updated, and the other when a query is made to the database.

Update Classification Extension

For all security levels L_1 and L_2 ($L_1 \leq L_2$) and all base relations R in the database (where L_1 is the basic_level of R), a tuple T being stored securely in a partition P (at level L_2) of R implies that the basic_level of any of the data of T stored in P is $\leq L_2$.

> **Definition:** The BASIC_LEVEL(T) of a tuple (or portion of a tuple) is the lowest level of the set of levels at which T can be securely stored.

For a discussion, see our policy report [Hon87c].

Informally, this means that we partition the data in the database by the base_level security level of the data. We use the enforcement of LOCK to provide most of the security, with the database extension mechanisms only handling special cases such as classification by context.

Response Classification Extension

For all responses R, and all objects O, a response R being written into object O implies that the security-level of the object O is in the group of levels defined by Admissible_Derived_Level_Set(R).

> **Definition:** The Admissible_Derived_Level_Set(R) is the set of all levels for which releasing the information in the response R at that level will not enable any user to infer any further information whose sensitivity level exceeds that user's level.

For a discussion, see our policy report [Hon87c].

Informally, this means that responses are written into ordinary objects (which afterwards can be shared in any arbitrary way, subject to normal system security constraints). The appropriate security level for the objects depends not only on the response, but upon what can be inferred by the response being released at that level.

Enforcement of Policy Extensions

The way LDV enforces the two policies is by three assured pipelines. There is one pipeline each for updates and responses; our particular design for handling metadata such as constraints means that we also needed an assured pipeline to manage the metadata. We discuss the pipelines in the next section.

The details of the DBMS security policy extensions are presented in our policy report [Hon87c].

5.3 Pipelines

The DBMS security mechanism for enforcing the update and response classification policy extensions is three assured pipelines. Assured pipelines originate in [YTBK86], and the pipeline integrity is itself enforced by the LOCK type enforcement mechanism. These pipelines pass through a number of subjects [2] in order to support encapsulation and the security and/or integrity policies. The three pipelines are:

- the query/response pipeline,
- the data input/update pipeline, and
- the database definition/metadata pipeline.

The first of these maps a query from the application domains to the DBMS, processes the query to produce a result relation, labels this result, and exports it to the user domain. This response pipeline runs untrusted in the early stages[3]; the portion which determines the classification label of the data to be released is an example of a trusted portion.

The second pipeline allows subjects executing in a special data input domain to prepare records for input to the DBMS, identify records to delete, etc., and transforms them into a data type readable by the DBMS domain.

This update pipeline also runs untrusted in the early stages; the portion which determines the data classification and where-to-write is trusted code.

The final pipeline provides the mechanism for defining a database structure, specifying relations, views, attributes, classifications, etc., and would normally be restricted to access by the database administrator and by the database system security officer. As with the others, the metadata pipeline allows untrusted code in the early stages; an example of a trusted portion is that which actually stores the constraint metadata.

The remainder of this section describes the organization of the response assured pipeline; the others are presented in [DOST88].

5.3.1 The Response Pipeline Design

This section describes the design of response processing as an assured pipeline of the LDV system. An introduction to the Response Pipeline, the major design issues considered in the design, and an overview of the design are presented. The structure of an assured pipeline is laid out, and the response pipeline is mapped to that structure. Some comprehensive

---

[2] A detailed list of the subjects, together with the types of objects that they act upon, and the kind of accesses allowed by each kind of subject to those objects, is found in the complete report [DOST88].

[3] For example, the SQL parser can be untrusted design/code, since the worst it could do would be to create an internal form of a SQL statement different than one that the human user could enter externally.

examples, and a detailed WELLMADE Design are separately presented in [DOST88].

The Response Pipeline is the query processor for LDV. Query processing for LDV is complicated by the fact that the databases being managed are multilevel. In LDV, the relational query language, SQL, is enhanced with constructs for formulating security assertions. These security assertions serve to imply sensitivity labels for all atomic values, contexts, and aggregations in a database. The data are partitioned across security levels, assigned to containers with dominating security markings or levels, and may only flow upward in level unless authorized otherwise. The assured Response Pipeline is a set of processes which execute multi-user retrieval requests, integrate the data, and output the information at an appropriate level.

Design Issues

The following design issues are addressed in the Response Pipeline design: data distribution across files, optimized recovery of distributed data, and assurance of the correctness of responses in spite of polyinstantiation. We summarize each of the issues here; they are discussed in more detail in [DOST88].

Data Distribution

The first design issue is how to distribute multilevel data so that a large number of authorized users may obtain needed information from the data. This issue arises because it is not sufficient simply to store data into the right containers. It is also important that the method of storage of the data does not allow even authorized users at a given level to infer information at a higher level.

The LOCK TCB, whose security mechanisms are available to LDV, already enforces a security policy which stipulates that "Data may only flow upward in level unless authorized otherwise" [Hon87a]. This policy is extended to LDV as follows: "Information may only flow upward in level unless authorized otherwise". In order to reduce the amount of trusted code in the DBMS, we have chosen to use the LOCK security mechanisms as much as possible and only augment those aspects that do not meet the requirements for information security. Since LOCK enforces its security policy on data stored in operating system files, LDV security assertions on data items must be transformed into LOCK security assertions on files. This transformation is carried out by two other assured pipelines, the Update Pipeline and the Metadata Pipeline, but is discussed here to illustrate the impact of the data distribution scheme on query processing as well as the need to incorporate extra mechanisms (inside the DBMS) that would augment LOCK's.

A DBMS retrieval request must be transformed into the corresponding

OS file requests to LOCK. Since there is only one attribute or subset of each attribute per file, malicious code or a Trojan horse would have difficulty substituting attributes that are not specified in the query into a response. This minimizes the amount of code to be assured/trusted. For context-dependent classifications, a process in the Response Pipeline must detect that attributes have been referenced together. This detection is safer at the file level than at a higher level of query processing, and simpler since less code must be trusted to function correctly. The scheme in conjunction with the File Manager that controls the opening of files eliminates the need to upgrade files that are involved in context-based constraints and consequently reduces the frequency of downgrades as well.

Optimized Recovery of Distributed Data

The second design issue is the correct and efficient reconstruction of distributed data. Two kinds of data partitions that determine the type of reconstruction required are:

Replicate Lower Level Data in Higher Level Files. The replication approach is advantageous in a retrieval-system with infrequent updates. A sequential scan property is achieved with minimal overhead since the synchronization of updates to the replicated data is not frequent. As an example, consider the files created for the EMPLOYEE relation of (Name, Salary, Address) where the levels may be U, S, or TS. The data in the Name-U file would have to be replicated for the S-users and again for the TOP SECRET users (TS-users); the data in the Address-S and Salary-S files would each have to be replicated for the TS-users.

The disadvantage of this approach is the complexity of the updates. In those few cases when data have to be updated, the security risks are not trivial. If there is a separation of physical media by level, then multilevel processes must be spawned and synchronized in order to update the replicated copies. In addition, the commit protocol requires each of these processes to signal success or failure back to some coordinating process resulting in a possible covert channel.

Strict Partitions. Using a partitioning approach, lower level data are not replicated in the higher level files. A recovery algorithm is needed to reconstruct the partial relation representing a view at a given level. The advantage of this approach is the simplicity of updates. The disadvantage of this approach is the performance penalty for retrieval requests for the recovery algorithm.

In LDV, the data partitions are strict, with no replication; the query processor must first reconstruct the response at a level from fragments stored in various files. This reconstruction must be efficient. The LDV reconstruction algorithm is an efficient way to accomplish the LDV equivalent of a sequential scan of a relation. The reconstruction scheme does not preclude the use of access path selection strategies such as those developed in [S+79] and which have been adapted for use in LDV (see WELLMADE design in [DOST88]).

Assuring the Correctness of Responses In Spite of Polyinstantiation

Updates to multilevel data in the face of non-interference and non-disclosure policies may lead to polyinstantiation and inconsistencies. Polyinstantiation is an update anomaly which violates such basic integrity constraints as primary key constraints or, more generally, functional dependencies [DLS+87]. For example, a U-user could inadvertently duplicate a primary key value that had been entered earlier by a S-user. Subjects must be shielded from such a phenomenon by enforcing the basic integrity constraints on the result of a query. For flexibility, the user should be allowed to specify which tuples are to be filtered away from the response using time-oriented constructs and level-oriented constructs, as well as data definition constructs that allow a user to derive the values of attributes of one tuple from those of another. For example, the S-user may choose to see only those tuples that were entered after a certain time or to derive his/her own tuples from those entered by a CONFIDENTIAL user (C-user) rather than a U-user. The SQL languagc described in [DOST88] has been extended in such a way.

The preferred LDV approach to polyinstantiation is to allow for such flexibility as well as to enforce basic integrity constraints such as primary key constraints at each level,[4] functional dependencies, and multivalued dependencies. Initially, we require that primary keys and functional dependencies be enforced, meaning that the relations must be in Third Normal Form (3NF). Later, in order to support consistent Fourth Normal Form (4NF) relations, primary key constraints, functional dependencies, and multivalued dependencies may be stipulated and enforced.

Design Notes

This section presents some notes on the Response Pipeline design. Name-dependent and content-dependent classification are handled by the LDV data distribution scheme. Views of each base relation must be reconstructed at a given level from the data distributed across files. In this process, the context-dependent classification constraints are considered. Constraints involving aggregate functions and general inference control are considered after the response to the query has been built. The LDV data distribution scheme, the reconstruction of a view for a given level, the enforcement of constraints involving aggregate functions and general inference control, an overview of the major modules, and an overview of the security critical modules are presented.

---

[4]Primary keys are enforced within levels and not across levels, thus allowing for polyinstantiation.

LDV Data Distribution Scheme

The basic scheme for data distribution across LOCK files is to assign a set of files per security level. There is no replication of data across levels. The Update Pipeline determines the appropriate assignment of data to files by examining the name-dependent, content-dependent, and context-dependent classification constraints. The view at any particular level is reconstructed by the MERGE operation described in [DOST88]. Since partial relations that are stored at each level may have numerous null values, these nulls can be squeezed out by padding each partial tuple with a tuple descriptor. A tuple descriptor is a bitstring whose length is the order of the relation. A '1' in a position indicates that a value exists for that attribute, and a '0' indicates that the field is null. A 'D' in the first position indicates that the tuple has been logically deleted. In addition to the tuple descriptor, a time-stamp and the level of the tuple are stored. The level of the tuple is the level at which the tuple was inserted. These three fields are not displayed to the user by default; they are manipulated internally by LDV.[5] However, the user may request the retrieval of the time-stamp and level fields. The tuple descriptor always precedes the tuple, followed by the time-stamp, level, and values for the attributes that have '1's in their corresponding positions in the tuple descriptor.

Reconstruction of a View for a Given Level

The query processor reconstructs a partial relation representing a given user view from the data distributed across files. There is one such partial relation corresponding to each base relation in the user's query. The remaining query processing (for example, join) is performed using these partial relations.

In order to reconstruct a partial relation at a particular level, the query processor must take into account context-dependent classification constraints, and merge tuples from different files with the same primary key. In the first step, the partial tuples are retrieved, based upon the query, the level of the user, and the attribute and content-dependent classification constraints. For the second step, an operator called MERGE is used. This operator works with a knowledge of the properties of the tuples in the different partitions of a relation. This operator is security-critical, and the tuple properties are authoritative. Later in the pipeline, any properties attached to the tuple become advisory only.

[5]To save space, the level is not actually stored in the tuple, but is derived from the level of the file when it is retrieved. It appears to LDV that the level was stored.

5.3.2 LOCK Pipeline Organization

The key to the assured pipelines in LOCK is that each pipeline is composed of a group of dispatchable subjects. Each subject, similar to a process in other operating systems, is constrained by its creation parameters:

- to execute in a particular execution domain,
- to execute a particular segment of object code,
- to run at a particular security level,
- to execute with particular discretionary attributes.

Subject Characteristics

By virtue of the domain in which it executes, a subject can only open objects of certain types. Even there it is constrained in the kind of access it may have to objects of those types. Most importantly, any particular execution domain will usually only have read access to a few types of objects, and write access to a few others. Thus no objects other than those of the specified types can be observed, modified, or created by subjects executing in a particular domain. This thwarts the problem of objects being observed or modified by subjects executing in some general domain. It also thwarts the subject that makes a back-pocket copy of data, intending to release it via some unauthorized way.

By virtue of being marked to execute in some particular domain, a subject is allowed to execute in that domain. This means that arbitrary subjects cannot run wherever they please, but are restricted to a certain "vanilla" domain. This thwarts the problem of subjects moving to a particular domain to gain the privileges of that domain, specifically to gain the ability to read or write objects of certain types, and thus construct their own private pipelines paralleling the public ones.

By executing at a given security level, a subject is restricted in which objects it can read or write. This means that it cannot (unless "trusted") bypass any of the mandatory security enforced by LOCK.

Because each subject executes on behalf of some (personal) user, with that user's characteristics, the subject will not be able to read/write data from/to objects not marked for that user. This thwarts the problem of subjects accessing data at their level, but for which they should not have access.

Controlled Data Movement

The characteristics described above allow the creation of groups of subjects, called pipelines, across types and domains. A general characteristic of such pipelines is that each subject takes data of a single type, and writes data of some other type. If one defines only one domain (say domain-p) able to read objects of type-1 and write objects of type-2, and if one further allows no other domain to read objects of type-1 or to write objects of type-2, then the group (type-1, domain-p, type-2) forms a pipeline between types 1 and 2. Furthermore, if one allows only one subject (say subject-s) to execute in domain-p, then there is extremely tight control over the pipeline. Provided that one defines a number of these groups of types and domains, it can then be proved that data can only reach the end of the pipe by passing through all the subjects and objects.

This has the beneficial effect that if one can control the format of the data by a process late in the pipeline, (say be a canonicalization of data) one can thus ensure that unvalidated subjects earlier in the pipeline cannot leak data through the format provided. For example, where earlier portions of a pipeline provide requests to be acted upon, and later ones provide the actual data, those earlier portions can be unchecked code.

5.3.3 Response Pipeline Organization

Figure 5.1 shows the general organization of the response pipeline.

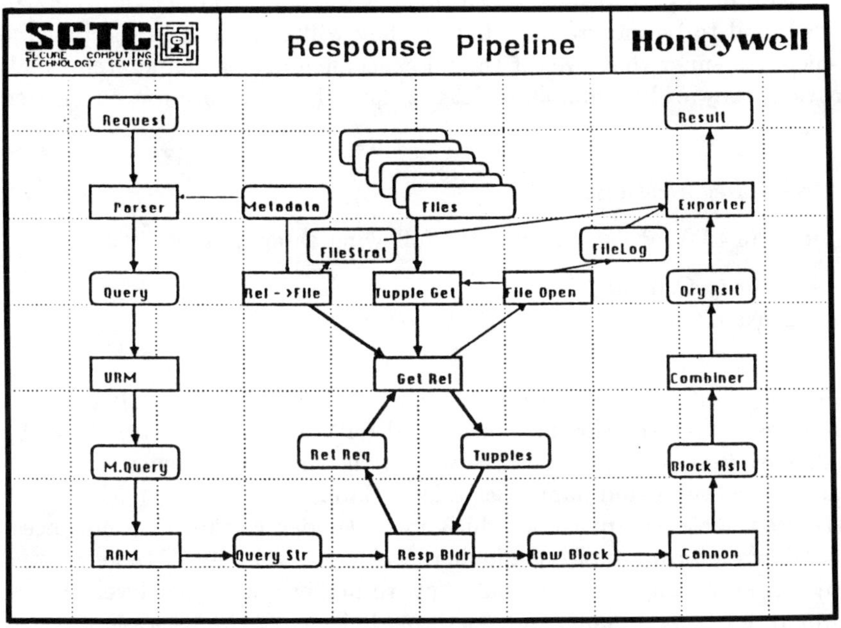

FIGURE 5.1. Response pipeline.

Subjects are shown as boxes with rounded corners, and objects as boxes with square corners. Dataflow between objects is shown as arrows. There are two kinds of arrows in the figure. Those shown as heavy lines represent the major flow of data within the response pipeline. Those shown as light lines represent auxiliary data entering the pipeline, control data provided by another pipeline, or auditing data written by certain functions within the pipeline.

Prevention vs. Detection

As with other areas such as programming languages, there is a controversy over whether prevention or detection of certain kinds of errors is better. Experience with programming languages shows that forbidding certain features and actions (such as label- and entry-variables in Ada) in order to prevent certain problems also prevents the use of those items in situations where those features are helpful. In LDV, we have taken a balanced assurance view towards both correctness and security properties. Certain subjects will be "shown to be correct". That is, we will perform a FTLS (Formal Top-Level Specification) [Hon89] of the design, and our implementation will be tested to show that it follows the design. Other subjects will be "allowed to be incorrect". That is, they will be placed in the pipeline in such a manner that even if they do (accidentally or deliberately) malfunction, they will be unable to release data that they are not authorized to release.

Subject Categorization

Subjects in LDV are assigned to the following categories:

- Security-Critical
- Trusted
- Ordinary

Security-Critical subjects are those whose malfunction could result in the release of information not authorized for release, either directly, or by modification of control structures within the database in such a manner that such release could happen at a later date.

Trusted subjects are those which must (under certain circumstances) write-down information from a higher level to a lower one. Without trusted subjects, eventually all data would flow to higher and higher levels, where it would not be accessible, and thus would effectively be useless.

Ordinary subjects are those that do ordinary things, such as change the form of a user-request from human-readable in ASCII characters to one of that is efficiently machine-processable in terms of lists, trees, and bit-codes.

The assured pipeline mechanism allows the mixing of these three kinds of subjects. It allows us to devote more time to the assurance of the first two kinds. Without such a mechanism (or a similar control method), one would have to provide detailed assurance about all of the database to have confidence in its non-bypassable operation; this is effectively impossible due to the sheer size of the design and code.

Response Pipeline Constituents

The response pipeline has seven constituents, each separated from the other. They are:

- Input
- Parsing
- Reordering
- Retrieval
- File Management
- Exception Control, and
- Output.

The Input and Output constituents isolate the database from the rest of LOCK. Requests can enter LDV only though the input constituent; Information can leave LDV only through the output constituent. This performs the isolation of LDV from the rest of LOCK, and thus ensures that the work done by LDV is both isolated and non-bypassable. Input and Output are ordinary subjects, since their function is merely to isolate, and not to transform the data.

Parsing can be done as an ordinary subject by code reused from some other database system. Since the only possible error would be that the request would be transcribed differently, this would be similar to a user making a typing error. If we were more suspicious, we could also require this constituent to log both its input and output for examination by Exception Control.

The next constituent is the reordering of the query. In database terminology, this is often called optimization. The objective is to transform the request into one that can be executed using less system resources. This can again be an ordinary subject, as it does not require processing of any sensitive database structures. Note that because of the level at which it runs, it would not be able to pass back information to a lower-level user process.

The area of "level-determination" is an interesting one. Here we look at the metadata in the database, and determine at what security level the query must eventually run. The subjects here are security-critical, as they read metadata of varying security levels. Of special interest is the subject that passes the determined-level to a (often just-created) subject running at that level. This must be a trusted-process, one trusted to write-down from its high level (where it can see all the needed metadata) the true level at which the query must run if it is to make sense. This level is the query-level, and it is from hereon that security-critical items will be checked via Exception Control.

During Retrieval, the retrieval mechanisms open the files whose identification they have been given at their own level. If a subject tries to open and read a too high-level file, it will be killed. The exception-control will eventually notice the absence of a result; the "result" provided to the user will thus be "No information can be provided about your query". Since identification of all files that are opened will be recorded, a subject that attempts to open a file not in its authorized set will eventually have its result nulled-out by exception control and replaced by a "No information" message.[6]

File Management is a set of security-critical subjects. Because of the domain-mechanism that enforces roles, only File Management can open the files that are the database proper. Whenever it opens a file, and makes it available to the rest of the database, it logs an identification of the file for exception control.

Exception Control is security-critical also. It has a simple job. It reads log-files created by various parts of LDV. It makes simple comparisons about what should have been done and what was done. If there is not a match, it refuses to allow any data that might have been generated as a result of the database retrieval to leave the database. However, note that this can be a simple program, since it need not decide if the results are correct, but merely if the right set of objects has been consulted in producing the result.

Output takes the result from Exception Control, and writes it into an object that can be read outside of the database. This object can indeed be of a higher level than the user who entered the request, as might be normal if a clerk was performing a retrieval on behalf of some other person whose level and clearance were different from the clerk doing the retrieval.[7]

5.3.4 Pipeline Implications

The implications of a pipeline organization may be not obvious, however, we believe that our organization allows us to

- Separate Security-Critical and Trusted Processes from Ordinary
- Isolate for reliability (correct answers or none)
- Provide for Non-Bypassable Operations

---

[6]While this function (mandatory category separation) is already provided by LOCK, LDV requires this to a finer degree of granularity. That is why LDV depends on LOCK for the coarse level, but does its own enforcement at the fine level.

[7]Note that the identification of the object must either be provided by the original requester, or another trusted-path must be provided by LDV in order to provide the requester with the identification of the object. Again, this may be a very necessary trusted-path (of a very special kind) the content of whose downgrade must be carefully scrutinized.

in a way or cost not practical in other organizations for databases that provide less or more poorly controlled separation.

5.4 Conclusions

We have shown the need for a security policy for a database system that builds upon the classical security policies for operating systems. We have described our policy for LDV and shown how it builds on the policy for LOCK. We have described how our pipeline organization helps to minimize the amount of design and code that must be trusted and/or verified.

Our complete report [DOST88] describes additional challenges we faced, and the approach we are taking towards solving them.

5.5 References

[Cen85] National Computer Security Center. Department of defense trusted computer system evaluation criteria. *Technical Report DOD 5200.28-STD*, Department of Defense, December 1985.

[DLS+87] D.E. Denning, T.F. Lunt, R.R. Schell, M.Heckman, and W.R. Shockley. A multilevel relational data model. In *Proceedings of the 1987 IEEE Symposium on Security and Privacy*, April 1987.

[DOST88] P.A. Dwyer, E. Onuegbe, P. Stachour, and B.M. Thuraisingham. Secure distributed data views—implementation specification for a DBMS. *Interim report a005*, Honeywell Systems Research Center and Corporate Systems Development Division, May 1988.

[Hon87a] Honeywell. B-level design specification for the LOCK operating system. *Technical Report CDRL A009*, Contract MDA 904-87-C-6011, Honeywell Secure Computing Technology Center, St. Anthony, Minnesota, June 1987.

[Hon87b] Honeywell. Secure distributed data views—SAT formal security policy. *Technical Report Interim Report A003*, Honeywell Systems Research Center and Corporate Systems Development Division, April 1987. prepared for the Rome Air Development Center, Contract F30602-86-C-0003.

[Hon87c] Honeywell. Secure distributed data views—security policy extensions. *Technical Report Interim Report A002*, Honeywell Systems Research Center and Corporate Systems Development Division, April 1987. prepared for the Rome Air Development Center, Contract F30602-86-C-0003.

[Hon89] Honeywell. Secure distributed data views—formal top level specifications. *Technical Report Interim Report A004*, Honeywell Systems Research Center and Corporate Systems Development Division, March 1989. prepared for the Rome Air Development Center, Contract F30602-86-C-0003.

[oD77] Department of Defense. Security requirements for automatic data processing (ADP) systems. *Technical Report* Directive Number 5200.28, May 6 1977.

[oD79] Department of Defense. ADP security manual. *Technical Report 5200.28M*, June 25 1979.

[oD84] Department of Defense. Information security program regulations. *Technical Report 5200.1R*, October 2 1984.

[S+79] Pat Griffiths Selinger et al. Access path selection in a relational database management system. In *Proceedings of ACM SIGMOD*, Boston, Massachusetts, May 1979.

[YTBK86] W.D. Young, P.A. Telega, W.E. Boebert, and R.Y. Kain. A verifed labeller for the secure Ada target. In *Proceedings of the 10th National Computer Security Conference*, 1986.

6

Sybase Secure SQL Server

Helena Winkler[1]

6.1 Introduction

Sybase and TRW have been working together to produce two secure relational database products that meet the guidelines set forth in the Department of Defense Trusted Computer System Evaluation Criteria (DoD TCSEC). A B1 version of the Sybase Secure SQL Server is being developed that will run on a B1 secure UNIX operating system. The B2 Sybase Secure SQL Server will run on bare hardware, avoiding the need for an underlying B2 operating system. The B1 and B2 systems contain the same security features, such as mandatory and discretionary access controls, auditing, and trusted paths for performing security relevant activity.

The B2 system provides greater security assurance by enforcing task isolation and memory protection at the hardware level. It protects the Trusted Computing Base (TCB) and its security-related data by partitioning it into its own address space, completely separate from the untrusted code address space. The B1 and B2 implementations present the same interface to users, System Security Officers and Database Owners. Only the degree of assurance differs, because of the B2 system's security architecture.

This paper gives an overview of the security features that are common to both systems. When the design differs, the specific system being discussed is explicitly mentioned.

6.2 Terms and Definitions

Primary Object In the Sybase Secure SQL Server a primary object is defined as a row. A primary object (i.e. row) is the smallest unit of information that can have a security label associated with it. Primary objects are protected by mandatory access and integrity control mechanisms.

Mandatory Security Mandatory security protects primary objects. A

[1]Sybase

user can access a row in the database only if the user's login security level dominates the security level of the row.

Secondary Object Secondary objects are defined as databases and tables in the Sybase Secure SQL Server. Secondary objects are protected by discretionary access control.

Discretionary Security Secondary objects have associated access control lists. Users can access an object only if their logins or their groups are in the object's access control list. Discretionary access can be granted to any number of individuals or groups, or to all users based on the specific database operations SELECT, INSERT, UPDATE and DELETE. This differs from UNIX where only the owner, the group that the owner belongs to, or all users, can be granted permission to access an object.

System Security Officer The System Security Officer (SSO) is responsible for security-related operations. These include adding, deleting and changing user accounts, specifying which events will be audited, and writing-down data.

System Administrator The System Administrator (SA) has system-level responsibility for database functions, such as device management, creating and altering databases and killing processes.

Database Owner The Database Owner (DBO) has database-level responsibilities. These include changing the owner of a database, adding or removing users and groups from a database, dumping a database and its transactions, and granting or denying users permission to create tables.

6.3 Objectives

The overall objective of the project is to produce a commercially-viable relational DBMS that complies with the "DoD TCSEC," Division B, classes B1 and B2 requirements. A direct result of meeting this objective will be placing a commercially available, multilevel secure DBMS on the NCSC's Evaluated Products List at Classes B1 and B2. In addition to the security requirements, the Sybase systems will meet industry requirements by providing users with a friendly interface, state-of-the-art relational database capabilities and high performance. Our specific objectives are as follows.

Provide B-Level Functionality. B level functionality includes mandatory security, discretionary security, auditing of security events, trusted write-down, and a logical division of work among the System Security Officer, System Administrator, database owner and user.

Provide B2 Level Assurance. B2 level assurance requires a security design built around a TCB operating in a domain separate from untrusted software. The TCB is always invoked, self protecting and small enough to examine and test. It is designed in accordance with the principle of least privilege, structured design and possesses well-defined interfaces.

Minimize Performance Degradation. The Sybase Secure SQL Server will have a minimum amount of performance degradation. The goal was to build a secure DBMS that has performance comparable to non-secure relational database systems. This was accomplished by basing the Secure SQL Server upon a very high performance DBMS, namely the Sybase SQL Server.

Provide Integrity Assurances. In addition to the necessary security features, the Sybase Secure SQL Server provides integrity assurances. Each page in the database contains a Cyclic Redundancy Check (CRC) which is used to verify that the page has not been altered after it was written to the disk. Internal checks are used throughout the system to ensure the integrity of the database.

6.4 B2 Design Philosophy

A significant problem in developing a B2 level DBMS has been the large amount of code that may be designated as trusted. Historically, many relational database systems are hundreds of thousands of lines of code. The Sybase Secure SQL Server is based upon the Sybase SQL Server which is considerably smaller in size. A DBMS includes operating system and compiler technology as well as database-specific technology. Implementing a trusted compiler is a difficult problem, and it is a comparable problem to the implementation of an SQL translator. To date, no systems which contain trusted compilers have been submitted to the National Computer Security Center (NCSC) for evaluation.

The approach taken is to have untrusted code compile SQL statements into a query plan which is then executed within the TCB. The query plan is comprised of a small, limited binary instruction set whose security properties can be accurately delimited.

In the B2 system, the untrusted code is in one domain and the TCB is further divided into two other domains. One TCB domain contains low level operating functionality and the other contains security-relevant database code. This division implements the least privilege design principle. Each body of code runs in a separate hardware domain, which minimizes the ability of these three code bodies to interact and subvert the security and integrity controls.

6.4.1 Database Server On A Network

The Sybase Secure SQL Server is a database server on a network. It contains an interface that will enable it to provide private communications between itself and a client process on a host when network support for this functionality becomes available. The initial version utilizes an Ethernet and TCP/IP protocol. When multi-level secure (MLS) networks become commercially available they will be encorporated into the Secure SQL Server.

6.4.2 B2 Sybase Secure SQL Server

The B2 Sybase Secure SQL Server is being developed to run on bare hardware without an operating system. There are three benefits to this approach:

- No dependence on a secure operating system. This is important because there are currently no commercial operating systems, with at least a B2 level of assurance, that have sufficient performance to support an on-line transaction processing relational database management system. In addition, there are no guidelines explaining the interactions between a secure Operating System and large-scale system applications such as a DBMS.
- Isolation of the database from the user. There is no mechanism to enable a user to program on the same machine as the Secure SQL Server. The only means of communication is with SQL through the network, or through one of the trusted interface terminals directly connected to the Secure SQL Server. These types of communication use a well-defined set of protocols. This reduces the number of paths available for circumventing the DBMS.
- System performance. DBMS performance can be optimized to the hardware architecture. This is particularly important since security controls invariably impose performance overhead.

6.5 Flow of Control

Users log in to the Sybase Secure SQL Server and submit a query for processing. The TCB performs user authentication and all communications with the network. The query is parsed and compiled by untrusted code and is then submitted to trusted code for validation and execution. When execution is complete the TCB returns results to the user. An important aspect of this design is that information returned to the user goes directly from the TCB to the user. Since untrusted code in the Secure SQL Server does not have access to labeled results, this assures the correctness of the security labels returned with each result row.

Rows returned to the user are always labeled with the row's security level. This security level is the least upper bound of the security level of all of the rows accessed when forming the result row. The SSO may choose to have a CRC calculated for each row and returned to host applications.

6.5.1 Login

A request to log in comes over the network. A user logs into the Server through a private Server protocol. The login establishes the identity, login security level and role of the user. The user can log in at any security level dominated by his/her maximum clearance. A user's maximum clearance is set by the SSO and stored in the database. A user wishing to log in as an SSO can only do so from the SSO Trusted Interface.

Passwords may be set to expire after a certain time interval. The interval is set by the SSO. After a user's password expires, that user is able to log in from the User Trusted Interface for the purpose of changing his or her password. Passwords must be at least 12 characters long, and can be comprised of either letters or numbers.

The TCB reads the log in request from the network, identifies the user, authenticates the user by checking the password, insures that the login security level is dominated by the user's maximum clearance level and checks that the user is allowed to log in with the specified role. The TCB then creates an untrusted process on behalf of the user, at the user's requested login security level. Control is then passed to an entry point in the untrusted command interpreter. The user's untrusted process then blocks waiting for the next command from the user. Trusted code is now free to process other commands.

6.5.2 Parsing and Compilation

A command expressed in Sybase Transact-SQL arrives from the network and is passed by the TCB to the untrusted DBMS process acting on behalf of the user. The TCB enforces process separation between untrusted processes. The command is compiled, that is, translated from SQL into a binary internal form called a Procedure. The process which translates SQL into a procedure is a very large body of code in any relational DBMS. Both the SQL parser and compiler run as untrusted code. Once the query is compiled, it is handed to the TCB for execution. Note that the TCB handles all aspects of execution. This means that untrusted code has no contact with the data retrieved from the database on behalf of the user's query, though it does determine what data will be retrieved.

Untrusted code is comprised of the SQL parser and compiler. The SQL parser converts SQL queries into an internal tree structure. This is a mechanical process which does not require any interaction with the TCB except for requests for blocks of private memory. The TCB provides memory in 2048 byte blocks which are first cleared before allocation and then mapped only into the process's assigned memory space.

Compilation consists of converting the tree generated by the parser into a procedure by building an internal representation and translating the logical names into internal identifiers. To do this, the compiler requests Data Dictionary information from the TCB. All such requests pass through the TCB's reference validation mechanism so that the procedure will be compiled based only on Data Dictionary information which the user is allowed to see. The procedure is then passed to the TCB for execution.

6.5.3 Description of Procedures

A procedure is a complete description of a plan of execution of a query including the tables that the user referenced, the index chosen to access each table, the operations specified in the query (such as AND, EQUALITY, SUMMATION), and storage areas for accumulation of results. Control flow indicates the order in which statements are executed. The execution logic forms rows and either updates the database or sends the results back to the host.

6.5.4 Execution of Procedures

In the B2 system the TCB first maps the procedure out of the user's address space and into its own address space so that it cannot be altered or read by the untrusted code. For both systems, the TCB then validates the procedure to insure that internal structures and pointers are all contained within the user's address space and that the procedure contains only legal operations. Validation insures that the procedure operates within its own memory boundaries and cannot examine or store data outside of its boundaries. Thus, whether or not the procedure created by the untrusted code corresponds with what the user requested, no violation of security policy can occur. If any of the validation checks fail, the procedure is rejected, and the TCB returns an error message to the user, deallocates the procedure memory and audits this event.

The TCB provides mandatory protection for all primary objects in the database. Before a user is allowed read access to a primary object, the TCB confirms that the user's login security level dominates the object's security label. For database objects such as tables, views and procedures, the object's definition is stored as a row in the Data Dictionary, along with the object's overall security level. Therefore, if a table definition is labeled secret, then users logging in at secret or above can read from the table and write into it. Because of this the table can hold data that is secret or above. SSOs determine if successful access to rows should be audited.

The TCB then performs discretionary security checks. Discretionary access is checked against the tables used in the procedure. Discretionary access privileges are also stored in the Data Dictionary. The TCB examines each use of each table to make sure the user has authorization to perform the requested operations. If the procedure fails any of the discretionary security checks, the TCB audits the failure and reports that the procedure is not executable. If it succeeds, the procedure is passed on to be executed.

The TCB does not provide discretionary protection for database objects other than databases and tables. In the regular Sybase SQL Server a user can be granted privileges to execute a stored procedure, or use a view, but not have access to the tables that either the stored procedure or view reference. In the Sybase Secure SQL Server, the user must have discretionary access permission to all of the tables that the procedure or view references, in order to make use of the procedure or view. Objects other than tables and databases do not have discretionary access controls associated with them.

All data manipulation occurs as a result of procedure execution. All data accessed throughout the execution phase is passed through a reference validation mechanism which handles mandatory security for each row. If the user's login security level dominates the security label of the row it is passed to the execution logic; otherwise the row is ignored.

6.6 Trusted Operations

Trusted operations can be executed only over a trusted path. The Sybase Secure SQL Server includes two separate trusted interfaces, one to be used only by an SSO and one to be used by SAs, DBOs and regular users. Both trusted paths consist of a direct physical connection (not utilizing the network) between a terminal and the TCB of the Sybase Secure SQL Server.

When a user is interacting with the Sybase Secure SQL Server through either of the trusted interfaces, their requests do not utilize the untrusted parser and compiler but rather come directly into the TCB and are executed in a similar fashion as described above for procedures. All users are automatically logged on at their maximum allowable security level when they log in through either the SSO or User Trusted Interface.

6.6.1 SSO Trusted Interface

System Security Officers perform security-related operations. These include all login-oriented procedures such as account generation and deletion, setting a user's password, maximum log in security level, and role, and account lock out. System Security Officers can also write-down data, define auditable events, remove permanent tables, run load database and load transaction and choose the expiration interval of passwords. All of these operations are performed at the SSO Trusted Interface, a terminal dedicated to SSO functions.

6.6.2 User - Trusted Interface

System Administrators are responsible for general system functions. They use the User Trusted Interface for device management, such as formatting a physical disk or adding devices that can be used for making backup copies of a database or transaction log.

Database owners utilize the User-Trusted Interface to specify create table permission, to change the owner of the database, to create or delete groups within the database and to allow or disallow users access to the database. Database owners also use the User Trusted Interface to dump the database or transaction log.

Owners of tables (i.e. secondary objects) use the interface to assign discretionary access controls on these objects. They can allow or disallow SELECT, INSERT, UPDATE or DELETE permission on their tables for specific users or groups, or all users of the DBMS.

All users must change their passwords via the User Trusted Interface.

6.7 Auditing

The Sybase Secure SQL Server allows for auditing at the user, database, table, or row level. Auditing is performed by writing records both to a printer and a system table called Sysaudits. Sysaudits can be queried by SSO's using SQL. It provides a way to build SQL applications that can perform threat monitoring, a B3-level capability.

Security-relevant events that are due to system-level inconsistencies are always audited. Other security-related events can be audited at the discretion of the SSO. An SSO can choose to audit the actions of a particular user. The SSO can specify whether successful access to a table is audited. All discretionary access failures are automatically audited. The SSO can choose to have table auditing on read access and/or all other types of access (update, delete, and insert). The SSO can also specify by table if successful access to rows with a specified minimum clearance level is audited. Use of a database can also be audited. All operations performed at the SSO Trusted Interface, the User Trusted Interface or by an SA are automatically audited. Whenever a user logs in or logs out this is audited. If procedure validation fails, this event is also audited.

The information captured in the audit rows complies with the TCSEC standards. Examples of information that is included are the timestamp, the user's login name, the name and security level of objects accessed and the operation type.

6.8 Conclusions

The Sybase Secure SQL Servers will be commercially viable secure DBMS products. The B1 and B2 implementations present the same interface to users, System Security Officers and Database Administrators. Only the degree of assurance differs, due to the B2 system's security architecture.

The B1 system is designed to run on a UNIX operating system that is at least B1 secure. The B2 system runs on bare hardware. No other program, not even an operating system, can run on the same machine as the B2 Server.

The Sybase Secure SQL Servers have been designed to meet both government and industry requirements. The Sybase Secure SQL Servers contain state of the art database functionality as well as B1 and B2 levels of security assurance. They are designed to conform to the standards set forth in the NCSC's TCSEC, in anticipation of the forthcoming Trusted Database Interpretation. When the Trusted Database Interpretation is available, they will be modified as necessary to conform to those standards as well.

7

An Evolution of Views

Dorothy E. Denning[1]

7.1 Introduction

My work in the multilevel database security area began in 1982, when Marv Schaefer invited me to be on the steering committee for the Air Force Summer Study on Multilevel Data Management Security, to be held at Woods Hole. At the time, I was on the faculty at Purdue University, where I had spent the past several years working on the statistical database problem (protecting sensitive data released in the form of aggregate statistics). I had just finished my book and was glad to have the opportunity to see whether my earlier work would apply to the multilevel database problem. We had several committee meetings prior to the workshop, during which time we discussed the problem, determined whom to invite and how to structure the workshop, and listened to briefings from various government agencies. At first I found the meetings hard to follow; acronyms (RADC, CECOM, WWMCCS, Blacker, ...) were flying by at a rate faster than I could catch them, but gradually I began to make some sense out of them.

I remember one day we were discussing whether data should be classified at the granularity of a relation, tuple, attribute, or element; and how to deal with the problem of dynamic classification, where the classification of a tuple or element may change depending on changes to related data in the database. It occurred to me that we could solve the problem by assigning classifications to view definitions rather than to the individual elements, since the view definitions represent invariants about the underlying data. Thus, the data could change, but it would be unnecessary to reclassify any data because views could capture the invariant classification rules; for example, that a flight is classified SECRET whenever it is carrying the president. Views seemed to provide a powerful means of supporting classification by context and content (the latter through predicates in the view definition) and a formal means for addressing inference and aggregation problems.

I also recall Mike Stonebraker arguing that discretionary access controls should be at a high-level rather than on the underlying low-level data elements, and taking such an approach in Ingres. In addition, System R

---

[1]Georgetown University

placed their access controls on views (and base relations), and Peter Neumann, who was also a member of the steering committee, had outlined an approach to secure views in the PSOS report [NBF+80]. The steering committee decided that it was worthwhile to investigate whether views also could provide a mechanism for classifying data in multilevel systems, and charged Peter and me with the task of leading a group at Woods Hole that would investigate views in the context of finding a long-term solution to multilevel database security. Meanwhile, I wrote a paper which was distributed to all workshop participants before their arrival at Woods Hole. The paper outlined a general approach that went as follows: a view representing the entire database is classified at the highest level; views that filter out data are classified at lower levels, depending on how much information is lost by the filtering function.

At Woods Hole, I recall considerable skepticism about whether it would be possible to build a very secure system based on using views as the object of classification – it seemed that it would require trusting too much of the database system. Ted Glaser and Joseph Goguen both supported the view approach, at least in theory. Ted helped us clarify the rationale for views. Joseph developed some theoretical underpinnings for addressing inference and aggregation problems with the view approach, which he later presented at the annual Oakland meeting in a paper coauthored with J. Meseguer[GM84]. The study group recommended that the view approach be investigated further.

In 1983 I left Purdue and joined Peter Neumann at SRI. I had a grant from NSF to pursue the view approach, but progress was slow. Then in 1985, The U.S. Air Force, Rome Air Development Center (RADC) solicited proposals for research to design a secure multilevel database system that would be based on the view approach and meet the evaluation criteria for class A1. This was to be the follow-up study to the Woods Hole recommendation. However, whereas I and the others at Woods Hole had intended the follow-up to be a research project aimed only at investigating the approach, RADC wanted a formal model, formal top-level specifications, and implementation specifications for an actual system – in three years! The whole idea scared me to death. Then one day Roger Schell called me and invited Peter and me to bid on the project with him. I held Roger in considerable esteem, and was highly flattered that he would ask us to work with him. I also reasoned that Roger knew how to build secure systems, so if he thought we could do it, we could. I accepted his invitation and started thinking about how we would do it. The skeptics at Woods Hole were right; using views alone was going to require too much trusted code in the database system.

I then saw that we could approach the assurance problem by labeling the underlying data elements with one set of views, called classification views, and accessing the data through another set of views, called access views. Assurance would be obtained by making sure that the data elements were securely labeled when entered into the database and by using a security kernel to control access to the labeled data. Later we saw that the classification views were really just integrity constraints and named them classification constraints [DAH+87a].

The SRI and Gemini team won the contract, and we started work in the fall of 1985. In addition to Roger, Peter, and me, the initial project team included Mark Heckman of Gemini and Matthew Morgenstern of SRI. I led the project. Shortly thereafter, Teresa Lunt joined SRI and began working closely with me on the project. She was followed by Bill Shockley, who joined us on the Gemini side. Selim Akl of Queen's University also worked with us during his year's sabbatical at SRI. (Others have joined since my departure.) At some point, we named the project SeaView (for secure data views) in honor of our project lunches on the Monterey coast.

Although the initial task was to develop an informal policy at the user level, the assurance requirement drove our approach from the beginning. We decided early on that we would support labeling at the granularity of individual elements, and began looking at how we would store the data in order to get the needed assurance. Initially, we thought we would make elements the basic objects of protection, but found that this approach led to all sorts of difficulties because the elements of a tuple are not independent entities. At some point, I saw how multilevel relations could be automatically decomposed into single-level relations such that the decomposition supported our requirements for polyinstantiation [DLS+87]. The complete relation, or a view of the relation at a lower classification, could be restored using the relational operators. For example, a SECRET view of a relation containing both SECRET and TOP-SECRET data could be constructed by composing the single-level SECRET relations. With this approach, each single-level relation could be stored in a single-level segment managed by an operating system security kernel that partitions the data segments by their access classes. Our assurance was thus obtained from an OS kernel[DLS+88]!

In the fall of 1987, I left SRI to join Digital. Although the SeaView project had one year to go, I was confident that Teresa would lead it to a successful completion. It then occurred to me that SeaView had evolved from a state of enforcing both mandatory and discretionary security through security filters, namely views (including entire relations), to a state of enforcing mandatory security through partitioning and composition, and discretionary security through filtering. If we were to enforce both types of security by partitioning and composition, we could obtain a higher level of assurance for discretionary security and unify mandatory and discretionary security. I briefly mentioned this approach in my talk on the SeaView security model at the 1987 Symposium on Privacy and Security, and named it MeadowView. I do not know if it is a good idea; it may be that the requirements are inherently different and require different approaches.

In 1982 I had thought that the problems of inference and aggregation were best approached through views. By 1985 I seriously doubted the viability of this approach, although I was still convinced that the constraints inherent in view definitions provided a basis for addressing the problems. (A view definition can be regarded as a constraint relating derived data to other data that are stored or derived.) Matthew Morgenstern had seen the value of constraints as a general means of approaching the inference problem, so when the U.S. Army, CECOM asked me to investigate the application of AI technologies to database security, Matthew and I explored his ideas about constraints as well as a logic programming approach suggested by Neil Rowe. It soon became clear that constraints provided exactly the right basis for addressing the inference problem, because they represent the real-world semantic relationships among data, and it is those relationships that are exploited during inference. Our results were encouraging, showing that classification and integrity constraints, expressed either as statements in a logic programming language or in the constraint expression language developed by Matthew, could be analyzed to uncover inference problems [DM86].

In summary, I have shifted from views to constraints as a basis both for classifying data and for uncovering inference problems.

Acknowledgements: I am grateful to Teresa Lunt and Peter Neumann for their helpful suggestions.

7.2 References

[DAH+87] D.E. Denning, S.G. Akl, M. Heckman, T.F. Lunt, M. Morgenstern, P. G. Neumann, and R. R. Schell. Views for multilevel database security. *IEEE Transactions on Software Engineering*, 13(2), February 1987.

[DLS+87] D.E. Denning, T.F. Lunt, R.R. Schell, M. Heckman, and W.R. Shockley. A multilevel relational data model. In *Proceedings of the 1987 IEEE Symposium on Security and Privacy*, April 1987.

[DLS+88] D.E. Denning, T.F. Lunt, R.R. Schell, W.R. Shockley, and M. Heckman. The SeaView security model. In *Proceedings of the 1988 IEEE Symposium on Security and Privacy*, April 1988.

[DM86] D.E. Denning and M. Morgenstern. Military database technology study: AI techniques for security and reliability. *Technical report*, Computer Science Laboratory, SRI International, Menlo Park, California, 1986.

[GM84] J.A. Goguen and J. Meseguer. Unwinding and inference control. In *Proceedings of the 1984 IEEE Symposium on Security and Privacy*, 1984.

[NBF+80] P.G. Neumann, R.S. Boyer, R.J. Feiertag, K.N. Levitt, and L. Robinson. A provably secure operating system: The system, its applications, and proofs. *Technical Report CSL-116*, 2nd Ed., Computer Science Laboratory, SRI International, Menlo Park, California, May 1980.

8

Discussion: Pros and Cons of the Various Approaches

Dorothy E. Denning[1] and William R. Shockley[2]

8.1 Introduction

This report provides a summary of the issues raised in an afternoon discussion at the First Invitational Workshop on Database Security, hosted by SRI International in Menlo Park, CA. The topic of the discussion was to review the pros and cons of the various approaches to the design of secure database systems as described by the speakers that morning. However, the actual discussion quickly narrowed to the problems of aggregation and inference, particularly with regards to proposals for handling these problems in the systems described. Because these topics became primary areas of study throughout the workshop, the session described below must be regarded as only a preliminary discussion of issues that were explored in greater detail (and with greater collective insight!) in later sessions. For this reason, we have felt it appropriate to append a section entitled "retrospective," relating the preliminary topics raised during our discussion session with the insights gained later in the workshop.

8.2 Inference Problem

The inference problem arises in a multilevel database system whenever a user can deduce information about the state of a high-sensitivity datum from data of lower sensitivity. Although this definition encompasses such traditional information flow channels as model flaws and covert storage channels, it is specifically intended to describe inferences using common-sense knowledge about the real world that an unauthorized user might be able to make viewing only the low sensitivity data. Two problems amenable to technical analysis were identified: first, how to detect the potential for their existence given a complicated, multilevel data design; and second,

[1]Georgetown University
[2]Digital Equipment Corporation

what approaches might exist for dealing with them once they are found.

Statistical channels were mentioned, although there was little follow-up discussion regarding them. A statistical channel occurs when individual records of high-sensitivity can be deduced from statistical information about the entire collection of records, which is released at a lower sensitivity.

8.3 Aggregation Problem

The aggregation problem arises whenever the sensitivity of an aggregate of data is strictly higher than any of its parts. We will refer to such aggregates as "abnormal aggregates," to distinguish them from "normal aggregates," whose sensitivity is the "high-water mark" of its parts. Whereas normal aggregates are typically handled correctly without extraordinary measures by most proposed designs, abnormal aggregates, if supported at all, require specialized treatment.

A common approach for dealing with the aggregation problem is to declare any policy incorporating such a notion to be unsound. In effect, this position asserts that any sound policy for the classification of data will always classify any collection of data at the high-water mark of its constituents. The problem with this position is that classification authorities, in many instances, strenuously resist this position even though it is apparent that they understand the mathematical basis for it, and are unable (or unwilling) to provide a rationale for the classification policy. The alternate stance (which seemed to be the position of most of the discussion participants) was that if a technically informed sponsor and/or end user has a need for abnormally classified aggregates, then it is the responsibility of the designer to assume that the problem is real, however inconsistent it may seem at first. The problem may be obscured if it is not the aggregate per se that is more sensitive, but rather what can be inferred from it about information that may be external to the database.

Some ad hoc classifications of abnormal aggregations have been advanced in previous work by the participants. Hinke [Hin88], for example, distinguishes between "inference aggregation" (related to inferences using common-sense knowledge), and "cardinality aggregation" (the "phonebook problem", described below.) The Seaview project [DAH+87a] distinguished between "qualitative associations," which aggregate attributes of a database or records in different relations, and "quantitative associations," which aggregate records of the same relation (same as cardinality aggregation). All of these classifications are somewhat tentative, and there was no clear-cut acceptance by the group of any particular taxonomy for abnormal aggregates.

Statistical inference, as described earlier, is sometimes mistaken as an instance of abnormal aggregation in that it involves inferences of data from statistics computed over aggregates of data. However, the problem is actually the opposite of abnormal aggregation, because a statistic is released with a sensitivity lower than the data values from which it is derived. The aggregate is classified normally as the least upper bound of the classes of its constituent values, but the statistic is released at a lower level on the grounds that it loses enough information about the individual elements that inference is not possible.

8.3.1 Problem Instances

The group discussed several real-world instances of abnormal aggregates. The first instance discussed was what many call the "phone book problem." Many agencies handle their phone directories as sensitive, although individual phone numbers or small collections of phone numbers (in association with the individuals having those phone numbers) may be released as unclassified data. In the limiting case, it is admitted (by the classification authority) that an individual or collection of individuals might indeed, through diligent effort, collect all of the phone numbers, reconstructing the sensitive phone book from unclassified data. The phone book is an example of a cardinality aggregate; the operative policy appears to be an arbitrary limit on the number of phone numbers that may be released to a given individual at any one time. As Hinke observes, "it is not always clear why N elements of a set, such as a phone book, are classified at one level, while M elements are less classified, where $M \leq N$."

The phone book problem is aggravated by the difficulty of transfering a policy that seems plausible in a manual environment to the automated environment. The rationale for implementing such a policy in a manual environment seems to be that it would require a significant amount of effort for an uncleared individual to compile a significant section of the phone book from individually released phone numbers. In a computer system, it is difficult to see how a commensurate barrier can be erected, given the intrinsic capability of a computer to extract and compile information efficiently and rapidly. A Trojan Horse, for instance, could compile the complete phone book within a matter of seconds or minutes, given an unrestricted capability to query the system for individual phone numbers. Moreover, multiple users can operate in collusion to reconstruct the phone book.

It would appear that a parameter that is implicitly taken for granted in the manual system (that the available bandwidth is "low enough") must be made explicit for an equivalent automated system. Unfortunately, classification authorities have been reluctant to express a policy for what constitutes an acceptable bandwidth.

A similar instance of abnormal aggregation was identified by one of the military participants: an organization of an agency (e.g., the U.S. Army) is classified in aggregate, while the name or designation of any particular command is unclassified. The individual names are unclassified mainly because classification would require massive change to the message-handling and mailing systems. Yet the entire collection of names currently in use must be classified, because information can be inferred about current force levels, etc. Here again, the classification authorities seem to be weighing risk against work factor, although not precisely enough to be amenable to a straightforward policy transfer to computer systems.

A final example discussed was a technical data repository, in which a collection of technical documents (e.g., nuclear weapons data) contained in an archival repository might be highly sensitive in aggregate (i.e., only highly-cleared individuals might have direct access to the repository itself), although individual documents are each of lower sensitivity than the aggregate (that is, individual documents can be released by the archive librarians to individuals of lower clearance than the librarians themselves.) In this case, the aggregation problem might be solved by classifying the repository catalogue at a level higher than any of the individual documents. A user's request for an individual document might be freely honored, but the user is not given access to the catalogue of which documents are available.

8.3.2 Two Approaches

The group considered two general methods for supporting abnormal classification policies: classify the elements comprising an aggregate at the lower element level, marking up collections of data as they are released by the system, vs. classify the elements at the higher aggregate level, downgrading individual data elements as they are released by the system.

The Honeywell architecture [STD88] was a clear-cut example of the first sort of system, the SeaView formal security policy model [DLS+88] uses the second approach, and most currently planned near-term systems (including the SeaView near-term design [LSS+88]) do not provide explicit support for abnormal aggregates.

The consensus of the group appeared to favor the second approach on the grounds that it would be safer in the sense that the labels associated with the data would be conservatively high, reducing the risk that some exploitable flaw in the TCB interface would release raw data (unhandled by the regrader) to a subject with an inappropriately low label.

Several group participants recommended making different options available, ranging from simply accepting the risk, to reclassifying enough of the data contributing to the inference to block its availability. Intermediate ground exists: one could reclassify enough information to decrease the certainty of the inference without removing it altogether.

8.4 Retrospective

A few comments relating the topics discussed in this early session to the remainder of the workshop seem appropriate. These comments, of course, reflect the opinions of the authors and are not necessarily a group consensus.

In retrospect, one major topic seemed to emerge as the "theme" of the workshop: the problem of data classification. Traditional access control techniques for mandatory security do a good job of ensuring that unauthorized information flows do not occur once data in the system are properly labeled. However, they do not solve the problem of labeling data when they are entered into the system. It became increasingly obvious, as the workshop proceeded, that in order to effectively utilize a multilevel secure database system, the system must support the classification of new data through classification constraints or similar mechanisms for either automating and/or aiding the human responsible for establishing the classification of incoming data.

The traditional method for classifying new data entered by a user is to classify the data at the user's session level, requiring the user to change session level to enter data that has a different classification. Whereas this approach works fine for many applications, others would greatly benefit from automated or semi-automated classification methods for entering data that are not uniformly classified, particularly when the classification policy is complex.

The problems of aggregation and inference thus would appear to be but a small corner of a much larger context: what languages and techniques are appropriate for expressing and enforcing complex, and potentially inconsistent, classification guidelines? While it would be premature to claim much insight into this problem, some preliminary hypotheses can be stated:

First, it would appear inappropriate to use automated or semi-automated classifiers as the basis for mandatory access controls per se. That is, once a label has been determined for incoming data, existing technology (perhaps tailored to support database operations efficiently) would seem to suffice for the enforcement of access to the data. The division of the "secure database problem" into access control and classification constraint subproblems seems a fairly natural one in hindsight, but the understanding that these are distinct problems with potentially distinct solutions has come only recently.

Second, it would appear desirable to encapsulate the access control enforcement within a traditional security kernel so that the high assurance that can be attained for such a kernel is not disturbed by whatever is done to support the classification of new data. (The assignment of a label by an automated classifier, or upon the advice of such a classifier, is obviously security critical, but at least one can say with assurance that once a label is assigned, access to the data is enforced with a high degree of assurance.) In effect, one is separating assurance into two pieces – assurance that a label is correct, and assurance that access controls are correctly enforced based upon whatever the labels are.

Although the problem of analyzing classification constraints for consistency, completeness, and inference problems is likely to be an intractable problem in its fullest generality, the SeaView work shows that it is possible to attain consistency and completeness for a fairly general class of constraints [AD87,DLS+88], and Denning and Morgenstern have shown that it is possible to express and analyze constraints for consistency and inference problems [DM86,Mor88].

We believe that the data classification problem is the next key problem that should be addressed by the database security community. It is not at all clear that the techniques implied by the Trusted Computer System Evaluation Criteria are appropriate for the evaluation of automated classification tools: they are specifically designed to address the evaluation of systems enforcing access controls, and are effective primarily because the policy to be enforced is relatively simple. The indicated program for research in this area would seem to be one of describing, then prototyping, languages for the description of classification rules and constraints, and using the tools within the context of multilevel database systems that enforce mandatory access controls. Criteria for the evaluation of classification tools should wait until worked examples of such tools have been constructed and experience has been gained in their verification and usability.

8.5 References

[AD87] S.G. Akl and D.E. Denning. Checking classification constraints for consistency and completeness. In *Proceedings of the 1987 IEEE Symposium on Security and Privacy*, April 1987.

[DAH+87] D.E. Denning, S.G. Akl, M. Heckman, T.F. Lunt, M. Morgenstern, P.G. Neumann, and R.R. Schell. Views for multilevel database security. *IEEE Transactions on Software Engineering*, 13(2), February 1987.

[DLS+88] D.E. Denning, T.F. Lunt, R.R. Schell, W.R. Shockley, and M. Heckman. The SeaView security model. In *Proceedings of the 1988 IEEE Symposium on Security and Privacy*, April 1988.

[DM86] D.E. Denning and M. Morgenstern. Military database technology study: AI techniques for security and reliability. *Technical report*, Computer Science Laboratory, SRI International, Menlo Park, California, 1986.

[Hin88] T.H. Hinke. Inference aggregation detection in database management systems. In *Proceedings of the 1988 IEEE Symposium on Security and Privacy*, April 1988.

[LSS+88] T.F. Lunt, R.R. Schell, W.R. Shockley, M. Heckman, and D. Warren. A near-term design for the SeaView multilevel database system. In *Proceedings of the 1988 IEEE Symposium on Security and Privacy*, April 1988.

[Mor88] M. Morgenstern. Controlling logical inference in multilevel database systems. In *Proceedings of the 1988 IEEE Symposium on Security and Privacy*, April 1988.

[STD88] P. Stachour, B. Thuraisingham, and P. Dwyer. Update processing in LDV. In *Proceedings of the 11th National Computer Security Conference*, Baltimore, Maryland, October 1988.

9

The Homework Problem

Rae K. Burns[1]

ABSTRACT The following "homework problem," phrased below as a take-home exam, was the centerpiece of the workshop. The workshop participants broke up into three groups and worked late into the night on this homework problem.

HI-TECH University
Database Security I

Final Exam (Take Home)
Due Date: April 1, 1988

The example database for this exam is taken from our primary textbook, Date's *An Introduction to Database Systems*, Volume 1, Chapters 16 and 27 (p. 279 in the third edition). The description from the text is as follows:

> In this example we are assuming that the company maintains an education department whose function is to run a number of training courses. Each course is offered at a number of different locations within the company. The database contains details both of offerings already given and of offerings scheduled to be given in the future. The details are as follows:
>
> - For each course: course number (unique), course title, course description, details of prerequisite courses (if any), and details of all offerings (past and planned);
> - For each prerequisite course for a given course: course number and title;
> - For each offering of a given course: date, location, format (e.g., full-time or half-time), details of all teachers, and details of all students;
> - For each teacher of a given offering: employee number and name;
> - For each student of a given offering: employee number, name, and grade.

[1]MITRE Corporation

Each exam question is based on this database application; each succeeding question builds on the answers to the prior questions. You are advised to read the entire exam first, and then to proceed to answer each question in turn.

1. *(5 pts)* Develop a data model diagram or an entity-relationship diagram for the education database described above.

2. *(5 pts)* Design a relational schema for the database. Include primary keys, foreign keys, and attribute data types. Use an "SQL-like" syntax, with any extensions that seem appropriate.

3. *(30 pts)* Using an "SQL-like" syntax, express the following application security policy, based on the relational schema developed in question 2. The policy statements assume only two levels of security: unclassified and secret.

   (a) Some courses are secret; all information about a secret course (including details of offerings, teachers, and students) is secret.

   (b) All course offerings at location "Pentagon" are secret.

   (c) If a course has a secret prerequisite, then the course is also secret.

   (d) Course information may be inserted, modified, or deleted only by a course administrator. At least one course administrator is cleared for secret data.

   (e) A course clerk enters offering, enrollment and student grade information; however, once entered into the database, such information may be modified or deleted only by a course administrator. No course clerks are cleared for secret data.

   (f) If a student has taken a secret offering, then the student's transcript is secret.

   (g) A student's grade point average (GPA) is unclassified but may be accessed only by a course administrator.

4. *(10 pts)* Briefly discuss the implications and ambiguities of at least two of the security policy statements above.

5. *(10 pts)* Specify two additional, or alternative, security policy statements that would be appropriate for the corporate education database.

6. *(40 pts)* Informally map four of the application-specific security policy statements from the previous questions (3 and 5) to a general DBMS security policy model. Discuss the relative success of the DBMS model in expressing and enforcing the application-specific policy. Address at least one data entry operation.

EXTRA CREDIT!

The extra credit question is based on the article by Morgenstern ("Controlling Logical Inference in Multilevel Database Systems," *Proceedings of the 1988 IEEE Symposium on Security and Privacy*, pp. 245-255) which was discussed during our special seminar on the problems of inference within database applications.

Define the sphere of influence (SOI) for the corporate education database. Localize and describe the sources of inference channels. Revise the database schema design and security statements as needed to remove any open inference channels.

10

Report on the Homework Problem

Rae K. Burns[1]

10.1 Introduction

One evening during the workshop, the participants divided up into three small groups to discuss and analyze a database security "homework problem". The questions focused on the security requirements of an example database application. While the example itself is not particularly realistic, it exhibits a fairly typical database design and a set of security requirements that are characteristic of commercial and DoD applications. Its primary advantage over the examples that have been used in the security literature to date is that it represents a more complete application, and not just a single file or relation.

The challenge of the homework problem was to formulate the application's security requirements in terms of proposed security policies for database management systems. In other words, the problem was to use the expressiveness inherent in a DBMS security policy to state the policy for this particular application. However, most participants found that the database application design process itself was unexpectedly complex and challenging, particularly when security requirements were considered in conjunction with other basic application requirements. The attempt to derive a concise and correct statement of the application's security design revealed numerous issues that impacted the overall design of the application.

The remainder of this report summarizes the security issues, database design trade-offs, and DBMS security features that were discussed during the homework sessions. The "answers" to several of the questions have been expanded beyond what was discussed in the limited time available during the workshop. In particular, a list of generic application requirements, stated in terms of the relational data model, has been derived from the security requirements of the example database.

---

[1]MITRE Corporation

10.2 The Example Database

The example database for the homework problem was taken from Date's *An Introduction to Database Systems*, Volume 1, Chapters 16 and 27 (page 279 in the third edition). Date used this example to illustrate the different logical schemas that would be needed for the hierarchical, network, and relational data models and to provide an example application for his Universal Data Language (UDL). The description from the text is as follows:

> In this example we are assuming that the company maintains an education department whose function is to run a number of training courses. Each course is offered at a number of different locations within the company. The database contains details both of offerings already given and of offerings scheduled to be given in the future. The details are as follows:
>
> - For each course: course number (unique), title, course description, details of prerequisite courses (if any), and details of all offerings (past and planned);
> - For each prerequisite course for a given course: course number and title;
> - For each offering of a given course: date, location, format (e.g., full-time or half-time), details of all teachers, and details of all students;
> - For each teacher of a given offering: employee number and name.
> - For each student of a given offering: employee number, name, and grade.

The homework problem was composed of six questions and an extra credit question dealing with inference. Each question built on the answers to the previous question. The first two questions related to the basic database design, and the third introduced the application's security requirements. The fourth and fifth questions analyzed and extended the application's security requirements, and the final question related the application security policy statements to a general DBMS security policy. The "extra credit" question was included to focus on the need to address inference concerns within the database design process.

- **Question 1** *(5 pts)* Develop a data model diagram or an entity-relationship diagram for the education database described above.

Figure 10.1 is the basic E-R diagram that is suggested by the application description.

The process of defining an entity-relationship diagram brought out several questions and alternatives, independent of any security requirements.

It was determined that an OFFERING is a "weak" entity in that it cannot exist without a corresponding COURSE. The question of the status of GRADE was also a concern - is it a separate entity or an attribute of the STUDENT relationship? Finally, while there may be a conceptual difference between a past OFFERING and a future OFFERING, within the database the logical data is identical for both.

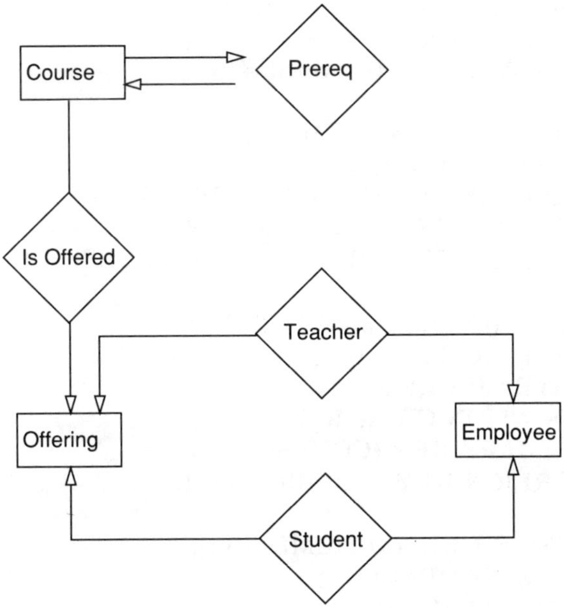

FIGURE 10.1. E-R diagram.

- **Question 2** *(5 pts)* Design a relational schema for the database. Include primary keys, foreign keys, and attribute data types. Use an "SQL-like" syntax, with any extensions that seem appropriate.

The following is the relational schema as presented by Date (p. 453). Primary and foreign keys are taken from the UDL schemas he presents (p. 456).

```
COURSE (COURSE# NUMBER(4),
     TITLE CHAR(30))
     PRIMARY_KEY (COURSE#);

PREREQ (COURSE# NUMBER(4),
     PRE# NUMBER(4))
     PRIMARY_KEY(COURSE#, PRE#)
     FOREIGN_KEY(COURSE.COURSE#)
     FOREIGN_KEY(PRE# COURSE.COURSE#);

OFFERING (COURSE# NUMBER(4))
     OFF# NUMBER(4),
     DATE CHAR(8),
     LOCATION CHAR(10))
     PRIMARY_KEY (COURSE#, OFF#)
     FOREIGN_KEY (COURSE.COURSE#);

TEACHER (COURSE# NUMBER(4),
     OFF# NUMBER(4),
     EMP# NUMBER(4))
     PRIMARY_KEY(COURSE#, OFF#, EMP#)
     FOREIGN_KEY(OFFERING.COURSE, OFFERING.OFF#)
     FOREIGN_KEY(EMPLOYEE.EMP#);

STUDENT (COURSE# NUMBER(4),
     OFF# NUMBER(4),
     EMP# NUMBER(4),
     GRADE DECIMAL(4,2))
     PRIMARY_KEY(COURSE#, EMP#)
     FOREIGN_KEY(OFFERING.COURSE#, OFFERING.OFF#)
```

```
    FOREIGN_KEY(EMPLOYEE.EMP#);

EMPLOYEE (EMP# NUMBER(4),
    NAME CHAR(30))
    PRIMARY_KEY (EMP#);
```

The workshop participants developed schemas that had slight variations from Date's schema, based on their interpretations of the database description. The main variation was the assumption that OFF# was unique, independent of the related COURSE#. This led to some simplifications, but could be taken as an implication that an offering could exist independent of any course. If COURSE# were not part of the primary key of the OFFERING relation, then the foreign keys of STUDENT and TEACHER would contain a reference to COURSE.COURSE# instead of OFFERING.COURSE#.

Another variation was an assumption that a student could take more that one offering of the same course. In Date's schema, the primary key of the TEACHER relation is (COURSE#, OFF#, and EMP#), while for the STUDENT relation, the primary key is only (COURSE#, EMP#). The implication of Date's key definitions is that an employee may teach several offerings of a course, but may take only one offering.

There were several other variations that were made; however these were determined by interpretations of the security requirements and will discussed as part of Question Four.

- **Question 3** *(30 pts)* Using an "SQL-like" syntax, express the following application security policy, based on the relational schema developed in Question 2. The policy statements assume only two levels of security: UNCLASSIFIED and SECRET.

    1. Some courses are SECRET; all information about a SECRET course (including details of offerings, teachers, and students) is SECRET.
    2. All course offerings at location "Pentagon" are SECRET.
    3. If a course has a SECRET prerequisite, then the course is also SECRET.
    4. Course information may be inserted, modified, or deleted only by a course administrator. At least one course administrator is cleared for SECRET data.
    5. A course clerk enters offering, enrollment and student grade information; however, once entered into the database, such information may be modified or deleted only by a course administrator. No course clerks are cleared for SECRET data.
    6. If a student has taken a SECRET offering, then the student's transcript is SECRET.

7. A student's grade point average (GPA) is UNCLASSIFIED but may be accessed only by a course administrator.

The "SQL-like" notation used by the participants resembled classification constraints and update triggers. In general, the expressions were longer and more complex than had been expected. The exercise of attempting to express the security requirements within the context of a relational language illustrated the difficulty of adequately formalizing the application's security requirements. The individual expressions that were generated will not be detailed here. However, the following is an example of the type of expressions that were derived for Requirement 3:

```
ON UPDATE PREREQ
        SET PREREQ.CLASS TO COURSE.CLASS
        WHERE PREREQ.COURSE# = COURSE.COURSE#;

ON UPDATE OFFERING
        SET OFFERING.CLASS TO COURSE.CLASS
        WHERE OFFERING.COURSE# = COURSE.COURSE#;

ON UPDATE TEACHER
        SET TEACHER.CLASS TO COURSE.CLASS
        WHERE TEACHER.COURSE# = COURSE.COURSE#;

ON UPDATE STUDENT
        SET STUDENT.CLASS TO COURSE.CLASS
        WHERE STUDENT.COURSE# = COURSE.COURSE#;
```

Implicit in most of the expressions was the use of tuple-level labels, rather than element- or relation-level labels. For this application, it is generally the identification of a tuple (i.e., the tuple's primary key) that reflects the classification of the entire tuple; therefore, tuple-level labels provide adequate granularity.

- **Question 4** *(10 pts)* Briefly discuss the implications and ambiguities of at least two of the security policy statements above.

The discussion groups found much ambiguity, incompleteness, and potential information leakage with description of the application's security requirements. Some of the discussions resulted in a reformulation of the relational schema in order to close leakage channels and clarify the application requirements. In order to better understand the security requirements, each of the requirements will be discussed here.

1. Some courses are SECRET; all information about a SECRET course (including details of offerings, teachers, and students) is SECRET.

There was some confusion as to what constituted "all information"; however, the general need to classify the data from several relations based on the course number was clear. It was not apparent exactly why some courses would be SECRET—presumably the decision is made by the course administrator when the course is defined.

An issue that is not addressed in the requirements is the question of constraining the enrollment in a SECRET offering to only those employees who are cleared for SECRET. Certainly this could be handled manually; however, to automate the constraint would require the addition of a clearance attribute for EMPLOYEE.

2. All course offerings at location "Pentagon" are SECRET.

   There was some question as to whether or not location should be a separate "entity", since it participated in a specific security context. However, it does not actually represent an "application entity"; conceptually, the LOCATION is simply an attribute of an OFFERING. For this requirement, the value of the LOCATION attribute impacts the classification of other attributes, specifically the attributes of the primary key. The implication, then, is that even the existence of an offering at the Pentagon is SECRET. This would mean that the primary key attributes of an OFFERING tuple must be SECRET if the location is the Pentagon. (See Question Five for a discussion of an alternative requirement based on LOCATION.)

3. If a course has a SECRET prerequisite, then the course is also SECRET.

   This requirement could also be expressed as: "The classification of a course must dominate the classification of all of its prerequisite courses." If a course were initially UNCLASSIFIED, but subsequently a SECRET course were added to its list of prerequisites, then either the update would have to be rejected or the course would have to be upgraded to SECRET (resulting in a "disappearing course" for non-SECRET users). In the context of this application, it would be more appropriate to create a new, different, course which would be SECRET, and phase out the old course by simply not offering it.

4. Course information may be inserted, modified, or deleted only by a course administrator. At least one course administrator is cleared for SECRET data.

   This requirement reflects the need for discretionary access controls based on the role an individual assumes within the application's context. Requirement 5 defines the additional role of a clerk, so that there are only two fundamental classes of users for this application.

5. A course clerk enters offering, enrollment and student grade information; however, once entered into the database, such information may

be modified or deleted only by a course administrator. No course clerks are cleared for SECRET data.

The role of the course clerk is significantly more constrained than that of the course administrator; the clerk may only insert information into the database and may not change it once it has been entered. The stated requirement does not delineate clearly what information a clerk would enter, as opposed to the information that a course administrator would maintain. There is an implicit assumption that information available to a course clerk is limited, and that therefore inferences about SECRET courses would also be limited.

Since a clerk is not cleared for SECRET data, another implication inherent in the requirement is that some information about SECRET courses is not actually classified until it enters the database. In particular, the COURSE# and OFF# in themselves could not be SECRET; otherwise it would be a security violation for an uncleared clerk to even be aware of them. The procedural solution, "Clear the Clerk", was advanced frequently during the workshop discussions; however, there were aspects of the requirement that could not be solved simply by having a clerk that was cleared for the data.

Much of the data entered by the clerk is "out of context" until it actually enters the database. For instance, an employee's grade would be entered with only a COURSE#, OFF#, and EMP#. Other "real world" examples of this type of data included an individual billing record of the amount of fuel loaded on a particular (SECRET) aircraft, or a weekly time record of an individual working on a (SECRET) project. The classification of the information does not occur "in the field", but rather when the data is collected together and made available in the context of a logical database.

An additional issue of batch processing of input data is reflected in this requirement. Some functions of the course clerk may actually be performed by a batch program. For instance, grade information might be recorded on machine-readable tab cards by the course instructor. The course clerk then would simply run a program that loads all of the grade information into the database.

A cryptographic alternative to "clearing the clerk" was also discussed. This involved generating a key that bound the student's EMP# and the OFFERING cryptographically. The key could then be UNCLASSIFIED and used by the clerk for all data entry that related to the employee's enrollment.

6. If a student has taken a SECRET offering, then the student's transcript is SECRET.

The intended definition of a "transcript" is not clear in this requirement. It might be simply the final piece of paper containing an employee's grades, or it could be interpreted more broadly as any retrieval of an employee's grades.

There are several problems with this requirement. First, there is the inference relationship with the next requirement that the employee's GPA be treated as UNCLASSIFIED. Second, there is the problem that occurs when an employee takes his/her first SECRET offering. Does the record of all grades need to be upgraded? A disappearing transcript might be an interesting occurrence to be monitored by hostile intelligence organizations. Third, if all grades, not just from SECRET courses, are to be considered SECRET, then access to retrieve any of the employee's grades must be constrained by the high-water mark of the set of offerings attended.

One alternative proposed was to generate (or maintain?) two GPAs, one for just the UNCLASSIFIED courses, and one that included all courses. This would negate requirement (7), since each of the GPAs would reflect the classification of the data from which it was derived. However, a course administrator would have to be cleared to SECRET in order to generate the "true" GPA for an employee who had taken SECRET courses.

7. A student's grade point average (GPA) is UNCLASSIFIED but may be accessed only by a course administrator.

   The GPA is a statistic that is generated based on the contents of the STUDENT relation. Since it would be possible to infer information about a grade in a SECRET course from a GPA containing all courses and a transcript containing just the UNCLASSIFIED courses, there is a potential inference channel if the UNCLASSIFIED portion of the transcript were available.

- **Question 5** *(10 pts)* Specify two additional, or alternative, security policy statements that would be appropriate for the corporate education database.

During the workshop sessions there was little discussion of alternative or additional requirements except as needed to clarify the requirements and address the "holes" in the requirements. However, there are several requirements that are interesting in that they exemplify additional generic database security requirements. These will be discussed here briefly.

1. The fact that employee "Smith" is one of the teachers for an offering of (unclassified) course "Encryption Technology" is SECRET.

   This requirement illustrates a relationship between two application entities that is more highly classified than either of the entities themselves. The TEACHER relationship may be classified higher than either the EMPLOYEE or OFFERING entities.

2. Assuming a CLEARANCE attribute in the EMPLOYEE relation, the CLEARANCE of an EMPLOYEE must dominate the classification of all OFFERINGS that he/she teaches or enrolls in.

   This requirement simply states that an employee must be cleared for all of the appropriate offerings.

3. The location of all courses taught at the Pentagon is SECRET.

   This requirement differs from Requirement 2 since only the location, not the offering itself, is classified. With element-level labeling, this requirement could be expressed by classifying the LOCATION attribute independent of the classification of the tuple's primary key. With only tuple- level labeling, a separate OFF-LOC relation would be needed that contained only the OFFERING primary key attributes and the LOCATION attribute. Then all tuples having a LOCATION of "Pentagon" could be labeled as SECRET in the OFF-LOC relation, and a view joining the OFFERING and OFF-LOC relations would provide the equivalent of element-level labeling.

4. Employees are authorized to query the database for information (locations, grades, instructors) about the courses and offerings they are enrolled in or have taken.

   This is one of a number of additional roles which would be appropriate in an actual database application, particularly as the scope of the database was expanded.

- **Question 6** *(40 pts)* Informally map four of the application-specific security policy statements from the previous Questions 3 and 5 to a general DBMS security policy model. Discuss the relative success of the DBMS model in expressing and enforcing the application-specific policy. Address at least one data entry operation.

Only one of the discussion groups (a really determined group!) addressed the applicability of a general DBMS security policy model to meeting the security needs of this application. For the purpose of this report, each security requirement, and some of the alternative requirements from above, will be restated in terms of the relational data model. A generic statement of the requirement is included to illustrate the types of security requirements that will need to be supported by a multilevel secure DBMS. The term "access class" is used to indicate a sensitivity label or data classification.

It should be noted that only a few of the generic statements are directly supported by any currently proposed DBMS security policies.

1. Some courses are SECRET; all information about a SECRET course (including details of offerings, teachers, and students) is SECRET.

This security requirement involves the extensive use of foreign keys. In particular, the course number is a foreign key in all of the associated relations that must be uniformly classified:

> **Foreign Key Dependency:** The access class of a tuple's primary key is determined by the access class of a particular foreign key.

2. All course offerings at location "Pentagon" are SECRET.

   Since even the existence of an offering at the Pentagon is SECRET, the value of the LOCATION attribute determines the classification of the primary key attributes of the OFFERING relation:

   > **Attribute Value Dependency:** The access class of a tuple's primary key is determined by the data value of a specific attribute.

3. If a course has a SECRET prerequisite, then the course is also SECRET.

   In relational terms, this requirement could be interpreted as stating that a tuple may be inserted into the PREREQ relation only when the classification of the foreign key tuple for COURSE# dominates the classification of the foreign key tuple for the PRE# attribute. In this case, the classification of the primary key attributes of a PREREQ tuple (COURSE#, PRE#) is constrained to be dominated by the classification of a single foreign key tuple, the one referred to by the COURSE#:

   > **Key Dominance Constraint:** The access class of a tuple's primary key is constrained to be dominated by the access class of a specific foreign key.

4. Course information may be inserted, modified, or deleted only by a course administrator. At least one course administrator is cleared for SECRET data.

   Individual users of an application generally function in several distinct roles:

   > **Role-based DAC:** The discretionary access requirements are based on the role of the user within the application.

5. A course clerk enters offering, enrollment and student grade information; however, once entered into the database, such information may be modified or deleted only by a course administrator. No course clerks are cleared for SECRET data.

   In database terms, this requirement reflects a need for the automatic upgrade of the classification of data as it is entered into a database. Once the data is within the logical context of the application's database, it can easily be related to other information. Therefore, the data being entered may actually become more highly classified than the user or process that enters it.

In this example, the COURSE# provides a reference to a foreign key tuple. The access class of that tuple can be used to automatically upgrade the OFFERING, STUDENT, and TEACHER tuples as they are entered by the course clerk:

> **Automatic Upgrade:** The access class of data is determined by its application context, not strictly by the access class of the subject inserting the data ("write-up").

6. If a student has taken a SECRET offering, then the student's transcript is SECRET.

   If a "transcript" is viewed as a select statement that retrieves all of the tuples of the STUDENT relation that pertain to a particular employee, then this requirement prohibits the retrieval of only the UNCLASSIFIED tuples whenever there are SECRET tuples. In other words, if an uncleared user attempts to produce the transcript of an employee who has taken a SECRET course, then that user should not even see the data for the UNCLASSIFIED courses:

   > **Tuple Set Dependency:** A subject's access class must dominate the highest access class of the set of tuples to be accessed.

7. A student's grade point average (GPA) is UNCLASSIFIED but may be accessed only by a course administrator.

   The STUDENT relation contains COURSE#, OFF#, EMP#, and GRADE. Note that all of the attributes except GRADE form the primary key, and, in addition, are foreign keys. When GRADE is associated solely with EMP#, it is UNCLASSIFIED (e.g., even a sequence of grades, not associated with individual courses, could be UNCLASSIFIED). When a GRADE is associated with the COURSE# and OFF# of a SECRET offering, it is SECRET. When viewed in this manner, the issue is not simply one of aggregation, but rather one of association. It is the association of an employee with a SECRET offering that is classified:

   > **Entity Association:** The access class of the non-key attributes of a relation that represents an association among two or more application entities, of varying access classes, is determined by the access class of the entity being referenced.

8. The fact that employee "Smith" is one of the teachers for an offering of (UNCLASSIFIED) course "Encryption Technology" is SECRET.

   This requirement classifies an individual fact that relates two foreign keys:

   > **Relationship Dominance:** The access class of a tuple's primary key may strictly dominate the access classes of related foreign keys.

9. Assuming a CLEARANCE attribute in the EMPLOYEE relation, the CLEARANCE of an EMPLOYEE must dominate the classification of all OFFERINGS that he/she teaches or enrolls in.

   If each employee's clearance were maintained within the database in a format compatible with the DBMS classification format, it could be used as a security parameter:

   > **Access Class Attribute:** The access class of a tuple's primary key is constrained to be dominated by an access class attribute in a particular foreign key tuple.

10. The location of all courses offered at the Pentagon is SECRET.

    In this alternative requirement, it is only the location attribute that is classified, not the primary key attributes:

    > **Attribute Classification:** The access class of an attribute value is determined by the attribute/value pair.

11. Employees are authorized to query the database for information (locations, grades, instructors) about the courses and offerings they are enrolled in or have taken.

    This requirement establishes an association between the users of the database and particular data (e.g., employee number) within the database:

    > **User Identifier Attribute:** Discretionary access controls include references to user identifiers as attribute data values.

- **Extra Credit!**

  The extra credit question is based on the article by Morgenstern ("Controlling Logical Inference in Multilevel Database Systems", *Proceedings of the 1988 IEEE Symposium on Security and Privacy*, pp 245-255) which was discussed during our special seminar on the problems of inference within database applications.

  Define the sphere of influence (SOI) for the corporate education database. Localize and describe the sources of inference channels. Revise the database schema design and security statements as needed to remove any open inference channels.

Clearly the answer to this question is beyond the current state-of-the-art in controlling database inferences. However, several types of potential inferences and possible counter- measures and schema revisions were discussed at the workshop.

A fundamental inference exposure in the corporate education database, as defined, is the potential for a course clerk to infer information about SECRET courses. An additional exposure is inferences concerning individual employees based on their course enrollments and grades. Since the sphere of influence for the application includes information about employees that may not directly exist within the database, a course clerk has additional data upon which to base inferences. For instance, knowledge of a teacher's speciality (or department) could provide an inference concerning the content of a classified course. Similarily, the location of a teacher may indicate the location of classified courses.

One proposed solution to the inferences problems asssociated with the student's transcript was to initially classify the transcript based on the student's 'major' or speciality. This classification would be independent of courses actually taken. A more constraining solution would be to uniformly classify all information about an employee, based on the employee's maximum clearance.

While the workshop participants did not derive any definitive statements of the inference exposures for this application, it was clear that potential inferences must be considered during the database design effort. In addition, the the application risks associated with each potential inference exposure must be weighed against the application costs of eliminating the exposure.

10.3 Summary

In total, there were eleven generic security requirements apparent in this example database:

1. *Foreign Key Dependency:* The access class of a tuple's primary key is determined by the access class of a particular foreign key.

2. *Attribute Value Dependency:* The access class of a tuple's primary key is determined by the data value of a specific attribute.

3. *Key Dominance Constraint:* The access class of a tuple's primary key is constrained to be dominted by the access class of a specific foreign key.

4. *Role-Based DAC:* The discretionary access requirements are based on the role of the user within the application.

5. *Automatic Upgrade:* The access class of data is determined by its application context, not strictly by the access class of the subject inserting the data ("write-up").

6. *Tuple Set Dependency:* A subject's access class must dominate the highest access class of the set of tuples to be accessed.

7. *Entity Association:* The access class of the non-key attributes of a relation that represents an association among two or more application entities, of varying access classes, is determined by the access class of the entity being referenced.

8. *Relationship Dominance:* The access class of a tuple's primary key may strictly dominate the access classes of related foreign keys.

9. *Access Class Attribute:* The access class of a tuple's primary key is constrained to be dominated by an access class attribute in a particular foreign key tuple.

10. *Attribute Classification:* The access class of an attribute value is determined by the attribute/value pair.

11. *User Identifier Attribute:* Discretionary access controls include references to user identifiers as attribute data values.

The example of the corporate education database is only one of many examples that can help to illumine the basic semantics of database security. While not all of the generic statements for this application reflect essential security features for a secure DBMS, they give a good indication of the kinds of statements database designers are going to be making in order to capture the security semantics of their applications.

There were two fundamental conclusions that all participants in the workshop discussion session would agree with:

1. Even such a "simple" application as the corporate education database is conceptually complex and difficult to design as a multilevel secure application.

2. The database security research community needs a "test-bed" of database applications that can be used as examples to compare and validate DBMS security approaches.

11

Classifying and Downgrading: Is a Human Needed in the Loop?

Gary W. Smith[1]

ABSTRACT This paper asserts that output products from a multilevel secure database environment should be classified at a level which accurately reflects, at the data semantics level, the contents of the product. The paper further asserts that for certain classes of data, "the system" can effectively determine the classification of the output product such that no human is required in the loop. For other classes of data, the paper asserts that we can not explicitly state the database security requirement; therefore, we cannot hope to implement a system that enforces those requirements and a human is required in the loop.

11.1 Introduction

The concept of multilevel security (MLS) has recently gained considerable emphasis and momentum in the research and operational communities. Command and control applications, which have traditionally operated in a "system high environment," are a main driver of this need and most certainly will be a prime user of multilevel secure systems. One significant issue in this area is "can the system be trusted to downgrade and/or properly classify outputs from the system, or must a human be in the loop?" There are really two dimensions to this question. First, can we explicitly articulate the database security requirements for classifying/downgrading in a way that can be represented and, therefore, have some hope of enforcing them? And second, once we can explicitly represent the database security requirements, can we then build "trusted software" (in the Orange Book sense [Cen85b]) to enforce those requirements? This paper addresses only the first dimension.

[1]National Defense University

11.1.1 Underlying Concepts

Before addressing the issue at hand, there are three fundamental concepts that form the foundation for the discussion which must be presented. They involve classifying outputs at the correct level, approaching the problem from a semantic level, the relationship between classifying and downgrading.

11.1.2 Classifying Outputs

The fundamental concept upon which this work is based is that output products from a system should be labeled at a level which accurately reflects their contents. What should not happen is that a report, which only contains unclassified data, be classified as TOP SECRET just because it "touched" a TOP SECRET object or came from a system operating in a TOP SECRET system high environment. To accomplish this data (and the associations between data) must be classified at a level that accurately reflects its real classification. This is as opposed to some artificial level such as a high water mark label or the security level at which the user happened to be logged on during the update. This principle extends to objects: objects not necessary in the Orange Book sense for operating systems, but objects in a database sense which occur at a lower level of granularity (i.e., records, tuples, elements, etc.).

The literature is silent on this concept except for [Wood87] which states very succinctly that Department of Defense data often becomes overclassified and is reflected in the labels of output products. Today's classified systems use a high water mark approach to labeling database objects: the whole file or database is classified at the level of the highest classification contained in the file or database. Thus all reports generated from these database objects must be marked at the high water mark level even though they contain only unclassified or lower level data. Although this approach is convenient and about the only way to do business today in a system-high environment, a multilevel secure environment must classify "things" at a level which accurately reflects the contents. Of course, there may be exceptions, where it is appropriate to use a high water mark approach: but they should be just that–exceptions, implemented only when absolutely necessary.

11.1.3 Semantic Level Approach

The second important concept is to approach the problem from a semantic level. That is, it is really important to understand and represent what makes things classified, i.e., "security semantics." In particular, security semantics are very application dependent; therefore, what we should be looking at and attempting to understand is the "security semantics of application."

The security semantics of an application encompass everything from simple relationships that are covered in mandatory access control to the difficult, but essential, security semantics that are referred to by the general titles of inference and aggregation. Effectively, anything that causes data to be classified is included in the security semantics of the application.

11.1.4 Classifying and Downgrading

The simple statement of this concept is that downgrading a report in a system high environment is logically the same as classifying a report in a multilevel environment–both attempt to mark a report at the classification level that accurately reflects the contents of the report.

In a system operating in a system high mode, all reports must be marked at the system high level. This means that all reports generated by the World Wide Military Command and Control System (WWMCCS) which operates system high at the TOP SECRET level, for example, are marked TOP SECRET even if they contain only unclassified data. The reports must be handled as TOP SECRET data until a human reviews the report and marks the report (downgrades the report) to the proper classification.

In a system operating in a multilevel mode, "the system" must determine at what level to mark the report. This process, called classifying, also attempts to mark the report with the proper classification. Thus classifying in a multilevel environment is logically equivalent to downgrading in a system high environment.

11.2 The Issue

Given that the goal of a multilevel secure database environment is to classify outputs (reports, temporary files, etc.) at the level that accurately reflects their contents, can the system do this? Or must a human be in the loop to ensure the correctness of the marking?

11.3 The Answer

The answer is either yes or no depending on the type of data contained in the output. Specifically, if the output contains structured data (that which we normally see in data processing system using a database management system) then the answer is *yes*. If, however, the data is free form text, then the answer is *no*. The following paragraphs describe the rationale that generated this answer.

11.4 Structured Data

Structured data is loosely defined as the type of data that has been traditionally included in data processing (including command and control) applications since the first programs were written and files designed. Systems engineers concentrated on accounting data, logistics data, personnel data, and so forth. Data elements were defined, had specific edit criteria to verify valid values, and were usually organized into file structures with one of the data elements as the primary key. Advances in technology allowed sequential files to migrate to index sequential files, random files and then to more complex database models used by database management systems. Generally speaking, these file structures and data models are not used to store, update, and retrieve text; the are not used to store the strings of words and phrases found in document-oriented systems.

Research has been conducted in the past three years on database security as it relates to the use of database management systems in a multilevel environment. Most research is directed toward database systems based upon the relational model as opposed to the network or hierarchical models [DLS+87,DH86,DOT88,RS87]. These research efforts concentrate on how to represent security and enforce mandatory access controls (MAC) and discretionary access controls (DAC) in a multilevel environment. Very little, if any, efforts have been expended to address the classification of queries whether generated on paper or on a video display.

In each effort, the researchers present a list of the types of security that must be represented. The next section presents a detailed summary of security semantics. The fact that all researchers in the area are able to articulate the semantics by which data in the database must be classified, indicates that classification of queries consisting of structured data can be automated.

This effort, however, will not be without challenges. Aggregation (combining data at one security level resulting in the combined data having a higher security level then any of the parts) and inference (using data at one classification to infer data which is at a higher classification) are two areas which are difficult because they are application-specific. An excellent and rigorous treatment of the inference problem can be found in [DM86]. Each of the database researchers cited above addresses both aggregation and inference and provides mechanisms to solve the problems. For example, SeaView uses aggregation and sanitization "views" to specify and enforce aggregation and inference constraints [DLS+87].

Although aggregation and inference are significant challenges, their implications can be explicitly included the security semantics of an application and, therefore, enforced.

The conclusion: We can understand and explicitly represent the inherent security semantics of structured data; thus we can automate the process of classifying queries involving that structured data.

The next section presents an overview of the security semantics of structure data that can be used to understand why data is classified.

11.5 Security Semantics of an Application

There are many "reasons" for data to be classified. These reasons have to do with values of data and associations between data and are usually dependent on the application. Several database research efforts have published a description of the types of data security problems (semantics) that they address. The purpose of this section is to present, in one place, a taxonomy of the generic types of security semantics of an application.

There are actually three dimensions to a security semantic; hence we will present a multidimensional taxonomy. The three dimensions are:

- *Content* - the actual instance of a security semantic that must be protected. Example: Flight #123 is classified because its destination is Iran.
- *Description* - the statement of the security semantic or classification rule. Example: the fact that flights with destination equal to Iran may or not be, by itself, classified.
- *Existence* - the fact that an instance of the security semantic exists in the database. Example: we may not want anyone to know of the "existence" of a flight to a classified location even though the destination is unknown. On the other hand, we may not care that anyone knows the flight exists–we just don't want them to know it destination.

The *content* dimension is always presented in discussions of database security. The other two dimensions are usually not explicitly discussed. A taxonomy of the generic types of content security semantics will be presented below.

The *description* dimension, which can be viewed as a statement of the "rule" that describes the security semantic, may not be classified, even though the content dimension is highly classified. In many cases, it may be common knowledge (even conforming to common sense) that a particular "thing" is classified. A good example is an employee's salary. In this case, the "fact" that "salary" is classified in the database is not important nor classified.

In other cases, it will be very important that the rule be protected, because the rule contains classified data or data from which classified information can be inferred. For example, the rule "flights to Iran are classified TOP SECRET" includes the information that we have flights going to Iran which, by itself, may be considered TOP SECRET.

The *existence* dimension is a binary decision: to let the user know that there is classified data they cannot see, or to hide the existence of the classified data from the user. The latter is normally assumed—that some data may be hidden. Hiding the data may always be the required response in the highly-classified intelligence world. However, it may be an unnecessary complication in the more business-oriented systems of both the government and private sector.

When analyzing the data security requirements for a particular application, it is essential that all three dimensions be addressed–not just the content dimension.

11.6 Types of Security Semantics

The following is a list of the different generic types of "content" security semantics that populate the content dimension. Only security semantics that relate to a single query or access are considered. The types of inferences that can be gained through multiple accesses are not addressed.

- *Value-Dependent.* Classification is based upon an actual value of an attribute. Example: 'Gemini' as a Project Name is classified TOP SECRET. That is, just the word 'Gemini' by itself is classified.

- *Attribute-Dependent.* The attribute is classified no matter what its contents may be or how it relates to other data. This may be the result of the name of the attribute being classified. Example: The Investigative Status of an employee may be considered so sensitive that the attribute is classified SECRET.

- *Attribute-Value Association.* Classification is based upon the association of the name of an attribute with a specific value or a range of values. This type of security semantic is normally assumed when attributes are classified. Example: The association of the attribute Project Name with a value, for example 'Gemini,' is classified TOP SECRET. Other values may have different classifications when associated with Project Name; for example, ISTAR could be SECRET while some associations could be UNCLASSIFIED.

- *Multi-Attribute Associations.* The association of attributes, and their values, among different entities, objects or relations (and even within these structures) is the real challenge of understanding the security semantics of an application. These challenges normally come under the topics of inference and aggregation. Example: The attribute Salary is not classified (the existence of something called Salary is not critical) and the values "100,000" or "25,000" are certainly by themselves not sensitive. In a similar manner, the attribute Employee Name is not classified nor are its values. However, when you combine the two attributes and their associated values, the result normally is considered sensitive and therefore is classified at some level.

- *Unique Functional Dependent Associations.* When one attribute is uniquely functionally dependent, that is, a one-to-one relationship exists between the attributes such that one attribute is uniquely determined by the other attribute and vice versa, then associations with both attributes should be at the same classification level. [SuOz87] gives a detailed discussion on inference problems due to functional dependencies.
- *One-to-Many Functional Dependent Associations.* When the functional dependency between two attributes is a one-to-many relationship, this becomes a concern when the "many" side of the dependency is a small number.
- *Temporal Associations.* The classification of an object may vary with time. This is especially the case in military command and control systems. Example: The data stating when and where the friendly forces will attack will be TOP SECRET before the attack, but may not even be classified after the attack has ended. Another particularly difficult temporal example is that certain data may be classified at one level (or unclassified) during normal peacetime operations, but it is classified higher or lower during a crisis.
- *Quantity Aggregation.* Often the result of an aggregation of several of the same data objects is classified at a higher level than the classification of the data object. Example: The name and telephone number of an employee is UNCLASSIFIED. But a list of all, or even a certain percentage or a certain number, of the employees and their telephone numbers is classified CONFIDENTIAL.

11.7 Textual Data

Although we can understand and represent the security semantics of structured data, the understanding of the meaning of text continues to be a problem. From the advent of the first computer, the dream has been to automate the understanding and translation of textual documents. There was early excitement that this capability would quickly be implemented. For example, the government spent millions of dollars on machine translation research in the 1950s and '60s. However, expectations far exceeded any real useful results.

We currently have capabilities that do a reasonably good job of literal interpretation of English sentences in static contexts and in limited, well-structured domains. Systems with this level of capability are called natural language database front-end, natural language interfaces for operating systems (help facilities), text filters and summaries, machine-aided translation systems, and grammar checkers and critics [Wal83].

The fundamental problem then, and now, is that text contains ambiguous references. Human cognitive powers can easily resolve these, but so far no way has been found to automate that capability fully for free form text. Researchers in many disciplines (natural language processing, computational linguistics, machine translation, and even speech recognition) have been and continue to look for a solution to this problem.

There has been little published research into automated classifying or downgrading of text. The system proposed by McHugh [McH85] provides only online assistance to a human to downgrade text. The only published paper on automatic classifying/downgrading of text is that by Lunt and Berson [LB87]. This paper proposes an expert system to classify and sanitize text based upon content, context or information source. The examples used to illustrate the expert system's capabilities (keyword oriented and associations within a sentence) do not reflect the difficult associations and ambiguities found in most textual documents. These are the types of difficulties that have stood in the way of the successful implementation of natural language understanding or machine translation systems for text which has not been disambiguated.

In 1983, document understanding—reading documents and assimilating their information into a larger framework of knowledge—was considered a long way off [Wal83]. Even in 1988 the basic problem remains. As Kohonen states, "Machine interpretation of complete sentences is a difficult task; it has been accomplished only when the syntax has been artificially limited." [Koh88]. Although solutions for limited domains of disambiguated text are possible, the solution to understanding free form text is not here today, nor will it be here in the near future.

The conclusion: Since we cannot automate the understanding (and, therefore, the security semantics) of free form text, we cannot expect to automate the classification or downgrading of that text.

11.8 Summary

We can only accurately classify or downgrade "things" for which we can explicitly articulate the rules (i.e. the security semantics) by which they can be classified or downgraded. If we can precisely articulate the security semantics then they can be represented such that the classification and downgrading functions can be automated.

We can articulate and present the security semantics for databases consisting of structured data; therefore, we can automate the process and indeed allow the system to classify automatically and/or downgrade this type of output; no human is required in the loop. (The ability to build "trusted software" for this capability still remains as a road block to successful implementation in an operational environment.)

Technology does not yet allow the security semantics of free form text to be automatically understood, therefore, we cannot trust the system to classify automatically and/or downgrade this type of output; the human must remain in the loop to ensure classified data is not released at a lower level.

11.9 References

[Cen85] National Computer Security Center. Department of defense trusted computer system evaluation criteria. *Technical Report DOD 5200.28-STD*, Department of Defense, December 1985.

[DH86] B.B. Dillaway and J.T. Haigh. A practical design for a multilevel secure database management system. In *Proceedings of the Second Aerospace Computer Security Conference*, December 1986.

[DLS+87] D.E. Denning, T.F. Lunt, R.R. Schell, M. Heckman, and W.R. Shockley. A multilevel relational data model. In *Proceedings of the 1987 IEEE Symposium on Security and Privacy*, April 1987.

[DM86] D.E. Denning and M. Morgenstern. Military database technology study: AI techniques for security and reliability. *Technical report*, Computer Science Laboratory, SRI International, Menlo Park, California, 1986.

[DOT88] P. Dwyer, E. Onuegbe, and B.M. Thuraisingham. Design of a query processor for a multilevel secure relational database management system. *Technical report*, Honeywell Systems Research Center and Corporate Systems Development Division, 1988.

[Koh88] T. Kohonen. The "neural" phonetic typewriter. *IEEE Computer*, March 1988.

[LB87] T.F. Lunt and T.A Berson. An expert system to classify and sanitize text. In *Proceedings of the Third Aerospace Computer Security Conference*, December 1987.

[McH85] J. McHugh. An EMACS-based downgrader for SAT. In *Proceedings of the 8th National Computer Security Conference*, October 1985.

[RS87] P.A. Rougeau and E.D. Sturms. Sybase secure dataserver: A solution to the multilevel secure DBMS problem. In *Proceedings of the 10th National Computer Security Conference*, September 1987.

[Wal83] D.L. Waltz. Helping computers understand natural languages. *IEEE Spectrum*, November 1983.

12

Session Report: The Semantics of Data Classification

Gary W. Smith[1]

12.1 Introduction

This session addressed classification of data from a semantic level. The object was to approach database security from a semantic level—to look at why data objects are classified. The importance of this approach is summed up by Bill Shockley's comments after the session. Shockley believes that the current research efforts have reduced access control mechanisms to engineering problems. He believes that the next set of research problems to be attacked are at the semantic level, most of which involve database design issues.

The implicit significance of Shockley's comments is the need for designers and developers of applications to deal with database security issues that are application-dependent. The semantics of data classification are intimately connected to both the database design, application system design *and* the security policy—that is, a security policy at the semantic level and not at the security-model level. Not only must the designers deal with the technical issues of implementation, they must also first determine the security requirements of the user application. Indeed, these requirements are very dependent on the specific application *and* operational environment.

The homework problem devised by Rae Burns (see Chapter 9) was a dramatic example of the challenges and problems that people will face as they attempt to design and implement real systems. The homework problem was much more effective than any presentation or session discussion could ever hope to be—everyone experienced, first hand, the security policy and design issues that must faced to actually build a real multilevel secure application.

Although many database security problems can be satisfied through database design, there are others that will have to be approached through capabilities provided by the database management system, operating systems and even the application software. This is a new problem because in the past we have not had to really worry about the "semantics of data

[1]National Defense University

classification". We dealt with the database security problem by classifying databases and files at the highest level of the data they contain. We did not need to know why things were classified, only that a particular grouping of data, normally a file, had been determined to be classified at a certain level.

The multilevel secure environment brings us to a new level of requirements. Now, if we are to give data a classification that accurately reflects its meaning, then the designer, analyst, and security officer must understand, at the data semantic level, what relationships, properties or folklore make the data classified.

The notion that data should be classified at their "real" level was generally accepted, although it was not at all clear how this could be accomplished across all systems.

The discussion of the semantics of data classification was accomplished in the context of the presentation preceding this session, called "Classifying and Downgrading: Is a Human Needed in the Loop?" (See Chapter 11.) In particular, the taxonomy of "security semantics" presented in that paper was used as a basis for much of the discussion by the group.

The concept of "value-dependent" security semantics generated a lot of discussion—as may have been expected based upon previous experience with the subject. Value-dependent security semantics were defined to mean that a value of a data element, for example Gemini, is by itself classified. This means that a particular string of characters would be classified independent of its contextual association with attribute names or other attribute name-value pairs. Most people found this type of security semantic to be counter-intuitive. Tom Hinke asserted that information always has a context, albeit implicit. According to Hinke, there is always an implicit context such as "the information came from system X" or "it was included in report Y" or even, "Joe says this." These types of implicit contexts and/or associations are always present and must be considered when establishing the classification semantics. For example, the classification of a fact that is contained in a report issued by the Joint Chiefs of Staff may be higher than if the same fact were reported in the Washington Post. (Credibility is another issue!)

Even ignoring the implicit contextual associations, many researchers do not believe that there are data values that, by themselves, are classified. An example from the past could be "Manhattan." During World War II the Manhattan Project was highly classified. Most certainly, to combine the words "manhattan" and "project" into one sentence would be also highly classified. Because of the extreme sensitivity of this project it may even have been the case that just the word "manhattan" by itself (with the implicit contextual associations—from a government system or employee) would also be classified.

Marv Schaefer told the story of a crossword puzzle writer who got into a lot of trouble because he used a highly sensitive word in one of his crossword puzzles. He had no idea he was using a highly classified word—but he was questioned and investigated just the same.

Matt Morgenstern brought up the case of self-describing data. Such data could conceivably be classified on its own, independent of its context (in a sense it supplies its own context!)

When pressed for a current example of a value-dependent classification, the response has to be "I'm sorry, I can't tell you, because that is classified!" Seriously, knowledgeable individuals in the intelligence community indicate that there are real-world examples of this classification semantic—they do exist, but most of us do not see them.

The discussions continued on more complex semantics involving associations between the attribute name and the attribute value (called attribute name-value pair) and also among two or more attribute name-value pairs. An example of a single attribute name-value pair would be association of the value "manhattan" with the attribute name "project-name" being classified. In this case, the value manhattan would not by itself be classified. Only when combined with the attribute is there any classified data.

There are many examples of associations between two attribute name-value pairs: the association of the attribute name-value pair "destination" and "iran" with the attribute name-value pair "mission-number" and "195" would be classified even though each attribute name-value pair is individually unclassified; in a similar manner, both the attribute name-value pairs "employee-name" and "smith" and "salary" and "100,000" are individually unclassified, but when they are combined the association is classified.

The two types of classification semantics just described are called by various names. For example, the work by Honeywell talks about "content-dependent" and "context-dependent" classification. SRI's SeaView project calls them "value-dependent," "time-dependent," "context-dependent," and "history-dependent" [LDN+88].

The essence of this issue is that data are normally classified when they are combined with other data or metadata (e.g., attribute names). Single and multiple attribute name-pair relationships must be identified at the database schema level so that possible inference and aggregation threats can be identified. It is possible, as pointed out by the SeaView project [DAH+87a,Lun89], to reduce and/or eliminate inferences through the use of database design techniques.

The homework problem provided a good example of how database design techniques can be used to solve an apparent database security problem. In this example, the accounting system, which is unclassified, keeps track of financial resources expended by projects. Another system addresses project management and mission-oriented information for these same projects. The latter system is classified because of the project data. These two systems operate on different computers in today's "system-high" environment. The challenge is how to interface the two applications or databases on the same computer in an multilevel secure environment. The design approach is to keep the unclassified project data in an unclassified file using some project ID which is unclassified, while classifying and protecting the relationship or "mapping function" between the unclassified project ID and the classified project name or ID used for the classified project data. This is an effective design approach for separating classified and unclassified data even within one application system.

Inferences can also result from data which are functionally dependent on other data. Included are one-to-one dependencies and one-to-many dependencies. As the "many" part of one-to-many gets closer to "one," the potential problems are encountered. For example, there is a one-to-many dependency between area code and city. It would, however, be difficult to infer one's city just from the area code. On the other hand, the inference in the other direction can be accomplished without any ambiguity.

Temporal semantics, i.e., those classification rules that are time-dependent, can be particularly difficult. Time can affect classification in both directions; this data can become either classified at a higher level or at a lower level. Perishable data, that loses its value or importance after a certain event or specific amount of time, causes the classification level to be lower. This can best be illustrated by examples. A departure time for a flight may be considered classified until it actually takes off, after which the departure time is unclassified. As another example, in tactical battlefield operations, the time of an attack is classified until the attack begins.

Temporal semantics can also result in the classification becoming higher with time. As an example, in the command and control arena, data which are unclassified during normal peacetime operations may be classified at a higher level during periods of crisis. This type of wholesale change of classification based upon some "readiness criteria" poses really difficult challenges for labeling of objects, whether operating system or database objects. The difficulties stem from the inevitable covert channels that are introduced if the wholesale changing of dozens or hundreds of security labels is performed. Many felt that although this might be required for some systems, it could not be achieved with greater than B1 assurance.

The group also discussed the relationship between the semantics of classified data and integrity constraints on the same data. The group acknowledged that there is a relationship between the two. Unfortunately, as Dorothy Denning pointed out, there was no formalism for integrity nor for integrity constraints implemented with a database. Although many think that integrity constraints are simple, there are, in fact, many types of integrity constraints that are difficult to implement. In particular, in a multilevel secure environment, additional complexity is added since integrity is enforced for each security level and thus not all data are visible to the subject enforcing the constraint.

A considerable part of the session was spent discussing automatic classifying and downgrading. At issue is whether a system can (or should be allowed to) automatically downgrade or classify data without human intervention. Shockley pointed out that there is an implicit assumption in the argument that the system can automatically classify or downgrade; namely that there is no Trojan Horse that can corrupt the data as presented by the database system. Schaefer agreed that for this application one would like to assume "honest users" and "honest programmers"—in other words, a non-hostile environment. This concept was later named the "honest world assumption." Schaefer believes that this assumption can hold for environments that would use automatic classifiers. Unfortunately, the honest world assumption may not be appropriate for today's systems.

There are other disadvantages to automatic classifying/downgrading. Peter Neumann stated there are many ways to signal through a database that cannot be detected by the expert system. Covert channels come in two types: storage and timing. In the database context we are normally concerned with storage channels. Storage covert channels occur when a high-level user can cause low-level data to change or has an impact which can be observed by a low-level user. One case where this can happen is if there is an integrity constraint which affects more than one classification level. There is also a classification constraint which says that some cargo is classified and an unclassified user can only see the unclassified cargo. A high-level Trojan Horse could use the payload field to signal information to a low level user by periodically changing the amount of classified cargo. The low level user can query the payload field and determine the maximum unclassified payload to obtain the information encoded by the Trojan Horse.

Also as Shockley pointed out, untrusted subjects in the classification system could inadvertently (or even maliciously) alter the classification rules; this has implications for modifiability and maintenance of the rule base.

Schaefer stated that one clear advantage to automatic classifying/downgrading is consistency. The "system" will always classify/downgrade the same data the same way. Classi, an automated text classification system proposed at the December 1987 Aerospace Computer Security Conference by Teresa Lunt and Tom Berson [LB87], was cited by Schaefer as an example of an expert system which should be pursued to provide consistency. Humans have proven to be inconsistent in two ways: first, because of the biases that can be seen between different persons; and second, because of the influence of various factors (such as mood or fatigue). In fact, it has been shown that for some domains, expert systems can be at least as good as humans in making these kind of decisions [LMCar].

Denning countered that relying on machines could give a false sense of security, especially if the inconsistency of humans can be attributed to rules that were not captured by the expert system.

Morgenstern pointed out that humans provide an additional robustness in two ways. The first is that the system can only handle precisely-defined actions and will have difficulty (or cannot) deal with a task which is beyond the scope that the system knows. Specifically, the human knows how to say "I don't know," whereas the system may not have this capability. The second is the continuity of the answer. For example, if the response is predicated on five inputs and one of the inputs changes a little, does the expert system's response only change a little?

Other reasons for using an expert system were also discussed. In addition to consistency, Cathy Meadows added that using an automatic facility such as this could make up for the lack of sufficient numbers of qualified people to classify/downgrade documents. Another reason, of course, is related to time and quantity of data required to classified/downgraded. For example, in intelligence systems (and even command and control systems) there is a tremendous amount of data which must be dealt with in a time-constrained environment. An automated capability could handle periods of peak loading where there are not enough personnel to accomplish the mission.

The "advisor paradigm" for an expert system was also discussed. In this case, the expert system serves only in an advisory capacity to the human, and the human can accept or reject the advice. Unfortunately, it has been shown that a human accepting an expert system's advice only when he or she thinks it is appropriate results in poorer performance than if the expert system made all the decisions or if the "suboptimal processor" (the human) made all the decisions without the aid of the expert system [LMCar].

One participant noted in that in one operational system the human was punished if the expert system was ignored and the problem was not successfully solved. On the other hand, if the human took the advice of the expert system and the problem was not successfully solved, then there was no punishment. Some thought that there should be a way to "punish" the expert system if it were wrong.

Lunt noted that we need to look into how to achieve a high degree of assurance for AI systems, such as CLASSI, that are used to assign access classes to text or data. In the absence of high assurance, a human may still be needed in the loop. But as Shockley noted, putting a human in the loop is not an answer either.

The area of semantics of data classification proves to be interesting and an extremely appropriate research topic for the immediate future. As multilevel secure database management systems become available, the community will need to deal with design issues—which ultimately means that semantics of data classification must be addressed.

12.2 References

[DAH+87] D.E. Denning, S.G. Akl, M. Heckman, T.F. Lunt, M. Morgenstern, P.G. Neumann, and R.R. Schell. Views for multilevel database security. *IEEE Transactions on Software Engineering*, 13(2), February 1987.

[LB87] T.F. Lunt and T.A Berson. An expert system to classify and sanitize text. In *Proceedings of the Third Aerospace Computer Security Conference*, December 1987.

[LDN+88] T.F. Lunt, D.E. Denning, P.G. Neumann, R.R. Schell, M. Heckman, and W. R. Shockley. Final report vol. 1: Security policy and policy interpretation for a class A1 multilevel secure relational database system. *Technical report*, Computer Science Laboratory, SRI International, Menlo Park, California, 1988.

[LMCar] P.E. Lehner, T.M. Mullin, and M.S. Cohen. *When Should a Decision Maker Ignore the Advise of a Decision Aid?*, forthcoming.

[Lun89] T.F. Lunt. Aggregation and inference: Facts and fallacies. In *Proceedings of the 1989 IEEE Symposium on Research in Security and Privacy*, May 1989.

13

Inference and Aggregation

Matthew Morgenstern,[1]
Tom Hinke,[2], and
Bhavani Thuraisingham[3]

13.1 Introduction

The *inference problem* recognizes that sensitive information must be protected not only from direct retrieval but also from indirect disclosure. Information flow analysis addresses such indirect disclosure within the system, such as signaling, observation of resource utilization, and other covert channels.

Recently, increasing attention has been directed at *logical* inference problems, in which *logical deduction* (e.g., by an untrusted user) is utilized to uncover sensitive information. We can further distinguish two related categories. The first category utilizes only universally accepted 'laws' such as the rules of mathematics, or the laws of general physics. A simple example is that if values A and B are individually not sensitive, but we want to protect their total C, then we must not release both A and B. In many cases, such problems can be resolved by appropriate database design and careful assignment of classification labels to the data.

This example is related to what also has been called the *aggregation problem*, wherein individual values are not sensitive but a *large enough collection* of individual values is considered sensitive. The classic example is the "phone book" for a military installation: individual phone numbers may be released, but no one should obtain more than, say, ten such numbers.

The second category of *logical inference problems* involves data and/or specialized knowledge that is *external* to the system—such as application data or knowledge about how the application or its environment operates. For example, finding out what week a person's contribution to Social Security Tax is no longer being deducted might at first appear to be not sensitive (only a date is being released, not information about salary values). However when combined with external knowledge of tax laws, such seemingly

[1]Xerox Advanced Information Systems
[2]University of Alabama at Huntsville
[3]The MITRE Corporation

benign information can be utilized to *infer* the approximate salary of the individual.

The following material begins with written submissions by each of the three panel members, including the chairman, and is based upon their presentations during the workshop. Section 13.2 is by Tom Hinke, Section 13.3 is by Bhavani Thuraisingham, and Section 13.4 is by Matthew Morgenstern. Following this material, selected portions of the group discussion among the workshop participants are presented in Section 13.5.

13.2 Database Inference

This section describes a graph-based approach to recognizing inferences in a database. The graph contains the semantic relationships of the data contained in the database as well as common knowledge associated with the database data.

13.2.1 The Problem

Unauthorized disclosure of data can occur in two ways within a secure system, such as a secure database management system. It can occur through inadequate protection or inference.

Sensitive data can receive inadequate protection, either because of vulnerabilities in the system, or because of incorrect application of the protection mechanisms. An example of misuse of protection would be the incorrect labeling of top secret data at the secret level. An example of exploitation of system vulnerabilities would be an access control mechanism that can be broken or circumvented such that certain unclassified users gain access to top secret data.

Even if each data element is adequately protected, classified data still may be vulnerable to unauthorized disclosure if other visible system data can be used to reveal the more sensitive data. For example, if various bits of unclassified data can be combined to reveal secret data, then the secret data has been compromised through inference. This problem is of special concern in databases since they contain large amounts of interrelated data. This interrelationship could lead to compromising inferences, even in a system that has been successfully evaluated at the highest levels of security assurance.

13.2.2 A Solution Approach

The first step in addressing the inference problem is understanding what constitutes an inference. This section provides a short introduction into the subject. It is based on work that has been reported earlier [Hin88,HGWng].

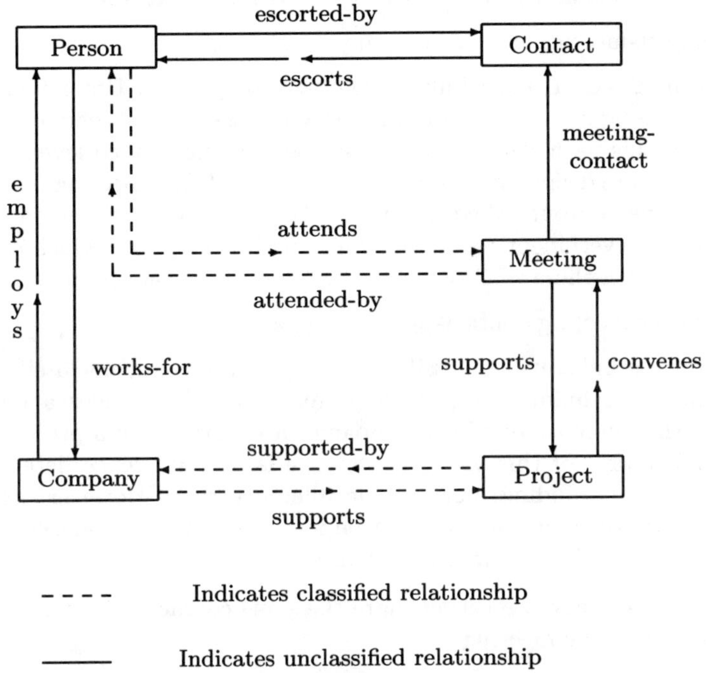

FIGURE 13.1. Example semantic relationship graph.

The basis for this work is the recognition that while data in isolation is not sensitive, the relationship of one piece of data to another may be sensitive. For example, neither a company name in isolation nor a project name in isolation is sensitive. However, a company name associated with a secret project might very well be secret. Figure 13.1, taken from [Hinke88] illustrates an example of this. In the figure, sensitive (classified) relationships are indicated with a dashed line, while non-sensitive (unclassified) relationships are indicated with a solid line. For example, the fact that projects have meetings or that a person works for a particular company is unclassified. However, the association of company and project is considered sensitive.

In terms of the graph, the inference problem can be stated as the problem of finding a second path. For example, in the figure, the project-company relationship is classified and is thus a target for an inference attack. This attack is successful if a second path linking project to company can be found such that all of the links that comprise this second path are unclassified.

Consider first the fact that projects convene meetings. Meetings are attended by people and people work for companies. Thus the path

project-meeting-person-company

could form a second path linking company to project. Unfortunately, as shown in the figure, the relationship between meeting and person is classified, hence this path can not be followed at the unclassified level.

Looking more deeply at this problem, it is noted that meetings are scheduled by some person, called a contact. Likewise, when a person visits a company or government research facility, he has a contact which serves as his escort. With these relationships, the following second path is provided:

project-meeting-contact-person-company

Each of these links are unclassified and hence a second, unclassified path has been found linking project to company, which provides a means of allowing the inference of which companies are working on a project.

One advantage of this view of inference is that inference detection requires only path finding, not specific inference rules. However, based on the path, the rules of inference can be identified. In the example, the following rules of inference are implicit in the path:

1. If a person and a meeting share the same contact, then the person is attending the meeting

2. If a person attends a meeting for a project, then the company for which the person works is supporting the project.

The basis for this approach is to describe both the data in the database and related common knowledge in a semantic relationship graph. The semantic relationship graph can be viewed as a variant of the entity relationship graph with no distinction made between entities and attributes. In this graph, the double arrow indicates a 1:n relationship. For example, a project convenes multiple projects, hence the double arrow between project and meeting. But, for this example, it is assumed that a meeting supports only a single project, hence only a single arrow.

This approach to inference can also be used to identify potential inference problems. For example, assume that a new relationship is added to the figure. This new addition is the banks-with relationship, that relates person to the company with which the person banks. This has the form

person-company.

Now, we have two person-company relationships, the works-for and the banks-with relationships. This can lead to a false inference that has the following second path:

project-meeting-contact-person-company (with which a person banks).

In [Hinke88b] some approaches to addressing this problem are addressed.

13.3 The Inference Problem

Security violation via inference occurs when users acquire unauthorized information from various sets of information that they have legitimately acquired. Solutions to the inference problem have been proposed in [Mor87, Mor88,Thu87,Hin88] among others. Morgenstern [Mor87,Mor88] has established a framework to study the inference problem. Inference rules are specified in a constraint language and the intent is to design the database in such a way that security violations by inference cannot occur. While Morgenstern's approach focuses on database design tools, Thuraisingham's approach [Thu87,KTT88] is to classify the responses so that a user only gets the response he/she is authorized to know. Hinke [Hin88] has developed algorithms to detect logical inferences on the extensional data. This note briefly summarizes the solutions proposed in [Thu87,KTT88] which were discussed in a special session on database inference at the workshop.

In [Thu87], an architecture for a secure DBMS augmented with an inference engine is proposed and algorithms are given to detect certain inferences before responses are released to users. More formally stated, a response R can be classified at security level L without violating security if the following condition is satisfied:

For every Level L^* which is not dominated by L (i.e. $L^* \geq L$ or is comparable to L), Level(Infer($E(L^*) \cup R$)) $\leq L^*$ where $E(L^*)$ is the environment associated with the level L^* (note that the environment consists of everything that a user at level L^* has seen so far), Infer ($X \cup Y$) is the set of all information that can be logically inferred from X and Y, and Level(X) is the security level of the information X.

Security constraints expressed in logic are used to assign security levels to information. The information includes the data in the database as well as external data.

In [KTT88] another algorithm is given to detect inferences. It applies Sadri and Kowalski's [SK88] constraint satisfaction method to consistency checking to detect inferences. The essential points of the argument are as follows:

The query evaluation process is viewed as updating the environments. That is, whenever a response is released into $E(L)$ all environments $E(L')$ where $L' \geq L$ are updated. In most cases the update consists of only the insert operation. When the environment is updated, the extended SLDNF proof procedure is applied. If the empty clause is derived then a security violation by inference has occurred. The response is then not released to the user. Note that an empty clause will be derived only if the constraints are not satisfied. Therefore a security violation occurs only if the environment does not satisfy the constraints. This is stated in the result below:

Result: Let a response R be released into the environment $E(L)$. Let the extended proof procedures be applied to $E(L')$ ($L' \geq L$). If the empty clause is deduced, then security violation by inference has occurred.

Proof: First note that whenever a piece of data is released into an environment L, all the environments associated with level $L' \geq L$ need to be checked for security violation (i.e., it has to be ensured that from any subset of $E(L')$, it is not possible to deduce data at level $L'' > L'$).

Now suppose that the response R is added to the environment. If an inconsistency occurs, (i.e., if the empty clause is deduced) then one or more constraints are violated by the inclusion of R. This is only possible if the level of some data, which was classified at a Level $L'' \leq L'$, is now increased to a level $L+ > L'$. Therefore if the response R is released into $E(L)$, a user at Level L' will infer information at level $L+ > L'$, to which he/she is not authorized. This is a security violation.

13.4 Analysis of Logical Inference Problems

Much of the work in security is concerned with enforcement of the barrier between the user and the system. However, this barrier only protects data which is known to the system. A smart user can circumvent these security mechanisms by going around the barrier—that is, by going outside the system.

If we want to prevent the user from obtaining information about some stored data element C, then we need to be concerned about the fact that the user can make logical deductions. In addition to the retrievable data, the user may have additional information which is external to the system. With this additional information, the user may be able to *infer* the classified data C, or at least something important about C.

In order to represent the knowledge which is external to the system, I have borrowed from my work on Intelligent Database Systems. In particular, I find it useful to represent such application knowledge in terms of logical constraints among the relevant data objects.

13.4.1 When Classifying a Rule is Worse than Useless

A humorous but useful example helps to show how classifying an inference rule can turn out to be *worse than useless.* We will say that classifying a rule is *useless* if doing so does not prevent the release or inference of data, compared to not classifying the rule. We would probably also agree that the process of classifying the rule higher is *worse than useless* if doing so can lead to release or inference of more data compared to not classifying that rule.

The example deals with a tax preparation agency that treats the gross income of its clients as classified. Now the management of the agency decides to increase its security measures by also classifying the rule which relates tax bracket to gross income, because they do not want people to be able to deduce gross income.

The marketing department wants to attract more clients, and so they would like to boast about the clients the company already has. The marketing department sees that the rule relating tax bracket to gross income has now been classified so as not to be visible. They therefore believe that releasing the high tax brackets of certain clients would no longer reveal the gross income of those clients, as this rule is now classified.

However, people already know that rule, so the result of classifying the rule within the system led to misguided actions which actually made possible inferences about secret data—thus releasing more information than before the rule was classified.

A significant conclusion from this example is that if we classify an inference rule inappropriately, we can have a similar effect. While the rule will then appear classified to the system, in fact, people outside the system will already know the rule. Subsequent decisions in the system, based upon the assumption that the rule is classified, then can lead to inadvertent release of just that information we were trying to protect.

13.4.2 Sphere of Influence Analysis

The Sphere of Influence analysis is described in my paper [Mor88]. The basic idea is that if you start with some set of data at one or more classification levels (call this the *core data*), then the *Sphere of Influence* (SOI) is just that set of data which is inferable from this core data.

Inherent in this analysis is a representation of relevant application semantics which could be utilized singly or in combination to make possible inferences. For this purpose, I utilize a constraint-based representation of the application knowledge. Each constraint serves to represent several potential inferences. Alternatively, one can use horn clause logic or predicate calculus expressions.

It is particularly important that we deal effectively with *partial inferences.* Informally this means that we know some but not all of the information. For example, we may be able to reduce the range of possible values through inference—e.g., we may be able to infer that someone's salary lies between $40K and $45K even if we cannot determine it exactly. To this end, we use an information theoretic inference function which ranges between zero and one, where one means exact inference. It incorporates earlier work by Denning [DM86], and is defined in terms of the *uncertainty* or *entropy* of y, denoted $H(y)$, and the *relative uncertainty* of y given x, denoted $H_x(y)$, as follows:

Inference Function:

$$\begin{aligned}\text{INFER}(x \to y) \;&:=\; [H(y) - H_x(y)]/H(y) \\ &\qquad\qquad \text{if } [H(y) - H_x(y)]/H(y) > \epsilon \\ &:= 0 \quad \text{otherwise .}\end{aligned}$$

If x discloses no information about y, then $H_x(y) = H(y)$ and $\text{INFER}(x \to y) = 0$. If x discloses full information about y (its exact value), then $H_x(y) = 0$ and $\text{INFER}(x \to y) = 1$.

When this *degree of inference* exceeds some preset threshold value ϵ, then we consider this partial inference to be of importance, and include the inferred data in the SOI. Setting this threshold ϵ to be greater than zero allows us to ignore trivial inferences.

Formally, the Sphere of Influence (SOI) is defined in terms of the above INFER function:

Sphere of Influence:

$$\text{SOI(core)} := \{ \text{ Y} \mid \exists \text{X} \subseteq \text{core} \wedge (\text{INFER(X} \to \text{Y)} > \epsilon) \}.$$

At times we find it useful to use a geometric interpretation for the SOI, where a high degree of inference is represented by data objects being close to the core, and further distance from the core represents a lower degree of inference.

The Sphere of Influence analysis can be used relative to any (sub)set of data, though it is most useful relative to particular choices of core data. For example, the *Safety Test for a Classification Level* [Mor88] can be used relative to a classification level l to determine whether classification labels have been assigned consistently with the application semantics. If not, then application semantics could be used to infer higher level data from data visible at that classification level.

The Safety Test relative to classification level l chooses the core data ($core_l$) to be all data at and below this classification level l. If the SOI relative to this core does not include any data outside this core, then the classification labels have been assigned consistently. Thus level l is *safe* if this SOI yields a *fixed point*, that is: $\text{SOI}(core_l) = core_l$.

If we determine that the SOI is *not* a fixed point, then we need to determine the *Inference Channels* to higher level *Target Data* T. We see that $\text{T} = (\text{SOI}(core) - core)$. In [Mor88] we characterize the *Source* of these inferences, that is, the subset of the *core* data which gives rise to these target inferences.

One of the techniques we could use to eliminate the inference channel is to reclassify to a higher level the source data of the inference channel, so as to eliminate these upward inferences. However, care must be taken to analyze the consequences of doing so. When we classify such data to a higher level, we must also reanalyze the other data and their classification labels. In particular, we must now determine whether there are any inferences leading to the data which we have just reclassified to a higher level.

While these inferences would have existed previously, they would have been safe prior to this upward reclassification. One might argue that these secondary inferences *might* be less significant because they involve two levels of inference. However, until these new inferences are analyzed, one does not know whether they are significant. Thus eliminating one potential inference by an upward classification of data could create a pandora's box of new potential inferences to be analyzed. We are working on techniques for incremental analysis of such inferences. Also, there may be more than one way of eliminating a potential inference, and so it is desirable to analyze the consequences of each alternative, so as to choose the solution with least impact on the overall system.

13.4.3 Network of Constraints

In general, our design-time analysis of inferences can be seen as a process of satisfying the network of interdependencies and logical constraints among the data objects. A consistent set of classification labels for the data would satisfy these constraints. This means that the labels would make it impossible for someone who knows these constraints, by virtue of being familiar with the application, to infer higher level data from lower level data. Some of these constraints arise from the database schema, while other constraints arise from the semantics of the application.

There are a potentially large number of inferences, and an analysis could become bogged down in the combinatorics unless a careful strategy is followed. As we described, it is not sufficient merely to locate the source of an inference and classify that data higher, because doing so may create the potential for many other inferences—these too must be analyzed.

Looking toward the future, I believe that constraint analysis across the network of these logical constraints will be a good means of addressing this problem. Such constraint network analysis could provide a more direct attack on these inference problems than incremental raising of classification levels and iterative analysis of consequences of each of these changes.

In any case, we can see that computer-based tools will be needed to deal successfully with large multilevel databases which almost are upon us. With the increasing capabilities for data storage and computation, it is likely that our databases will continue to grow rapidly in size.

13.4.4 Questions

QUESTION: How does the system keep track of the consequences of each piece of data that it releases in response to queries? Such consequences may include the combined effects of several inferences.

M. Morgenstern: I'll answer that in two parts. First, the Sphere of Influence takes as its core all the data at and below a particular level, and considers the cumulative effects of the inferences derivable from this set of data — rather than looking at inferences from individual data objects.

Secondly, with this approach the analysis takes place initially at design time rather than at data release time. At design time we are looking at the potential release of data. Thus we are considering a worst case scenario for maximum protection. Consequently, we do *not* need a history of data which has been released in response to previous queries, nor do we need a run time analysis of this history before answering each query.

It is possible that the actual inferences may be less significant than in the worst case analysis. So *if* one wanted to add a run-time analysis selectively in the expectation that only some of the data would be requested, one could utilize an *aggregation constraint* on the data comprising the source of the inference channel. The run-time aggregation constraint would allow limited subsets of this data to be released, but not enough for the previously analyzed inference channel to become significant.

A particular advantage of our approach is that such run-time controls could be added quite selectively, or not at all, since the design time analysis provides maximum protection. Use of run-time controls simply allows somewhat more information to be released than would otherwise be the case. The opportunities for such run-time controls are determined during the design time analysis.

An important distinction between design time and execution time analysis is that the design time process ensures that the classification labels on the data protect that data from compromises of security arising from logical inference. Execution time analysis implies that the labels on the stored data may not fully protect the data, but rather that run time filtering of the responses also is needed.

13.5 General Discussion

QUESTION: What are the advantages of design-time versus run-time analysis?

T. Hinke: You have to have both approaches. There are potential inferences that you want to detect at design time. However, it could be the case that the actual inference might not arise because the relevant data was not actually entered into the system. So some inferences you may want to check for at run-time.

QUESTION: Could there be any inferences that you could detect at execution time which would not be possible to detect at run time?

M. Morgenstern: Design-time analysis should utilize a worst case analysis, so all potential inferences would be detected. For inferences that are value-based, the design time approach is to assume that all possible values could arise, thus covering all possible cases and giving full protection.

Although design-time analysis can detect all types of inferences which could be detected at run-time, it may overclassify some data in comparison with run-time tests. On the other hand, the value-based analysis achievable with run-time tests generally will be more computationally expensive, in total, than design-time analysis. Furthermore, since no results can be released until the run-time tests are completed, responses can be delayed substantially by costly run-time tests.

An intermediate approach between design and run-time analysis is also possible. Actually a spectrum of alternatives, with differing tradeoffs, exists. For example, reasonable assumptions could be utilized for design-time analysis, and then run-time checks would ensure that these assumptions held. If the assumptions were not valid—e.g., a larger percentage of data values where being requested—then restrictions (also derived at design-time) would be applied to the release of data. As another example, design-time analysis may determine that only a certain range of data values could lead to sensitive inferences, in which case run-time restrictions on release of these particular values might be sufficient, rather than classifying the whole set of data. Related issues also must be considered, such as trustworthiness of the software that must be relied upon by these run-time tests.

QUESTION: To what extent would performance be a consideration for run-time versus design-time analysis?

M. Morgenstern: Execution-time analysis generally would incur a substantially higher cost than design time analysis, and could cause noticeable delay in responding to the user. Design time analysis could be run overnight, so that there would be almost no run time overhead in response to actual queries and updates. One wants to do as much pre-analysis as possible. Even if some run-time checks are utilized, it is much better to simply check predetermined constraints at run time than to do the primary inference analysis while the user is waiting for a response.

M. Schaefer: I think there is an issue as to whether the database changes frequently or is relatively constant. If the database does not adhere to the initial design time assumptions, then additional analysis may be needed. For example, when you travel overseas you are given instructions to not travel the same route on consecutive days. However, particular conditions may reduce the set of alternatives which are available, and the probabilities associated with particular inferences. Also, one may be able to input particular patterns of data to force responses in a predictable manner.

M. Morgenstern: Especially for a changing environment, it becomes desirable to have incremental inference analysis techniques to determine the consequences of limited changes, rather than doing a full re-evaluation. This incremental reevaluation need not wait until queries arrive, but can be done as soon as the changes are known. When such changes are temporary, this process could generate and compile run-time rules that limit release of data during the temporary interval.

QUESTION: Are you looking at a particular semantic model to represent the inference channel analysis?

M. Morgenstern: I have a constraint expression language which I find useful, though the inference analysis approach could utilize other representations also. Semantic databases and semantic networks use nice graphical constructs, but these fixed sets of constructs are limited in expressiveness. The constraint language can capture the semantics of such network representations, and its constructs can be combined to represent other semantics not handled by network models. Also, the use of the constraint language allows the inference analysis to be relatively independent of particular database schemas, since the constraints can apply to relational, object/entity, CODASYL, and other data models. I hope to develop a graphical representation for visualizing these constraints and their interactions.

QUESTION: What if the multilevel data allows one to deduce a fact which is Secret but is not represented in the database?

M. Morgenstern: That is a good example of why I look at not just the database schema, but at what I call a *universe of discourse.* It provides an extended schematic representation of all types of data which are relevant to the application and its security. It includes the database schema as a subset, but extends beyond the stored data. This approach makes possible analysis of inferences about data which is outside the system.

QUESTION: When you do locate an inference, and there are several alternatives which would eliminate the inference, does the user get the opportunity to select the modification or does the system automatically pick?

M. Morgenstern: Inference analysis is intended as a tool to aid the security officer and/or database administrator. When the tool is implemented, the security officer would be consulted with the results of the analysis, and would have final discretion as to which actions are taken. There may be important tradeoffs to be made, including: reasonable availability of other data, and impact on system performance if elaborate run time checking is utilized.

T. Lunt: In your approach you are looking at potential inferences for all possible values of data with which you could populate your relations. So your result doesn't only show that there is a path from this relation to another relation. You could say that if there is a value in a particular range then there would be an inference. Then you could build a classification constraint or an integrity constraint to rule out those cases.

M. Morgenstern: Yes, that is how it is designed. The level of detail in the result will depend upon the level of detail in the original representation and analysis, of course.

G. Smith: The constraint expressions are meta-data. Earlier there was a comment that the rules (meta-data) which are utilized to classify data should not themselves be classified. Could we explore that further?

M. Schaefer: The values in question may be classified, but the rules may not need to be classified. Consider an analogy to protecting access to a system by using passwords, for example. The values of the passwords are classified. The way the passwords are used to authenticate users, and the fact that passwords are encrypted, are assumed to be public knowledge. The fact that a TCB is driven by tables that contain user IDs and clearances, and data IDs and classifications is well known. The particular values in the table may be classified.

By analogy then, you may have a set of rules which say that if the subject is any of the things in group A, and the object is in group B, then access will be restricted. The rule may be unclassified, but the particulars of groups A and B could be kept secret.

QUESTION: What thoughts do you have on the similarities and differences between inference versus aggregation?

T. Hinke: Dorothy Denning pointed out that the aggregation problem arises only when each piece of data in the aggregate could be classified individually at a lower level than the aggregate as a whole. If we had three pieces of secret data and one piece of top secret data, then the combination would be top secret, but this is not the aggregation problem because some of the data already was at that high a level.

Many so-called 'aggregation problems' seem to involve inference at some level. For example, the 'telephone book' problem, and its restriction as to the number of entries that can be released, probably arises from the concern not to give information about the structure of the organization, the employees of the agency, etc. Information may be available outside the agency about the skills and training of the employees, thus enabling one to deduce something about the types of projects being worked on.

M. Morgenstern: I agree that even the 'telephone book' example involves some inference as its basis, and perhaps a whole set of inferences, but these inferences are not sufficiently known or understood. So instead we use numeric or cardinality criteria to deal with what otherwise could be an elaborate and complex set of inferences which have not been made explicit. The cardinality-based *aggregation* constraint then can be seen as an *abstraction* of these underlying, and perhaps complex, inferences. This abstraction arises in the *analysis* of security requirements.

On the other hand, when we look at *implementation issues*, aggregation techniques provide a mechanism rather than an abstraction. The *aggregation mechanism* allows restricted release of some but not all data from a given set. It may be used for the typical 'telephone book' type situation, where potential inferences are not known explicitly. In addition, the *aggregation mechanism* may be used as a pragmatic tool to thwart real inference problems—that is, when we know the sensitive inferences—and we wish to use a simple run time mechanism to protect that data.

As an example of the latter, if we need to keep secret the total budget of a large project, we still may be able to release costs of particular parts—so that the standard billing process does not require highly cleared personnel. That works so long as we do not release costs of too many of the parts involved in the project. In this case, we know the classified target of potential inferences, i.e. the total budget, and we know the inference rules, just simple mathematics here, yet the *aggregation mechanism* may serve us well as an *implementation tool*. The aggregation mechanism also allows us to simplify run time analysis—from complex inference analysis (done during design time analysis) to relatively simple run time tests on particular subsets of data. Thus it seems useful to distinguish between aggregation as an abstraction for analysis versus aggregation as implementation tool.[4]

We must be careful about the differences between aggregation and inference. As one acquires more facts, one becomes better able to make logical inferences. With enough facts, substantial inferences often are possible. It would be misleading, however, to label this an aggregation problem simply because one needed to amass enough facts in order to make the inferences. From an analysis point of view, a key distinction is that these are *explicit inferences*, and thus this is an inference problem. In contrast, aggregation problems arise during analysis as the primary demonstrable abstraction of *implicit inferences* which may be unknown or poorly understood.

Furthermore, when we consider *explicit inference* problems, it is useful to further distinguish the sources of such explicit inferences. The structure and associations present in the database provides one source of inferences. For a relational database, attributes and keys within a tuple are directly related, and many other associations are easily derived by joining tuples from different relations based upon common join attributes. I would call these *explicit internal inferences*—they are *internal* to the database.

Clever database design often can eliminate such internal inference problems without over-classifying large amounts of data. As Dorothy Denning has previously suggested [LDN+88][5], sensitive associations among data, e.g. within the same tuple, can be eliminated by decomposing the relation into two (or more) joinable relations. Then one can classify higher only the relevant decomposed relation, or just the foreign key attribute(s) needed for the join.

In comparison with such *internal* inferences that derive from database facts, a user also may utilize knowledge and facts outside of the database to make inferences. I would distinguish this case as *explicit external inference* because some of the critical inferences rely upon knowledge that is *external* to the database. To detect and prevent such inferences, we must be able to model relevant application and environmental knowledge during the analysis process. Many types of 'common knowledge' for specific groups of users can be anticipated. While the completeness of representing such

[4]This distinction between abstraction and implementation is similar to the distinction between policy and mechanism. – P. Neumann

[5]Also discussed in Ray Burns' example in another workshop session.

external knowledge may not be provable, we will be *less* likely to detect the numerous trap doors and logical inference channels if we don't attempt to address such *external* inferences.

QUESTION: What are the different kinds of mechanisms which give rise to inference problems, in addition to association and aggregation?

B. Thuraisingham: Deduction is a basis for inference of course.

M. Schaefer: Reduction is another such mechanism.

An interesting example arises from the fact that the list of people in the US Army is not classified. After the Grenada incident occurred, the Army admitted that a secret unit did exist. So if one could ask the right questions about members of unclassified units, then one could derive the membership of units that are not publically identified. This is the opposite of the NSA phone book example [because here only particular small subsets are classified, whereas the whole list of Army members is not classified]. It is closer to census bureau issues of statistical inference, wherein smaller subsets may be more sensitive because of the potentially greater information they give about the few members of the small subset.

M. Morgenstern: Another type of inference arises from patterns of activity over time. Such 'time-based inference' is an interesting area that will require further study—in order to select a suitable temporal representation and, especially, to determine appropriate analysis techniques.

H. Hosmer: 'Cause and effect' provides another basis for inference. [We may be able to infer from the data that a cause and effect relationship exists. Alternatively, we may be able to infer more information and intent about observable events and actions if we know that they are related by cause and effect. – M.M.]

M. Morgenstern: With the goal of designing the most effective *inference control tool* possible, I'd like to invite suggestions for research issues and, especially, for what capabilities you feel we should be putting into a *classification tool* to aid the security officer and the database designer?

The suggestions put forth by the participants included:

1. We should be able to look at the database design at different security levels.

2. Graphical ways of representing security characteristics, and the ability to visualize security constraints among the data would be useful.

3. When different alternatives to close an inference channel are presented to the user (security officer), information such as performance implications should be presented. For applications where performance is critical, one may wish to tolerate a modest probability of inference.

4. Some inferences can be made with greater certainty than others. The 'degree of certainty' measures should be included in the analysis tool.

5. We should be able to start with a more basic conceptual representation than the database schema — for example, database dependencies and more general constraints.

6. We need to be able to represent how the data is manipulated and the types of operations on the data. Transaction definitions are important, but would not be sufficient if ad hoc queries are to be processed also.

13.6 References

[DM86] D.E. Denning and M. Morgenstern. Military database technology study: AI techniques for security and reliability. *Technical report*, Computer Science Laboratory, SRI International, Menlo Park, California, 1986.

[HGWng] T.H. Hinke, C. Garvey, and A. Wu. A1 secure DBMS architecture. In T.F. Lunt, editor, *Research Directions in Database Security*, forthcoming.

[Hin88] T.H. Hinke. Inference aggregation detection in database management systems. In *Proceedings of the 1988 IEEE Symposium on Security and Privacy*, April 1988.

[KTT88] T.F. Keefe, W.T. Tsai, and M.B. Thuraisingham. A multilevel security model for object-oriented systems. In *Proceedings of the 11th National Computer Security Conference*, October 1988.

[LDN+88] T.F. Lunt, D.E. Denning, P.G. Neumann, R.R. Schell, M. Heckman, and W.R. Shockley. Final report vol. 1: Security policy and policy interpretation for a class A1 multilevel secure relational database system. *Technical report*, Computer Science Laboratory, SRI International, Menlo Park, California, 1988.

[Mor87] M. Morgenstern. Security and inference in multilevel database and knowledge-base systems. In *Proceedings of the ACM International Conference on Management of Data (SIGMOD-87)*, May 1987.

[Mor88] M. Morgenstern. Controlling logical inference in multilevel database systems. In *Proceedings of the 1988 IEEE Symposium on Security and Privacy*, April 1988.

[SK88] F. Sadri and R. Kowalski. Theorem-proving approach to database integrity. In *Foundations of Deductive Databases and Logic Programming*. Morgan Kaufmann, 1988.

[Thu87] M.B. Thuraisingham. Security checking in relational database management systems augmented with inference engines. *Computers and Security*, 6(6), 1987.

14

Dynamic Classification and Automatic Sanitization

Marvin Schaefer[1]

ABSTRACT This chapter contains a panel session summary of the panel entitled "Dynamic Classification and Automatic Sanitization." This chapter includes an expansion of topics discussed during the panel session on Dynamic Classification and Automatic Sanitization, and is reproduced from personal notes and a tape-recorded transcript. The panel was conducted in association with a panel on the closely allied topic of Aggregation and Inference. Earlier discussions had focused on the "homework" problem. This chapter attempts to integrate related topics discussed earlier in the workshop with those mentioned during the actual panel. The taped record indicates that several topics from the other sessions were referenced in context, but without detailed expansion. An attempt has been made to expand on those references and thereby unify the overall discussion.

14.1 Introduction

Sensitive data needs to be classified at the time of its creation in order to provide a basis for its continued protection. (Many data classifications are tentative until they have been reviewed by competent authority, i.e., by individuals who possess original classification authority.) A reference monitor needs to be able to determine the classification and dissemination constraints on data prior to releasing it. This panel session was intended to examine technical issues relating to the classification of data at the time of creation and at the time of release.

Problems relating to dynamic classification and automatic sanitization are very closely related to those of inference and aggregation. The basic issues derive from the desire and need to provide a population of users with access to only those portions of a database for which they are appropriately cleared and to which they have a need to know.

Analogies for automated trusted data processing applications are often drawn to their "paper-world" counterparts. In this article, paper-world analogues are discussed prior to examinations of the related requirements

[1]Trusted Information Systems, Inc.

for trusted automated data processing contexts.

Whole documents or files are classified based on an assessment of the potential damage to the national security that could be caused by unauthorised disclosure of the information contained therein. Such entities are required to be reviewed for sensitivity, based on content, coincident with their creation in order to provide for adequate protection and control. Classified entities are marked with classification labels and handling caveats that define their sensitivity and which may indicate a rationale for the original classification designation. Such physical markings provide an effective syntactic means to enable security officers who are not conversant with a specialised topic to determine whether to forward an entire classified entity to another named individual. They do not require that the security officer actually read the classified entity in order to decide whether or not to release the data.

In the paper-world, a document or other corpus of information is classified at the level of the most sensitive data contained therein. In general, not all of any classified document is equally sensitive. For example, the individual words of a classified document are [almost always] all unclassified, while concepts represented by specific combinations of these words may be classified to different degrees. It is often a practical requirement that less sensitive data be extracted from documents for release to individuals who lack clearance or the need to know for the entire document's contents. By statute, to ensure that security compromises do not occur, each request to see or distribute portions of a classified paper entity must reviewed by a competent authority consistent with established classification guidelines. The review process must guarantee that the material to be released has been properly "sanitized": that is, the data being released is not "contaminated" with more sensitive data that cannot be released.

The manual nature of such a system tends to limit the amount of data that is released, as well as the rate at which it is released, to each individual or organization. These decisions do require that the security officer actually read the classified entity.

A presumption behind such paper-world models is that the content and context of the extracted material can be understood by the security officer who determines the semantic classification of what is to be released. It appears generally to be assumed that the release authority can and will identify patterns of requests for information. The latter analysis may serve to identify an individual or set of individuals requesting a great deal of information on a specific topic. Such an analysis could potentially identify paper-world attempts to collect sufficient subsets of a classified entity to permit the collector to derive unreleased restricted data values without actually seeing them. It may or may not be possible to identify a group of individuals acting together in collusion to collect such data.

14.2 Sanitization

"Sanitization," as a concept, is necessary in several classified data processing contexts. As noted above, data to be extracted from classified documentation for release in less sensitive environments must have the more sensitive data "sanitized" from it. There are also requirements that classified data be produced in sufficiently "clean" environments and that the environments in which classified data is accessed be "cleansed" prior to becoming accessible to those not authorised for all of the sensitive information to which the environment had been exposed.

In the "paper world" a classified document is normally created, accessed and stored in an environment that is adequately isolated and protected to control access to the document. Personnel entering a classified environment are generally prohibited from bringing in recording devices; those exiting are generally prohibited from carrying classified data out of the protected environment. Especially if the classified area is to be accessible afterward by personnel who lack sufficient security clearance or need-to-know for sensitive data accessed in the facility, it is required that there be no remnants of the sensitive data when less authorised personnel are admitted to the area.

Sometimes documents and other data entities are found to have been assigned an improper security classification. Two cases are treated below: initial overclassification and initial underclassification.

14.3 Initial Overclassification

When the initial security classification is found to have been too restrictive, it is at least certain that the overly restrictive classification has prevented any unauthorised access to the data. Apart from needed modifications to accountability papers and receipts associated with the document, reclassification can be achieved by modification of the physical labels on the document's cover sheet, individual pages, and possibly on individual paragraphs.

In an automated data management context this requirement can be significantly more difficult to manage correctly than its paper world counterpart. The problem is sometimes called the "Downgrading Problem". In order to change the classification marking and protection accorded to an object, it is necessary to violate either the Bell-La Padula Model's $\star$- Property (copy the object's contents into a new object that is visible at a less restrictive security level) or the Bell-La Padula Model's Tranquility Principle (directly modify the classification attributes of the object).

To downgrade the classification of "large" simple objects (e.g., entire files), the problem can be resolved to one of ensuring that the object named (and its contents) is the only object whose classification is changed: thus, the security official must be capable of unambiguously communicating to the TCB the name of the object whose classification is to be changed and the classification to which it is to be reassigned. In addition, there must be assurances that the contents of the designated object are not modified by any untrusted subject during the reclassification transaction (i.e., the designated object must be isolated from Trojan horses while being manipulated by the security official).

To downgrade the classification of "large" complex objects (e.g., files stored on physical devices in structured file systems, entire single-level databases), the problem is made more complex because of the need to produce an information secure update to the computer system's central data structures (e.g., hierarchical directories, physical disk maps, etc., themselves potentially a multilevel database). While the direct violation of the $\star$-Property or Tranquility Principle may not cause a significant leakage of information, it is conceivable that side effects resulting from the reclassification could be used as part of a covert storage or timing channel. (Here also, it is found that an isolated trusted path mechanism is needed so that the security official can perform the required content reviews and classification assignments free from interference by untrusted subjects.)

A downgrade of the classification of "small" objects (e.g., individual pages, paragraphs or sentences of a document; or relations, records or fields of a database) appears to combine the requirements of downgrading the large objects discussed above. Even for small simple objects (e.g., an instantiation of a classified field in a single tuple of a database), it is potentially necessary to modify entries in various internal database dictionaries, hash and inversion tables, pointer chains, and so forth, both at the security level at which the data originally appeared and at the target security level. It is to be noted that the additional semantic richness surrounding the small objects complicates the nature of the previously required isolated trusted path mechanism, which must consistently and compatibly duplicate much of the functionality of the underlying multilevel application system. This suggests that either the trusted path mechanism cannot be isolated or that it must be part of the application's TCB. Taken together, these imply that the system TCB or the application TCB cannot be as small and simple as that of a trusted operating system.

14.4 Initial Underclassification

During a classification review, it is possible to find that data has been underclassified. Such a discovery raises the need to correct the mislabeling and to protect the data according to its established sensitivity. The correction will necessarily violate the Tranquility Principle; data consistency requirements may also necessitate the violation of either the $\star$-Property or the Simple Security Condition of the Bell-La Padula Model.

While pending review, the data may have been tentatively handled as though it had always been more sensitive, in which case the correction corresponds to an initial classification assignment from a processing environment protected to the determined sensitivity level of the data (in which case there is no real problem), or the data may have been produced in a more sensitive environment. In the latter case, the problem is really identical to the downgrading problem discussed above.

The classification reviewer may conclude that data has been tentatively underclassified but stored consistent with its initial classification assignment rather than with the more restrictive protection dictates of the higher classification. In this case, consideration must be given to a sanitization requirement: the underclassified data, the data necessary to its representation, and the entire processing environment from which it is reviewed all need to be purged from the more open environment and screened from potential continued exposure. A related consistency requirement, particularly relevant to database applications, pertains to the need to update all the internal data needed for the display or retrieval of the affected data.

Conceptually, a data upgrade (reclassification from a security level to a dominating security level) for a "large" simple object in the sense of the preceding section can be achieved in a sequence of steps: (a) isolate the underclassified object to preclude further unauthorised accesses; (b) create a receiving object at the target dominating classification level; (c) copy the underclassified data into the receiving object (the underclassified object could be read from the receiving level into the receiving object via traditional existing mechanisms); (d) delete the underclassified object and associated supporting data (e.g., gross directory entries). If the security officer can concurrently perform his function from the two different security levels, much of the compound operation can be performed by normal user-support functions (the isolation and sanitization operations being the principal exceptions for which strict trust requirements would exist). Reclassification between nondominating security levels would not be so direct. Trusted mechanisms would be required at every step of the process.

The trusted processing requirements are far more sophisticated for upgrading the classification of complex objects, especially those in database management contexts. This is because of the potentially large set of artifacts that may need to be created in order to represent, retrieve or support the retrieval of the object. Complications range from linked lists, indexing, and data inversions through the search strategy exported by the query optimiser. Artifacts of the underprotected data may also exist in recovery logs. While this structure needs to be purged completely in order to sanitize one environment, much of the same structure may need to be recreated in the receiving security level. Pointer manipulation may be particularly complex because of information flow exigencies.

14.5 Discovered Misclassification

In database management applications, new associations between data items can occur as a consequence of repeated application of the join, project and select operations. Examples can be constructed such that the classification displayed for the retrieved data would be incorrect. Such discoveries would have to be treated when they occur, and would entail essentially the same security and assurance issues as would those identified in the classification reviews described above.

14.6 Automatic Classification

Because of the semantic nature of data classification, it appears that many of the rules for data classification issues are complicated and sometimes conflicting or ad hoc. Many such issues were identified in the paper on Berson's and Lunt's proposed expert system application CLASSI [LB87].

The formulation for the homework exercise was found not to completely address the necessary data classification rules. In particular, there were several permissible state transitions that could lead to a need to reclassify a student's transcript in seeming violation of the Tranquility Property. Yet, since evidently certain information about the student could still be retrieved at the unclassified level, there were several available routes that would permit a potential interloper to derive (or infer) information about classified entries in the classified transcript. [For example, an interloper could periodically monitor each student's transcript. If at some time the transcript were to disappear from view, it would indicate that the student had enrolled in one or more classified courses. Several potential problems could result from this situation: (a) The grades received in the classified courses could be approximated based on the previously known grades and grade point average and the unclassified grade point average that would be accessible at the end of the term. (b) A hostile intelligence service could also derive a list of students who were just being introduced into a classified training program, information that could prove to be valuable with respect to students with low grade point averages—especially those students whose grade point averages had lowered as a consequence of enrolling in the classified classes.]

These apparent counterexamples to the desired security classification policy emphasised the degree of complexity that could be achieved in even a simple automatic classification problem.

14.7 References

[LB87] T.F. Lunt and T.A Berson. An expert system to classify and sanitize text. In *Proceedings of the Third Aerospace Computer Security Conference, December 1987.*

15

Presentation and Discussion on Balanced Assurance

William R. Shockley[1]

ABSTRACT This discussion, conducted by William Shockley of Gemini Computers, Incorporated, consisted primarily of a discussion of what balanced assurance means and the technical and management motivations for choosing to interpret the *Trusted Computing System Evaluation Criteria* (hereinafter referred to as the *Criteria*) [Cen85b] in this way. The material presented below summarizes the contents of his presentation.

15.1 Introduction

Balanced assurance is a concept applicable to appropriately-structured, complex trusted computing base (TCB) implementations (for example, a TCB architecture based on the *TCB subsets* concept [SS87]). It is based upon a designation, by the system sponsor, of those TCB subsets responsible for enforcement of the mandatory access control security policy, together with those TCB subsets upon which any such subsets depend. The designated subsets are collectively referred to as the "mandatory TCB". (The term "TCB subset" is meant to include Network Trusted Computing Base (NTCB) partitions[2], as described in the Trusted Network Interpretation of the DoD Trusted Computer System Evaluation Criteria (TNI) [Cen87].) It is emphasized that the notion of a TCB subset, as an independently evaluatable entity, is much stronger than that of mere software layering, and requires the enforcement of well-defined protection domains by the underlying reference validation mechanism.

Within the mandatory TCB, all applicable criteria for the targeted evaluation class (B2, B3, or A1) are to be applied in full. TCB subsets outside the mandatory TCB need only fulfill the applicable criteria for class C2, extended, however, to ensure that the expected functionality (not assurance) for audit, discretionary access control, and (in some cases), identification

---

[1]Digital Equipment Corporation

[2]The TNI defines an NTCB as follows: "The totality of mechanisms within a single network component for enforcing the network policy, as allocated to that component; the part of the NTCB within a single network component." [Cen87]

and authentication is provided for the targeted evaluation class. (For example, real-time audit alarms are a functional requirement at Class B3. If audit collection, storage, and review is provided by a TCB subset outside of the mandatory TCB, the audit subset(s) must incorporate a real-time audit alarm capability, although in most other respects only the Class C2 criteria need be met.)

The following rules expand upon this basic notion:

- There is no discernible difference between Class B1 and Class C2 systems except for the addition of functionality related to mandatory security. This means that the notion of balanced assurance is not, strictly speaking, applicable for this evaluation class. The composition of a Class B1 mandatory TCB with a Class C2 TCB subset supporting Class C2 functionality, is simply a Class B1 TCB with homogeneous assurance.

- A Class B2 mandatory TCB may be extended by a Class C2 subset or subsets to form a Class B2 TCB.

- A Class B3 or A1 mandatory TCB may be extended by a Class C2+ subset to form a Class B3, or A1, TCB, respectively. (Class C2+ is a term used to denote a system that meets the Class B3 functionality requirements, which are the same as the Class A1 functionality requirements, and the assurance requirements for Class C2 [Cen87]).

It is noteworthy that in the network case, the only difference defined between Class C2 and C2+ (the latter used only where balanced assurance is applied) is that the latter provides the equivalent of access control lists (ACLs) for discretionary access control functionality and real-time audit alarms. Configuration management, system architecture, documentation, etc. are all the same at C2 and C2+, and there is no notion of non-functional criteria being "selectively" applied. The insistence on ACLs and real-time alarms is intended to ensure that a B3 or A1 database management system with balanced assurance is a functional replacement for one with homogeneous assurance.

An example illustrating one motivation for balanced assurance is the following: we suppose that there exists a set of independent C2+ database backends, each being operated in dedicated mode at various sensitivities (some Secret, some Top Secret, and so on). The environment's document (the so-called "Yellow Book" [Cen85a]) would permit this. Next, we install a Class C2+ terminal controller for each group of backends of the same senstivity (that is, one for all of the Secret backends together, one for all of the Top Secrets together, etc.), allowing each terminal to be connected to any of the backends within a sensitivity "group" (but a terminal could not be used to access a backend outside of its dedicated sensitivity level). Clearly, this architecture is also consistent with Yellow Book guidance.

Finally, we replace all of the Class C2+ terminal controllers with a single Class A1 mandatory TCB acting as a secure terminal gateway, allowing any user to connect to any backend consistent with the user's clearance, which is registered in the mandatory TCB. C2+ discretionary access control is still enforced by the individual backends as before.

From the accreditor's standpoint, the new system is acceptable provided the range of sensitivities for the set of backends is compatible with the use of Class A1. From the user's standpoint, the new system is more useful. But if one were to insist on "homogeneous assurance," all of the Class C2+ backends would now have to replaced by Class A1 backends just because they are now part of a Class A1 TCB. It seems clear that an accreditor would have to be fairly persistent to convince the system sponsor that the system with Class C2+ backends had suddenly become "insecure" and that they should be replaced. A more likely result is a loss of credibility in the utility of evaluations.

The TNI adopted the balanced assurance point of view precisely so that this and similar system architectures could be evaluated as a Class A1 system (rather than forcing accreditors to treat them as accredited, interconnected systems with, at best, fairly broad guidelines for acceptability.)

It is important to note that, in the described architecture, there is no implied requirement to begin performing Class A1 configuration management, documentation, trusted distribution, etc. for the Class C2 backends—they may be managed just as always. If they were secure enough without these requirements in the original system, then they remain secure enough without them in the final system. Moreover, the failure to meet these architectural and documentation assurance requirements (the lack of an accurate DTLS, for example) does not have any impact on the correctness of the Class A1 gateway relative to the enforcement of the mandatory access control policy, although there *is* a certain risk that the system will work today, but not tomorrow when a new version of the database software for the database machine is installed. That risk, however, is not a security-relevant one and should not be addressed by an interpretation of the *Criteria.*

For completeness, the following short statement of the motivations for balanced assurance are included.

First, it is a technique that provides comparable evaluated ratings for architectures that provide comparable protection, from the accreditors' viewpoint. This motivation is illustrated by the example provided above. The next logical step might be described: to replace the Class A1 gateway and Class C2+ backends with multiple, isolated Class C2+ TCB subsets (one for each logically distinct database) supported by an underlying Class A1 TCB subset. Again, denying that this architecture meets the minimum requirements for Class A1 ultimately leads to the need to explain why a group of physically isolated Class C2+ dedicated database machines is not secure enough, from the accreditors' and users' viewpoint—when the Yellow Book says it is.

Secondly, balanced assurance stimulates the availability of usable products on the Evaluated Products List (EPL)[3]. In particular, it allows the use of existing database system designs (i.e., versions of commercial products tailored to meet the requirements for Class C2+ for execution on Class B3 or A1 TCB's) and thus ultimately provides the benefits of trusted systems for the community of database system users.

Finally, it is a technically appropriate decision. The "safety problem" [HRU76] for discretionary access controls (given an initial state, or set of authorizations, it is undecidable whether any given state can be reached; in other words, it is undecidable whether a subject S can ever obtain authorization for an object O) would seem to imply a choice between discretionary access controls which are highly-expressive (based on views) or which have high intrinsic strength of mechanism (such as, simple discretionary access controls, for example, an access matrix, for simple storage objects). The basic problem is that for a complex naming scheme (view-based, naming by content or context) the non-aliasing problem is undecidable: given a "complex" view, it is not generally possible to guarantee that the TCB can compute whether it "intersects" with another complex view. By supplying both a label-based mandatory policy with high strength of mechanism, and an expressive discretionary access control policy with low intrinsic strength of mechanism (for example, discretionary access controls for views) one can offer the administrators of a system the choice: mandatory controls where the concerns about access are sufficiently strong, discretionary controls where concerns are weaker and control by the users is appropriate or where a high degree of expressivity is desired.

15.2 References

[Cen85a] National Computer Security Center. Computer security requirements: Guidance for applying the Department of Defense trusted computer system evaluation criteria in specific environments. *Technical Report CSC-STD-003-85*, National Computer Security Center, June 25 1985.

[Cen85b] National Computer Security Center. Department of Defense trusted computer system evaluation criteria. *Technical Report DOD 5200.28-STD*, Department of Defense, December 1985.

[Cen87] National Computer Security Center. National computer security center trusted network interpretation. *Technical Report NCSC-TG-005*, Version 1, Department of Defense, July 1987.

[3] Appendix A of the *Criteria* discusses the commercial product evaluation process. The Evaluated Products List is a list of products, along with their assigned ratings, that have been subjected to formal product evaluation according to the *Criteria*.

[HRU76] M.A. Harrison, W.L. Ruzzo, and J.D. Ullman. Protection in operating systems. *Communications of the ACM*, 19(8), August 1976.

[SS87] W.R. Shockley and R.R. Schell. TCB subsetting for incremental evaluation. In *Proceedings of the Third AIAA Conference on Computer Security*, December 1987.

16

Some Results from the Entity/Relationship Multilevel Secure DBMS Project

George E. Gajnak[1]

ABSTRACT A multilevel secure version of the Entity/Relationship (E/R) data model has been developed. Its multilevel secure properties are based on three principles: the granularity principle, the dependency principle and the determinacy principle. These three principles are proposed as fundamental to the design of multilevel secure data models and databases. A comparison of the multilevel E/R model and the SeaView multilevel relational data model [LDN+88,DLS+87] reveals that the SeaView model violates determinacy. This violation, called referential ambiguity, comes from the interaction of polyinstantiation with the SeaView formulation of referential integrity. It is argued that referential ambiguity can produce undesirable side effects.

16.1 Project Goals and Assumptions

The history of multilevel secure database systems might be said to have begun with the now famous Summer Study of 1982 [AFSS83]. In this workshop, the participants examined the state of the art of database technology. The participants concluded that of the three major types of database systems available (hierarchical, network, and relational), only relational systems had the potential for being successfully adapted to the multilevel secure information processing environment. Accordingly, the Rome Air Development Center (RADC) funded a research project to examine relational views as the mechanism for enforcing multilevel security in a single database. This project, now known as the SeaView project, was awarded to SRI International.

The emphasis on the relational model in research on multilevel security makes sense, given the popularity of the model and its rigorous mathematical foundation. This emphasis, however, left open the question of what might result if a DBMS were designed "from scratch" for multilevel se-

---

[1]Digital Equipment Corporation

cure data. Accordingly, AOG Systems Corporation proposed a research project into the development a multilevel secure DBMS based on an Entity/Relationship (E/R) data model [Che81]. RADC accepted this proposal and the project was begun in 1986.

The project was conceived as being a complementary effort to the work in the relational model. The emphasis in the project was to be towards the short-term development (three to five years) of a multilevel secure DBMS at class B3 or higher. Accordingly, the more intractable problems (such aggregation and sanitization) would not be addressed. Furthermore, the data manipulation language (DML) proposed would be a call level DML, rather than an end-user query language. The hope was that by taking a different approach, three things might be accomplished:

- Earlier development of a simple, but usable, multilevel secure DBMS of level B3 or higher.
- Additional confirmation of results of other research by independent means.
- A different perspective that might shed light on the fundamental nature of multilevel data independent of the particular data model in use.

Additionally, we at AOG Systems had hoped to examine the hypothesis that a semantic data model, such as an E/R model, might have useful properties for handling multilevel data.

16.2 A Multilevel Entity/Relationship Model

The selection of an E/R model as an alternative to the relational model for multilevel data was based on the following considerations:

- Users find E/R models easy to understand, because they are used as a data design methodology.
- The additional semantics of an E/R model relative to the relational model might provide insight into requirements for multilevel semantic databases and/or multilevel knowledge bases.
- The soon to be declared American National Standard Information Resource Dictionary System (IRDS) is based on an E/R model. The IRDS does not address multilevel data, and the questions of management of multilevel metadata merited investigation. By choosing an E/R model for a multilevel DBMS, the opportunity presented itself to investigate the extension of the IRDS to handle multilevel metadata.

The immediate problem for the project was that, unlike the relational model, there is no single, generally accepted, rigorous E/R model. The approach taken was to generalize and formalize the E/R model found in the IRDS. The resultant model is called the Generalized Typed Entity/Relationship Model (GTERM) [CI88]. GTERM is rigorously defined by a set of primitives, definitions and axioms.

Rather than define a fully functional query language (like SQL), the project chose simply to define DBMS operations via a call-level interface. This decision was dictated by the near-term nature of the project. Of particular importance were the following considerations:

- A call-level interface could be precisely defined in a short period of time.
- A call-level interface could be used in a prototype implementation of the E/R DBMS.
- A call-level interface could be mapped more easily to the operations defined at the TCB interface.

16.2.1 Data Model Semantics

The purpose of this paper is to present what we believe to be some fundamental characteristics of multilevel data, rather than to describe GTERM *per se*. Nonetheless, a brief, informal description of GTERM is necessary to provide the background for the decisions made and the insights gained.

Basic Concepts

An entity is a data object which identifies a distinct thing or concept. The distinctness implies that the object can be named. The data model treats entities and their corresponding names as different data objects. We will discuss names later in this section. A relationship is a data object which associates two or more entities.

An E/R-item is a generalization of entity and relationship. In an E/R diagram, each polygon is an E/R-item. Each E/R-item has a single type. (In this sense GTERM is less than fully generalized because it does not accommodate any form of subtyping. This restriction was a necessary, if unfortunate, compromise in the model, dictated by the short-term goals of the project.)

A reference is a primitive component of a relationship which identifies one and only one participating entity. Note that a reference is not a replication of the entity's name. Rather it may be thought of as a "pointer".

References have a specific graphical interpretation in Entity/Relationship diagrams. According to Chen's conventions [Che81], an entity is represented by a rectangle; a relationship is represented by a diamond. As shown in Figure 16.1, the relationship "Jumped over (Quick Brown Fox, Lazy Dog)" is represented as a diamond with two arrows emanating from it, one pointing to a rectangle labeled "Fox", the other pointing to a rectangle labeled "Dog". A reference is a line connecting a relationship to a participating entity. We choose to emphasize the directionality by showing a reference as an arrow whose head points to an entity and whose tail emanates from a relationship. This directionality also expresses a logical dependency. A relationship is meaningless if a participating entity is non-existent. By regarding references as components of relationships, we recognize that the above relationship presumes the existence of both "the quick brown fox" and "the lazy dog".

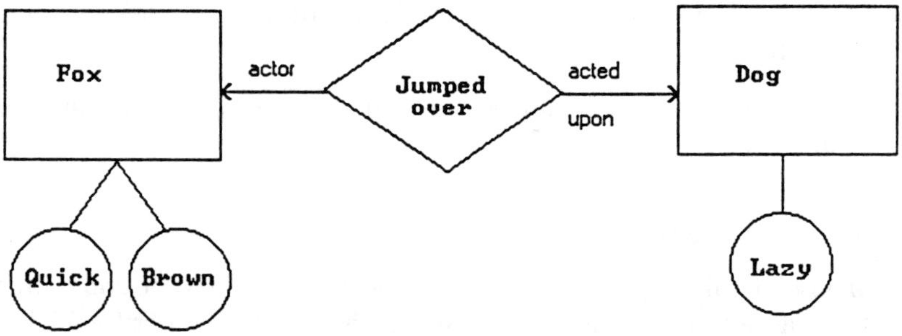

Entities:	**Fox, Dog**
Attributes:	**quick, brown, lazy**
Relationship:	**Fox jumped over dog.**
Roles:	**actor, acted upon**
	Fox assumes role of actor.
	Dog assumes role of acted upon.

FIGURE 16.1. An entity-relationship diagram for "The quick brown fox jumped over the lazy dog."

A role is a discriminant among references within a relationship. In the above example, it is obvious that the fox is the "actor" and the dog is the "acted upon". Were they to switch roles, the relationship would be very different indeed. From this it can be seen that not only the references themselves, but also their associated roles, are central to the meaning of a relationship.

A reference-set is the set of all references in an E/R-item that have a particular role. Each reference-set has a single type. Each reference set type is determined by the type of E/R-item which contains the reference set, and the role for that reference set. Reference set types also specify cardinality constraints. Mandatory references are defined by a positive minimum cardinality constraint on the corresponding reference set type; optional references are defined by differing maximum and minimum cardinality constraints.

For example, suppose we had a database of mortgages. A LOANS relationship type would have a reference set type for the role BORROWER. Since each loan must have at least one borrower, the corresponding reference set type would have a minimum cardinality of one. Since joint loans are possible, a maximum cardinality greater than one is possible.

Reference set types also specify the types of entities which may assume a particular role within a relationship. As shown in Figure 16.2, borrowers need not be only people. Companies or institutions (such as churches and foundations) can also have mortgages and thus assume the role of BORROWER in a LOANS relationship.

Attributes are (unordered) sets of values which are components of an entity, its name, or a relationship. Each attribute has one and only one corresponding type. We distinguish two classes of attributes:

- Property-set: a set of 0, 1 or more values (properties) that is a component of an entity or relationship.
- Designator: a set of 0 or 1 values which is a component of an entity's name but not the entity itself.

In most data models, the constructs corresponding to GTERM's attributes are singular, i.e., they can assume at most one value. The rationale for treating attributes as sets of values is twofold:

- Some programming languages such as Pascal and Ada support set data types. These data types can describe characteristics which are much more complicated than those described by single-valued data types. Consider, for example, the taste of wine. One wine's taste might be described as "dry, robust, fruity" whereas another might be described as "sweet, delicate, fruity". By describing all attributes as sets of values, GTERM directly supports such data types.
- Special "null values" for attributes are avoided entirely. Each null attribute is a null set. The semantics of the null set are well understood.

Mandatory/optional constraints for attributes can be expressed as simple cardinality constraints. Each attribute-type is assigned a minimum and maximum cardinality. Optional attributes are simply those whose type specifies a minimum cardinality of zero; mandatory attributes are those whose type has a positive minimum cardinality.

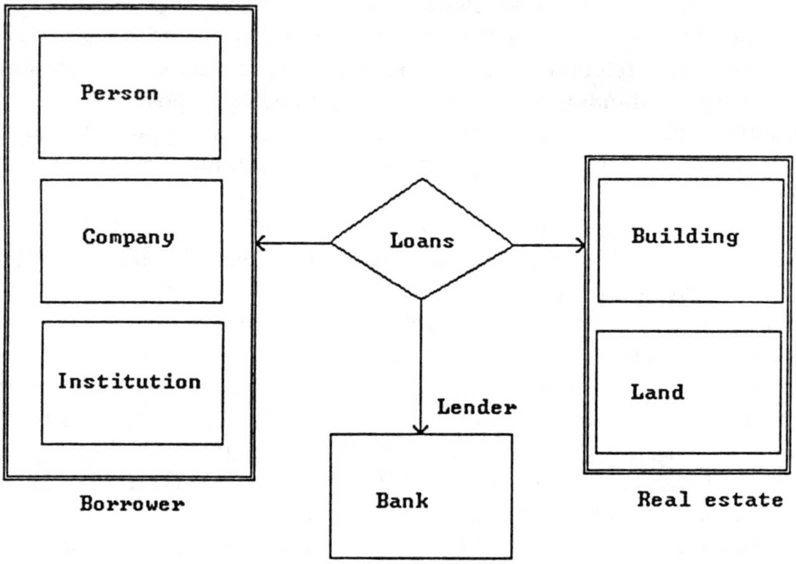

The reference-set-type for the role spans multiple entity-types.

FIGURE 16.2. An example of multiple entity-types assuming the same role.

Designators allow us to use characteristics of entities in naming which are not stored in the entity. Two common designators are access class and entity-type, neither of which is typically stored within a data object, but either may be necessary to identify such an object.

The name of an entity is an ordered n-tuple of singular property-sets and designators. Since each attribute in a name has a type, it is possible to construct the n-tuple of corresponding types. This n-tuple is called a namespace. Each namespace is associated with one or more E/R-item types. An E/R-item type with an associated name space is an entity-type. Each entity has a unique name in the namespace associated with its type.

To appreciate the distinction, consider a motor vehicle registration database. Such a database would contain descriptions of cars, trucks, and motorcycles. Each such vehicle might be named by its licence plate number. In GTERM, it is possible to treat "car", "truck", and "motorcycle" as different entity-types, and yet have a single namespace, composed of licence plate numbers, identify vehicles without regard to their type.

Other Characteristics

Some semantic data models are extensions to the relational data model, in that they attempt to classify relations and provide special relations to express more meaning. The GTERM data model does not do this. In fact, in specifying GTERM, we deliberately tried to be different. The reason for emphasizing differences was twofold:

- Some application schemas which would have clumsy relational representations have more elegant GTERM representations. This suggests that a DBMS based on GTERM or some other semantic data model might be more appropriate for certain applications than a strictly relational database system.
- By emphasizing differences, we hoped that a different mental framework might provide us with insights which we would not have obtained had our model been closer to the relational model.

The major differences of GTERM from the relational model are as follows:

- E/R-items do not necessarily correspond to first normal form relations; both attributes and reference-sets may be multivalued.
- The scope of a namespace is not restricted to a single type of entity. This is to be contrasted with the relational model, where keys ensure uniqueness only within a given relation.

- A reference set is not restricted to referencing only a single type of entity. This is to be contrasted to the (single level) relational model, where a foreign key identifies a single tuple in a single predetermined relation. In the SeaView model, a foreign key can refer to multiple tuples, but each tuple still belongs to a single (multilevel) relation [DLS+87].
- References are not name dependent. In the relational model, a foreign key repeats the key of the tuple in another relation.
- References are explicit. In the relational model, references are achieved by matching attribute values.

16.2.2 Multilevel Security Characteristics

The basic axioms of GTERM which relate to multilevel security are fairly simple. Each E/R-item is a potentially multilevel data-structure subject to the following constraints:

- Each E/R-item has a minimum access class. The access class of each of the components of the E/R-item dominates the minimum access class of the E/R item.

  For simplicity, we call this minimum access class the access class of the E/R- item.
- Each name has an access class. The components of a name are uniformly classified at the same access class as the name.
- The access class of an entity is the same as the access class of its name.

  The rationale for this is simple. Knowledge of the name of an object is equivalent to knowledge of the object itself.
- The access class of a relationship dominates the access class of each referenced entity.

  The rationale for this axiom is that a relationship is a statement about participating entities. When viewed as a statement of fact, it is apparent that the existence of a relationship is predicated on the existence of participating entities. A relationship presumes knowledge of the participating entities. Thus its secrecy classification cannot be any lower than the secrecy of its participating entities. Furthermore, since the relationship represents additional information about each of the participating entities, the integrity of the relationship cannot exceed the integrity of any of the participating entities.
- The access class of a reference equals the access class of the E/R-item which contains the reference.

The rationale for this axiom is that references are central to the meaning of a relationship. If a reference is added to or removed from a relationship, then the meaning of the relationship changes. (This is a difference from the multilevel relational model, where the access class of foreign key elements of a tuple can dominate the access class of the tuple containing the foreign key. In the multilevel relational model no distinction is made between foreign key elements and others insofar as their classification is concerned.)

- The access class of a non-naming attribute dominates that of the entity or relationship in which it participates.

  The rationale for this axiom is similar to that for the axiom of relationship dominance. Non-naming attributes represent additional facts about the entities or relationships in which they reside. As such, their existence is predicated on the fact represented by the E/R-item which contains them. Thus their secrecy must be at least as great as that of the base fact, and their integrity must be no greater than that of the base fact.

- An entity's access class is always the last component of its name.

  This axiom is basically a design decision, dictated by our desire for name uniqueness within a namespace. This effectively partitions a namespace by access class. If access class were not a required naming component, the access class would still be required to distinguish among multiple entities with the same name.

16.3 Results of Research

This project provided us with several insights which we think should be shared with other members of the research community. First, it has provided us with a rationale for rules of multilevel secure data structures. The rationale is based on viewing a multilevel database as merely a set of facts. This abstraction revealed an underlying simplicity which has applicability beyond the E/R DBMS. Second, this abstraction allowed us to propose three data model invariant principles for multilevel secure databases: granularity, dependency and determinacy. Third, it provided an alternative to the SeaView multilevel relational model. By comparing this alternative to the SeaView data model, we discovered that the SeaView model violated the determinacy principle. The consequences of this final discovery have yet to be fully appreciated. We will now discuss each of these points in detail.

16.3.1 The Underlying Abstraction

As can be seen from our axioms for multilevel data structures in GTERM, we have regarded a multilevel secure database as a set of associated facts, where a "fact" is merely an encapsulated unit of information. In a database, some facts refer to other facts, and a fact which refers to other facts is logically dependent on each referenced fact.

One of the nice things about this abstraction is that it corresponds to a graphic interpretation. If facts are represented by nodes of the graph, the logical dependencies are arrows emanating from dependent facts and terminating at base facts. It seems fairly obvious that a well-formed database interpreted this way should generate an acyclic directed graph.

As we have shown previously, the data structures of GTERM reduce to this simple abstraction. It is one of the ironies of this project that the more complex data structures of GTERM should lead to such a simple representation of multilevel data.

Principles of Multilevel Databases

With this simple abstraction for a database, we now consider what a multilevel secure database should be. The answer is very simple. A multilevel database is a set of associated facts, where different facts have different access classes. This leaves open the question of what constitutes a "well formed" multilevel database.

We propose three principles for multilevel databases:

- The Granularity Principle
- The Dependency Principle
- The Determinacy Principle

It is our contention that a well-formed multilevel database conforms to these three principles. We do not claim that these principles are exhaustive.

The Granularity Principle

The granularity principle merely states that in a multilevel secure database, the finest level of granularity for protection purposes should be data structures which correspond to atomic facts. This statement is perhaps surprising in its obviousness. The interesting thing is that it can lead us to some unexpected conclusions.

We have already shown how this principle applies to GTERM. If we apply this to the SeaView model, we see that keys within a tuple should be treated as atomic facts. That is, all the elements of the primary key of a tuple should be assigned the same access class. We also see that all the elements of the foreign key of a relation should also have the same access class.

We see that what constitutes an "atomic fact" might not correspond to single data elements even for non-key elements of a tuple. For example, in a missile targeting application, the TARGET-LATITUDE and TARGET-LONGITUDE might be individual attributes. However, the atomic fact to be protected for any target would be its location, which would correspond to both fields together.

In applying the granularity principle, we see that an Entity-Relationship interpretation of data also forces us into treating all references as essential for expressing a relationship. Consequently, all references are assigned the same access class. If we were to take strictly a relational view of data, we would be tempted to assign different access classes to different foreign keys in a relation, if those foreign keys were not part of the primary key.

The Dependency Principle

A database of unrelated facts is uninteresting. The dependency principle presumes that we can look upon a multilevel database as a set of facts in which the facts are associated by their logical dependencies. Let us hypothesize the fact that the U.S.S. New Jersey is carrying nuclear weapons. This fact is logically dependent on the fact that there is a ship called the U.S.S. New Jersey. The dependency principle simply states that the access class of a fact must dominate the access class of any fact that it depends on. In this simple case, we see that it is absurd to have the fact of nuclear capability of the U.S.S. New Jersey have a lower access class than the fact of its existence.

When applied to GTERM, it is the dependency principle that leads us to have the access class of a relationship dominate the access classes of the participating entities. It also permits us to have non-naming attributes whose access class strictly dominates the entity or relationship which contains them. The SeaView model has rules which correspond almost exactly to those in GTERM.

As a consequence of the dependency principle, we see that if a fact is deleted from a database, logical consistency would have us delete or augment all dependent facts. This is allowed, because the deletion or updates of dependent facts are "write ups" with respect to secrecy and "write downs" with respect to integrity. The handling of such a rippling effect is one of the major issues to be addressed in the implementation of a multilevel secure DBMS. The limitation of the degree of factual dependencies in a multilevel database is a legitimate question for a design methodology to address.

The Determinacy Principle

The determinacy principle states that factual dependencies should be non-ambiguous. This is implicit in our view of databases as repositories of associated facts. Obviously, we would like a database to avoid confusion. Given this, one might wonder why we elevate this concept to a stated principle for multilevel databases.

Databases with a single level of security automatically fulfill the determinacy principle. Consider the (single level) relational model. Applying the fact abstraction to the relational model, a tuple represents a set of facts about an object identified by the tuple's key. The tuple's key is equivalent to an existence fact about the object. Thus each non-key element of the tuple can be interpreted as a fact which is dependent on the key fact.

Referential integrity requires that a foreign key in one tuple equate to the key of another tuple in one relation. Since keys are unique within relations, only one tuple is identified. Thus a tuple which contains a foreign key can be viewed as a set of facts, each of which has a dependency on another fact identified by the foreign key.

Multilevel databases, however, present a difficulty not present in single level databases: polyinstantiation. Polyinstantiation is essentially a replication of facts at different levels of security. When such replication occurs, the question of its interpretation becomes critical. The determinacy principle does not eliminate polyinstantiation. It does, however, avoid an explosion of interpretations which can lead to tremendous confusion. In the next section we will show how this confusion can arise, and what some of the consequences are.

Referential Ambiguity

Referential ambiguity is a phenomenon which occurs in the SeaView model but does not occur in GTERM. It occurs in the SeaView model with polyinstantiated tuples. The SeaView model does not include a tuple's base access class as a required component of the key. Thus when a tuple is polyinstantiated, a matching foreign key in another tuple refers to several tuples in different access classes. This is a violation of the determinacy principle. It can have some interesting and serious consequences. Consider the following example.

An Example of Referential Ambiguity

Starfleet has a mission-tracking multilevel secure database, which identifies each of its starships and their missions. The mission-tracking database describes starships, personnel, and planets. Among the information retained are personnel assignments to starships, starship missions to planets, and planet intelligence information.

Figure 16.3 shows a partial schema for this database, first as an entity-relationship diagram and as a set of relations. Figure 16.4 shows a sample collection of tuples from this database. For simplicity, we have not shown the classification elements called for in the multilevel relational model, and have given each element the same classification as the tuple which contains it.

Using the STARSHIP-NAME as the key for the STARSHIP relation, we

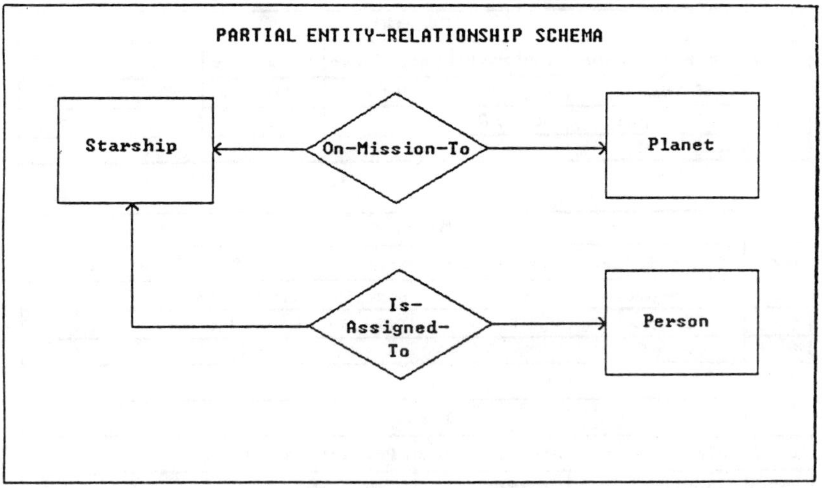

PARTIAL RELATIONAL SCHEMA

Starship

Starship-name	Contract	Ship-Class	Crew-size	...

Mission

Starship-name	Destination	Purpose	StartDate	...

Planet

Planet-name	Affiliation	Population	...

Personnel

Person-name	Rank	...

Assignments

Person-name	Starship-name	...

FIGURE 16.3. Starfleet mission-tracking database.

	Starship				
TupleAC	Starship-name	Contract	Ship-Class	Crew-size	...
Uncls	USS Enterprise	NCC1701A	Constitution	400	
Secret	USS Enterprise	NCC1701D	Galaxy	900	

	Mission				
TupleAC	Starship-name	Destination	Purpose	StartDate	...
TopSec	USS Enterprise	Talos IV	Bootleg Saurian Brandy	12/17/2488	
Secret	USS Enterprise	Rigel II	Diplomatic	12/15/2488	

	Planet			
TupleAC	Planet-name	Affiliation	Population	...
Unclass	Talos IV	Federation	5,000,000,000	
Unclass	Rigel II	Neutral	3,000,000,000	

	Personnel		
TupleAC	Person-name	Rank	...
Confid	James T. Kirk	Captain	
Confid	Jean-Luc Picard	Captain	

	Assignments		
TupleAC	Person-name	Starship-name	...
Confid	James T. Kirk	USS Enterprise	
Secret	Jean-Luc Picard	USS Enterprise	

FIGURE 16.4. Starfleet mission-tracking database: partial data display.

see that there are two tuples for the U.S.S. Enterprise. Furthermore, we see that two different captains are assigned to a ship called U.S.S. Enterprise, and a ship called U.S.S. Enterprise has two different missions, one to Talos IV and another to Rigel II. Suppose a top-secret user were to submit the query, "Who is the captain of the ship going to Talos IV?" In this case, he would receive the answer, 'James T. Kirk, Jean- Luc Picard". Similarly, it is impossible to get a definite answer to the question "Where in the universe is Jean-Luc Picard?".

Examining the database, the top secret user can have three possible interpretations of the data:

- The unclassified U.S.S. Enterprise is a cover story for the secret U.S.S. Enterprise.
- The existence of a secret U.S.S. Enterprise has been leaked.
- There are two ships, both named U.S.S. Enterprise.

Unfortunately, there is no way to choose among the cases based on the content of the database alone. One might argue that this is really a problem of key selection. However, one of the basic rules of multilevel data is that uniqueness constraints cannot span access classes. Thus, as long as there are starships in different access classes, the only ways to avoid information leakage are to either partition the key values by access class or polyinstatiate starships.

Assuming there are two ships, both named U.S.S. Enterprise, it still is impossible to tell who is the captain of each U.S.S. Enterprise and which U.S.S. Enterprise is on which mission. The confusion, however, does not stop there. One must consider the consequences of subsequent maintenance actions on the integrity of the database. For the sake of argument, let us assume that the "reality" of the situation is as follows:

The unclassified U.S.S. Enterprise is an aging museum piece. Its captain is the senile James T. Kirk, and the ship's top secret mission is to deliver 35,000 kegs of Saurian brandy to Talos IV for the centenary of that planet's joining the Federation. The secret U.S.S. Enterprise is a brand-new ship. Its captain is the pompous Jean-Luc Picard, and it is on a secret diplomatic mission to Rigel II. Figure 16.5 provides an E/R diagram which illustrates this "reality".

Now suppose James T. Kirk ran his Enterprise smack into a black hole. Obviously his mission would be scrubbed. However, in the database as shown in Figure 16.4, it is impossible to state with certainty which mission that is. According to the SeaView model's formulation of referential integrity, there would be no way to automatically delete the correct mission, because the correct mission is indeterminate. Thus the database would now reflect that the secret U.S.S. Enterprise is on a top secret mission to Talos IV. This is probably worse than the original case, because a previously

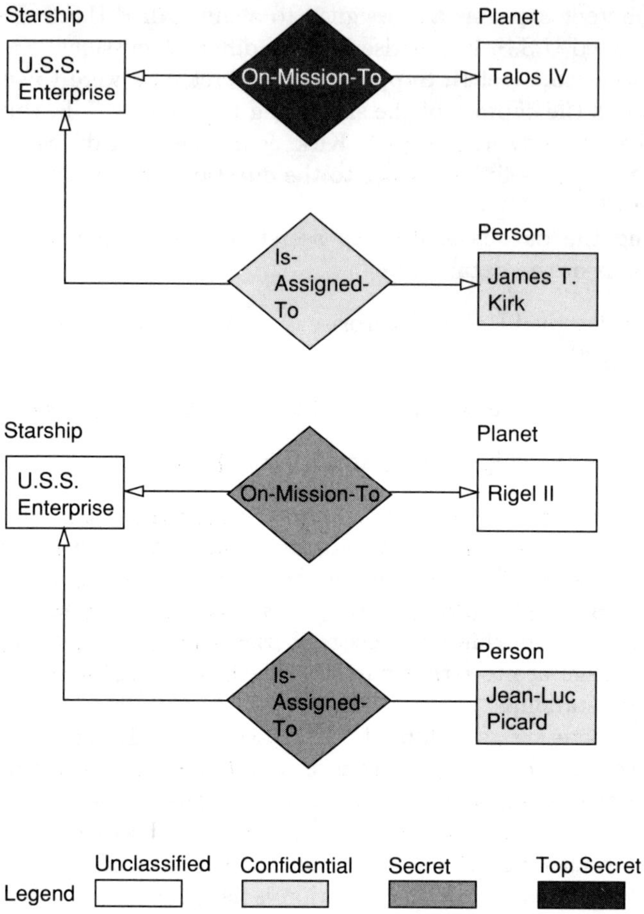

FIGURE 16.5. Starfleet mission-tracking database: a possible interpretation represented in an E/R diagram.

ambiguous reference to U.S.S. Enterprise in the MISSION tuple for Talos IV has been replaced by a non-ambiguous but incorrect reference!

GTERM avoids these difficulties entirely. In a GTERM database, all references are non-ambiguous. The GTERM DML requires the user to identify a specific entity explicitly when establishing a reference. This is facilitated by making each entity's base access class a required component of the entity's name.

The Relationship between Formal and Referential Integrity

The above example illustrates that a correct form of referential integrity is central to describing formal integrity for multilevel databases. It raises the basic question of whether or not one can have referential integrity in a database with referential ambiguity. The fact that the SeaView data model violates the determinacy principle raises the issue of whether the determinacy principle is fundamental to multilevel data models or not.

It is our contention that the determinacy principle is fundamental, and that one cannot have referential integrity with ambiguous references. Consequently, we think that the determinacy principle should be supported directly by multilevel secure data models.

One may take exception with this view. If so, the question becomes one of determining when ambiguous references are desirable and when they are not. This then becomes a question for multilevel database design methodologies to address.

16.4 Conclusions

From a data modeling perspective, the real insight is the interpretation of a database as an acyclic directed graph of facts and factual dependencies as the underlying abstraction. This leads us to the three principles of multilevel data: granularity, dependency and determinacy.

We believe that the proposed E/R model works precisely because we have been able to map its constructs to this underlying abstraction and because it directly supports these three principles. There is no suggestion that our proposed E/R model is unique in this respect. On the contrary, we believe that other data models can be developed which also map to this underlying abstraction. We suspect that such a mapping would be useful for Prolog and frame-based knowledge bases.

We recognize that the question of whether these principles should be embedded in every multilevel data model is controversial. Only time and the implementation of multilevel databases will determine the answer to this question.

Acknowledgements: This work was funded by RADC under contract number F30602-86-C-0117, contracting officer Joseph Giordano. The author wishes to acknowledge the following people. First, Dr. H. C. Lefkovits, who recognized the opportunity and provided leadership throughout the project. Next, the author wishes to thank Dr. Roger Schell of Gemini Computers, who kept us honest according to the Orange Book criteria, and Bill Shockley of Gemini Computers, who devised the graphic interpretation of the E/R model. Finally, the author wishes to recognize both Dr. Dorothy Denning and Teresa Lunt for their excellent and ambitious work on the SeaView multilevel relational model.

16.5 References

[AFSS83] Committee on Multilevel Data Management Security Air Force Summer Study. Multilevel data management security. *Technical report*, Air Force Studies Board, National Research Council, National Academy Press, 1983. For Official Use Only.

[Bib77] K.J. Biba. Integrity considerations for secure computer systems. *Technical Report ESD-TR-76-372*, USAF Electronic Systems Division, Bedford, Massachusetts, April 1977.

[BL76] D.E. Bell and L.J. LaPadula. Secure computer systems: Unified exposition and Multics interpretation. *Technical Report ESD-TR-75-306*, The MITRE Corporation, Bedford, Massachusetts, March 1976.

[Che81] P.P. Chen. *A Preliminary Framework for Entity-Relationship Models.* ER Institute, 1981.

[CI88] AOG Systems Corporation and Gemini Systems Inc. Multilevel secure entity-relationship DBMS. Draft, AOG Systems Corporation, May 19 1988.

[CM84] W.F. Clocksin and C.S. Mellish. *Programming in Prolog.* Springer-Verlag, second edition, 1984.

[DLS+87] D.E. Denning, T.F. Lunt, R.R. Schell, M. Heckman, and W.R. Shockley. A multilevel relational data model. In *Proceedings of the 1987 IEEE Symposium on Security and Privacy*, April 1987.

[Har85] M.D. Harris. *Introduction to Natural Language Processing.* Reston Publishing Co., 1985.

[LDN+88] T.F. Lunt, D.E. Denning, P.G. Neumann, R.R. Schell, M. Heckman, and W.R. Shockley. Final report vol. 1: Security policy and policy interpretation for a class A1 multilevel secure relational database system. *Technical report*, Computer Science Laboratory, SRI International, Menlo Park, California, 1988.

17

Designing a Trusted Application Using an Object-Oriented Data Model

Catherine Meadows and Carl Landwehr[1]

17.1 Introduction

Key problems in developing trusted application systems are defining the security requirements in a way that is comprehensible to the users and implementing the system in a way that makes it clear that these requirements are met. An object-oriented approach can help solve both of these problems because it permits describing the requirements in terms familiar to the users—objects can be mapped directly to real-world entities—and it permits identifying the parts of the system that enforce security requirements. In this paper we illustrate the usefulness of the object-oriented approach by considering from these two points of view the modeling of the NRL Secure Military Message System (SMMS) [Hei86,LHM84] as an object-oriented database system. Future work will address the problem of building such an application on top of a general-purpose trusted relational DBMS in much the same way that an object-oriented DBMS such as POSTGRES [Row87,SR87] is built on top of a relational database.

The SMMS was originally conceived as an example of a trusted application built to correspond to a security model written with that particular application in mind. Thus it has some security requirements beyond the access requirements of a trusted operating system. The most noticeable of these is the fact that each user can act in one or more of several roles, such as releaser, downgrader, or system security officer. Each role has a set of actions permitted to it, and each user is allowed to play only a particular subset of the set of all possible roles. Some of the integrity requirements of the system are also security-related. For example, the user of the system who receives an SMMS-message[2] should have some assurance that the

---

[1]Center for Secure Information Technology, Naval Research Laboratory

[2]We warn the reader that both the SMMS and the object-oriented database model involve the concepts of 'message' and 'object', defined in completely incompatible ways. In order to avoid confusion, from now on we will always use 'SMMS-messages' and 'SMMS-objects' when referring to objects and messages

SMMS-message has not been changed since it was sent. This is reflected in the requirements of the SMMS, which state that an SMMS-message marked 'sent' cannot be updated.

Previous attempts have been made to model the SMMS using the relational database model [AFSS83], but these attempts have not been wholly successful. This is partly because the concept of a tuple in a relation does not correspond perfectly with the notion of a military message, since a message may have an arbitrary number of paragraphs. Moreover, many of the operations provided in the relational calculus (e.g., join) are not needed for providing message system functions, while many of the operations that are needed (e.g., send) do not correspond precisely to relational operations. Finally, the relational model fails to reflect the hierarchical structure of the SMMS. It was possible to overcome all these difficulties, but at the cost of naturalness and ease of modeling. The object-oriented data model seems to capture the SMMS semantics more naturally.

17.2 The Object-Oriented Data Model

In this section, we present a brief description of the object-oriented data model. This is essentially a summary of the discussions given in [BCG+87] and [SB86].

In an object-oriented database system, all entities are modeled as objects. Each object has the capability of accepting and responding to a particular set of messages. The state of an object is defined by the values of a set of instance variables. In the case of composite objects, the values of the instance variables can themselves be objects. The behavior of an object is encapsulated in a set of methods. Methods are programs that manipulate or return the state of the object. For each message accepted by an object, there is a corresponding method that executes the response to that message. Only messages and their responses are visible from outside the object; methods and instance variables are hidden.

Most object-oriented systems allow three ways of organizing data. These are class objects and class hierarchies, composite objects, and related objects. At this point, the concept of related objects does not seem necessary to the development of the SMMS, and so we will restrict ourselves to discussion of class and composite objects.

The concept of classes and class hierarchies is introduced in order to prevent unnecessary duplication of methods and instance variable names. Objects with similar properties are grouped together into a class. Objects belonging to the same class are described by the same instance variables

---

as defined in the SMMS, and 'objects' and 'messages' when referring to objects and messages as defined in the object-oriented model.

and the same methods. Classes themselves are objects and may be members of classes. Thus it is possible to define hierarchies of classes. Objects that are members of a child class inherit the structures (instance variable names and methods) of the parent class. Objects may possibly be members of more than one class. In that case, rules must be developed for the handling of possible inheritance conflicts.

The object-oriented approach may also be used to model composite objects. A composite object is defined in terms of a set of dependent objects, which can themselves be composite objects. For example, a report may be thought of as an object that consists of a title page object and a text object. The text object consists of section objects, which in turn consist of paragraph objects. The title page consists of, say, the title object, the author(s) object, the date object, and so on. Subobjects of a composite object differ from subclasses of a class in that a subobject of a composite object does not inherit any properties of the parent object.

There are several aspects of the object-oriented model that seem promising for the SMMS. One of these is the idea of describing an object in terms of the messages it can respond to. This is particularly useful in the specification of roles. A role can be defined strictly in terms of such messages. For example, only the 'downgrader' role responds to the 'downgrade' message. Such a definition of security in terms of roles is used by Lochovsky and Woo [LW88] in the description of a hypothetical object-oriented office information system and Vinter [Vin88] in the development of the discretionary access control system for the SDOS secure distributed operating system being developed at BBN laboratories. The specification of security properties in terms of allowable messages is less helpful in the specification of the part of the system that handles multi-level security, since in this case allowed actions depend not only on the privileges of a user playing a role, but a comparison between the clearance of the user and the security label of the data. However, in future work we will show how an object-oriented system may make use of the protection provided by an underlying trusted relational DBMS.

Another feature of the object-oriented model that appears to be useful for trusted applications is the notion of hierarchical inheritance. Objects can inherit instance variables, messages, and methods from superclasses. Thus, in a system such as the SMMS, we can divide the set of objects into user class objects and entity class objects. The code for the handling of security labels and clearances can be written as message protocols and methods for these class objects which will be inherited by all subclasses. This will allow us to confine security enforcement to an identifiable set of software components.

However, we will also need to ensure that the inheritance property is strictly enforced. In other words, we need to be sure that, whenever a new object is created, it inherits all its security relevant message protocols and methods from a particular superclass. Thus strict enforcement of inheritance becomes a security requirement of the system.

Finally, the concept of a composite object corresponds naturally to the concept of a container in the SMMS. In the SMMS, a container is an entity that can contain other entities. However, the kinds of entities a particular container can contain depend on how the container is defined. For example, a file can contain SMMS-messages, or text, but not both, and it cannot contain directories. Thus it is straightforward to define, say, an SMMS-message file as a composite object consisting of an owner, a security label, an access list, and a set of SMMS-message objects. While the modeling of a container as a composite object is not directly security-related, much of the SMMS security model relies on the notion of a container; for example, a container cannot contain an entity unless its security label dominates the label of that entity. A natural and understandable means of modeling containers makes it easier to provide assurance that security requirements defined in terms of containers are enforced.

17.3 The SMMS as an Object-Oriented Database

We now present a brief outline of the SMMS security policy and describe how it can be re-stated using the object-oriented approach.

The SMMS includes users and entities. Each user has a clearance and authorization to assume one or more roles. Each role has a set of data operations permitted to it. Entities can be either containers or SMMS-objects. Containers can contain other entities; SMMS-objects cannot. Examples of containers are directories, which contain files, which can be either text files which contain text SMMS-objects or SMMS-message files which contain SMMS-messages, or SMMS-messages themselves. Examples of SMMS-objects are the components of a message such as addresses and paragraphs, and text objects. Each entity has a security label and an access list (although components of a message may not have access lists). Operations that can be performed by a user on an entity include insertion, deletion, display, downgrade, and release. The ability to perform some of these operations may depend upon a user's role (downgrade, release), upon comparison of clearances and security labels (insertion, deletion, display), or upon the entity itself (released messages cannot be updated; files cannot be released). A user can request access to an entity either directly, by giving the unique identifier of that entity, or indirectly, by giving an access path. If the user requests access directly, it is granted on the basis of the security label and access set of the entity, the clearance of the user, the security label of the terminal he is logged in from (which is also a container), the role or roles the user has assumed, and the nature of the entity itself. If the request is indirect, and one of the containers in the access path is marked CCR (container clearance required), then access to the entity requested also depends on whether the user's clearance dominates the security label of that container. For example, in the existing prototypes of the SMMS, all messages are marked CCR [HC85].

We begin by dividing the system into three kinds of objects: user objects, role objects, and entity objects. A user object is defined by three instance variables: the user name, the clearance, and the permitted roles. A role object is defined by the set of operations that a user playing that role is allowed to perform. At the moment we leave the question open as to whether the operations are values of an instance variable or messages to which the role object responds.

A user accesses the SMMS by logging in from a particular terminal and choosing a subset of the set of roles allotted to him. At this point a login object is created. The login object is assembled from the user object, the role objects corresponding to the roles chosen, and the terminal object (in the SMMS, terminals are entities). The login object consists of the user's ID, the user's clearance, the terminal's ID and security label, and of the names of the various roles he has assumed. The login object represents the user throughout that session. The user is able to modify the login object by adding or deleting roles that he is permitted to assume, but he cannot modify the login object in any other way except by logging out, in which case the login object is destroyed. The system is responsible for the correct assembly and use of the login object, and for its destruction when the user logs out.

An entity has at least three instance variables: the entity name, the security label, and the access set. It responds to the messages concerning creation, deletion, updating, and reading. The subclasses of the entity class object are the container object and the SMMS-object object. The container object is a composite object; its sub-objects are entity objects. The container object responds to all messages responded to by the entity object, and also responds to all messages concerning insertion and deletion of sub-entities. It is at this point that we define the methods that handle the security-relevant rules for insertion and deletion of subentities and the definition of CCR. The SMMS-object object responds to all messages responded to by the entity object, but cannot contain subobjects.

Container class objects can themselves be further divided into directories, text files, SMMS-message files, and SMMS-messages. Each of these responds to all messages responded to by the container class object, as well as some messages defined solely for it. The methods that implement the responses to the messages are also augmented. For example, it is at this point that we insert the rules governing which kinds of containers can contain which kinds of entities: directories can only contain files, SMMS-message files can only contain SMMS-messages, and so on. Some security-relevant rules are also introduced at this point: for example, in the SMMS prototype, all messages must be marked CCR.

SMMS-object class objects are divided into text and SMMS-message fields. SMMS-message fields are further divided into different kinds of message fields: address, sender, paragraph, and so on. Likewise, SMMS-messages are divided into two different kinds of messages: formal SMMS-messages and informal SMMS-messages.

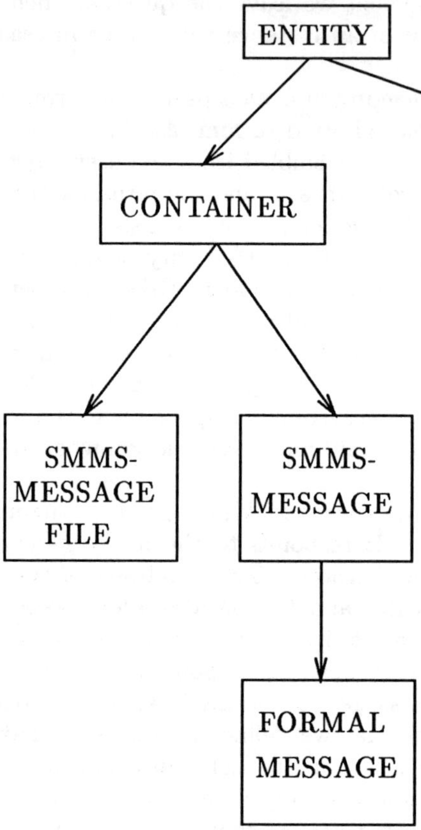

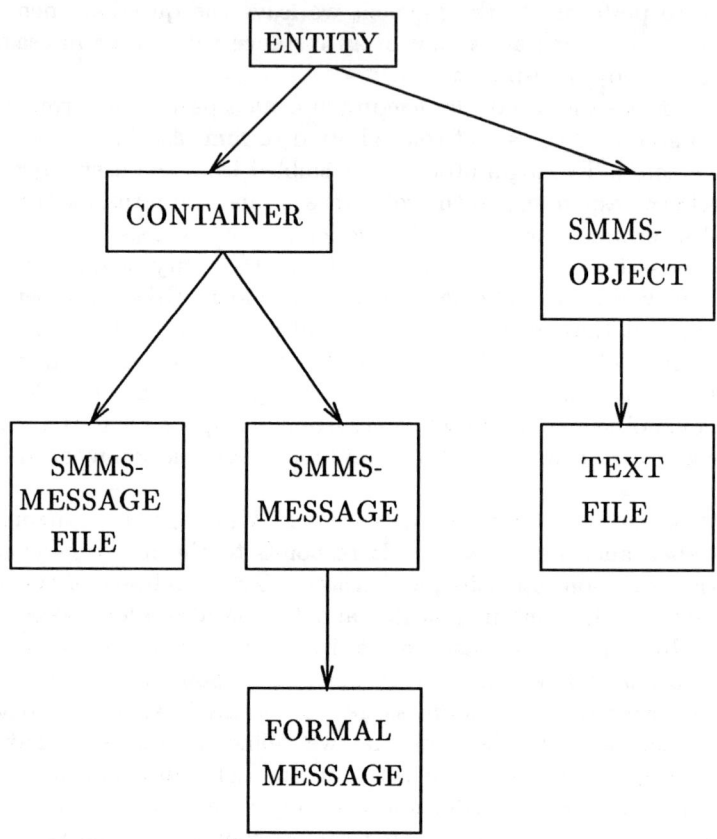

FIGURE 17.1. A portion of the SMMS class hierarchy.

We could continue in greater detail, but the general strategy is clear. Messages accepted by entities and the methods responding to them are defined at the highest possible level in the class hierarchy. An entity object inherits all methods and messages belonging to its superclass objects. However, it can also accept new messages, and the old methods can be augmented. (See Fig. 17.1).

17.4 Conclusion and Future Directions

In this paper we have set forth the SMMS as it would be modeled using the object-oriented approach. We have shown that the SMMS can be modeled naturally using this approach, and that the object-oriented data model can make the SMMS easier to understand. However, we have not yet addressed the issue of how to guarantee the security of a system built along these lines.

In order to do this, we need to do four things. First, we need to identify the set of security-related methods and ensure that they enforce the assertions of the security model. Secondly, we need to ensure that a given object responds only to the security-related methods associated with that object, and uses the security-related methods defined for that object. Next, we need to ensure that inheritance in the class hierarchy is strictly enforced. Finally, we need to ensure that methods and messages defined further down in the class hierarchy do not interfere with security-related methods and messages defined earlier. In future work, we will present an architecture for the SMMS as an object-oriented system, and show how this architecture can be used to enforce the security properties defined in this paper.

17.5 References

[AFSS83] Committee on Multilevel Data Management Security Air Force Summer Study. Multilevel data management security. *Technical report*, Air Force Studies Board, National Research Council, National Academy Press, 1983. For Official Use Only.

[BCG+87] J. Banerjee, H.-T. Chou, J.F. Garza, W. Kim, D. Woelk, N. Ballou, and H.-J. Kim. Data model issues for object-oriented applications. *ACM Transactions on Office Information Systems*, 5(1), January 1987.

[HC85] C.L. Heitmeyer and M. Cornwell. Specifications for three members of the military message system (MMS) family. *NRL memorandum report 5645*, Naval Research Laboratory, September 9 1985.

[Hei86] C.L. Heitmeyer. Requirements for the military message system family: Data types and user commands. *NRL memorandum report 5670*, Naval Research Laboratory, April 11 1986.

[LHM84] C.E. Landwehr, C.L. Heitmeyer, and J.McLean. A security model for military message systems. *ACM Transactions on Computer Systems*, 2(3), August 1984.

[LW88] F.H. Lochovsky and C.C. Woo. Role-based security in data base management systems. In C.E. Landwehr, editor, *Database Security: Status and Prospects.* North Holland, 1988.

[Row87] L.A. Rowe. A shared object hierarchy. In M. Stonebraker and L.A. Rowe, editors, *The POSTGRES Papers, Memorandum No. UCB/ERL M86/85.* Electronics Research Laboratory, College of Engineering, University of California, Berkeley, 1987.

[SB86] M. Stefik and D.G. Bobrow. Object-oriented programming: Themes and variations. *The AI Magazine*, Winter 1986.

[SR87] M. Stonebraker and L.A. Rowe. The design of POSTGRES. In M. Stonebraker and L.A. Rowe, editors, *The POSTGRES Papers, M86/85.* Electronics Research Laboratory, College of Engineering, University of California, Berkeley, 1987.

[Vin88] S.T. Vinter. Extended discretionary access controls. In *Proceedings of the 1988 IEEE Symposium on Security and Privacy*, April 1988.

18

Foundations of Multilevel Databases

Bhavani Thuraisingham[1]

ABSTRACT In this paper, formal logic is used as a basis for establishing concepts in multilevel databases. Issues covered include: model and proof theoretic approaches to formalizing multilevel database concepts, environments associated with security levels, the inference problem, handling negative information and the inclusion of formal semantics of time. Finally, issues related to the theory of multilevel relational databases, consistency and completeness of security constraints and assigning security levels to data are also briefly addressed.

18.1 Introduction

A multilevel database is a database with data at different security levels. Thus a multilevel database management system (MLS/DBMS) ensures that users cleared for different levels can still access and share data without compromising security. Since achieving prominence at the Air Force Summer Study in 1982, MLS/DBMSs have received much attention. Many attempts are being made to design these systems (see for example [ST,Thuar,DAH+87a,DLS+87,DOST88,KTTar]), and the operation of such systems appears to be in the not too distant future. However, the present state of development of MLS/DBMSs is comparable to the state of DBMSs of the early 1970s. That is, the theoretical foundation of MLS/DBMSs is still in its infancy. Consequently most of the designs are ad hoc in origin and highly dependent on the characteristics and functions of the trusted computing bases on which they are hosted.

But a better understanding of MLS/DBMSs can be achieved by exploring the foundations of DBMSs themselves as well as introducing advances in some of their techniques to MLS/DBMSs. This discussion paper relates multilevel database concepts to formal logic in the same way database concepts have been related. Consequently this approach provides a basis for MLS/DBMS by formalizing their concepts. In particular, since the seman-

---

[1]At present with the MITRE Corporation. The work was done while the author was at Honeywell, Inc.

tics of logic are well defined, the counterparts in MLS/DBMS can also be well defined.

This paper explores the applicability to multilevel databases of a set of issues that has been under active research during the past 15 years in the database community. The introductory material on logic and databases can be obtained from [GM78]. This reference consists of a collection of papers presented at the first workshop on this topic in France in 1977. Recently another workshop on this topic was conducted in Maryland. The papers presented at this workshop are published in [Min88]. The workshop shows how the subject has evolved over the past decade. Much of the work at both workshops has concentrated on the relational model of databases. However, logic has been used in the past to formalize database concepts based on other models as well. Since most of the discussion on multilevel databases is also focused on relational databases, this paper also focuses on the relational model. For a discussion on databases and on the theory of relational databases, the reader is referred to [Ull88] and [Mai83].

The organization of this paper is as follows: Section 18.2 gives definitions that are required to understand this paper. Sections 18.3 and 18.4 describe the model and proof theoretic approaches respectively to formalize multilevel databases. As stated in [Fro86], in the model theoretic approach, the knowledge that constitutes a database and its schema is viewed as defining a complete relational structure plus an associated formal theory. In the proof theoretic approach, the knowledge is regarded as defining a formal theory only. The model theoretic approach is the one used most often in formalizing concepts in conventional databases whereas the proof theoretic approach is generally used in formalizing aspects of deductive database systems. The results stated in Sections 18.3 and 18.4 are influenced by Frost's discussion on logic and databases [Fro86].

Section 18.5 introduces the notion of an environment associated with a classification level and discusses the applicability of the results in Tarski's fixed-point theory of lattices to environments. Subsequently a characterization of a specific environment called the least-fixed-point environment is given for a multilevel database. The results stated in this section are influenced by Lloyd's work in logic programming [Llo84].

Section 18.6 discusses the "inference problem" and the attempts that are currently being made to solve this problem. It then shows how some of the recent developments in deductive databases and logic programming may be applied to detect inferences. Treatment of negative and indefinite information in multilevel databases is discussed in Section 18.7. Counterparts to Reiter's closed-world assumption [Rei78] and Clark's Negation by Failure rule [Cla78] are proposed. Section 18.8 discusses the inclusion of the formal semantics of time in multilevel databases.

Section 18.9 briefly discusses some of the other topics in multilevel databases that may require formal treatment. Specifically, issues related to the theory of multilevel databases, consistency and completeness of security constraints and assigning security levels to data are discussed. Finally, conclusions are presented in Section 18.10.

18.2 Definitional Preliminaries

In this section the following concepts are defined to aid the reader with the rest of the paper:

Multilevel Database A multilevel database consists of a set of one or more multilevel relations.

Multilevel Relation A multilevel relation R is expressed as $R(A_1, L_1, A_2, L_2, ...A_n, L_n)$ where $A_1, A_2, ..., A_n$ are the attributes and for each $L_i (1 \leq i \leq n)$, L_i is the level assigned to A_i values [DLS+87]. This multilevel relation R is represented graphically in Figure 18.1. (Note that U, C, S, and TS are the respective levels Unclassified, Confidential, Secret and Top Secret with the following ordering: $U < C < S < TS$).

A1	L1	A2	L2	.....	An	Ln
a1	U	a2	S	.....	an	C
b1	U	b2	U	.....	bn	S
.	.	.	.	.	.	.
.	.	.	.	.	.	.
.	.	.	.	.	.	.
.	.	.	.	.	.	.
.	.	.	.	.	.	.
.	.	.	.	.	.	.
.	.	.	.	.	.	.
g1	U	g2	TS	.....	gn	C

FIGURE 18.1. Multilevel relation R.

Relational Structure A relational structure [Fro86] is a quadruple $U = < E, N, R, H >$, where:

1. E is the set of entities $\{e_1, e_2, ...\}$ called the *domain* of U;
2. N is the set of distinguished entities $\{n_1, n_2, ...\}$ such that N is a subset of U;
3. R is the set of relations $\{r_1, r_2, ...\}$, each of which is defined on E;
4. H is a set of functions $\{h_1, h_2, ...\}$, each of which is defined on E.

An example of a relational structure is

$$<\text{Nat}, \text{Zer}, \{=, <, >\}, \{+, \star\}>,$$

where Nat is the set of all natural numbers, Zer is the singleton set {0}, R consists of the equality/inequality relations, and H consists of addition and multiplication functions. Note that this structure is an interpretation of the theory of arithmetic.

Multilevel Relational Structure A multilevel relational structure is a quintuple $U = < E, N, L, MR, MH >$ where E and N are as before; L is a set of classification levels $\{l_1, l_2, ...\}$ such that L is a subset of E; MR is a set of multilevel relations $\{r_1, r_2, ...\}$, each of which is defined on E; and MH is a set of multilevel functions $\{h_1, h_2, ...\}$, each of which is defined on E (multilevel functions are defined analogously to multilevel relations).

Security Constraints Security constraints are rules that assign classification levels to data [DJT87]. The types of constraints include simple, content, aggregate and related data classification constraints. Examples of these constraints are given below.

- *Simple constraint:* Classifies entire attribute, relation or database, e.g., the attribute A_1 in R is secret (i.e., all A_1 values will be Secret).
- *Content-based constraint:* All A_1 values that satisfy the condition P are Secret.
- *Aggregate constraint:* A collection of A_1 values (say ten or more) is Secret.
- *Related data classification constraints:* Classifies relationships between relations, attribute names, and data elements. (Note that the context-constraints described in [DJT87] are a special type of related data classification constraint.)

18.3 Model Theoretic Approach

There are two ways to formalize multilevel databases using the model theoretic approach. In the first one, which is called the system-high world method, the multilevel relations are regarded as being equivalent to the multilevel relations in some slice of reality. This slice of reality is regarded as a complete multilevel structure, for example W. In other words, the multilevel relations are regarded as constituting a complete multilevel structure, say V, which is isomorphic to W. Both V and W are models of a first-order theory whose proper axioms are the schema rules. The schema is regarded as a set of well-formed formulas (wffs) in a Language L, which is the language of the multilevelrelational structure V.

In the model theoretic approach, all schema rules are considered to be integrity constraints. Therefore new facts cannot be deduced by inference rules. This could also apply for inferences across security levels. For example, suppose the following security constraint is enforced: The salary of a scientist is secret. Suppose the following integrity constraint is also enforced: A scientist's salary is 60K. If this integrity constraint is enforced as an inference rule, then it will be of the form: If the job title is scientist, then salary is 60K. Therefore, if an unclassified user knows that the job title of an employee is scientist, then from the integrity constraint enforced as an inference rule, he can deduce the salary, which is secret. However, in the model theoretic approach, the integrity constraint is not enforced as an inference rule; rather, it will be enforced as follows: either job title is scientist or salary is not 60K. In this case, if an unclassified user learns that the job title of an employee is scientist, then he cannot infer that the salary is 60K. Therefore, in the model theoretic approach, since inference rules do not exist, new facts cannot be deduced; that is, if a tuple is not stored as a member of a multilevel relation in database D, then it is assumed not to be a member of the equivalent relation in W. This is the closed-world assumption (CWA).

To summarize this method, it is assumed that there is only one world operating at the highest possible level. This world consists of data at various classification levels. Those persons at the lower levels have access only to the data that they are authorized to know. The illustration of this method, adapted from [Fro86] for multilevel databases, is shown in Figure 18.2.

In the second method, to formalize multilevel databases using the model theoretic approach, called the per-level world method, it is assumed that there is a world corresponding to each level; that is, there is a complete relational structure W_i for each level i. The database consists of a set of relational structures U_i for each level i, and W_i is isomorphic to U_i. Both W_i and U_i are models of a first-order theory whose proper axioms are the schema rules at level i and below.

Alternatively, in this method one can view the database as a complete structure that includes a set of entities E and a set of worlds W. Thus the denotation of an expression can be given with respect to a structure V, a valuation, and a world W_i. These concepts are influenced by a logic that has been developed by Montague [Mon73] called intensional logic.

Both the system-high world and the per-level world methods will be considered in the following discussions on query evaluation and database updates.

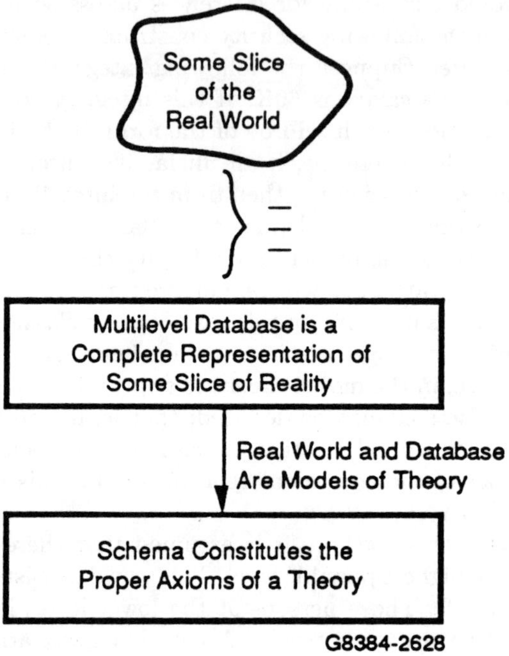

FIGURE 18.2. One World.

18.3.1 Query Evaluation

System-High World Method

Queries could be either closed or open. As stated in [Fro86], a closed query is a query whose answer is either True or False and an open query is a query whose answer is a set of zero or more tuples. Both types of queries are expressed as formulas of the language of the multilevel relational structure

V. If the database D consists of the relation EMP shown in Figure 18.3, examples of closed queries posed by unclassified, secret and top-secret users respectively are:

$$\text{EMP}(s_1, U, n_1, U, 40k, U, d_1, U)$$
$$\text{EMP}(s_4, U, n_4, U, 20k, U, d_4, S)$$
$$\text{EMP}(s_5, U, n_4, TS, 60k, U, d_3, S)\ .$$

SS#	L-SS#	Name	L-Name	Sal	L-Sal	Dept	L-Dept
S1	U	N1	U	40	U	D1	U
S2	U	N2	S	60	U	D2	S
S3	U	N3	S	100	U	D3	S
S4	U	N4	U	20	U	D4	S

FIGURE 18.3. Multilevel relation EMP.

Query evaluation amounts to evaluating the truth or falsity of the above formulas in the language of the multilevelrelational structure V. The answers to the first two queries are "True," while the answer to the last query is "False." Note that the levels specified in the query are at or below the level of the querying user, as they should be. This will prevent, for example, an unclassified user getting the correct response to queries such as, "Is the salary of N2 60K?"

An example of an open query posed by an unclassified user might be

$$\{X_2 :|\ \exists X_1, L_1, X_3, L_3 EMP(X_1, L_1, X_2, U, X_3, L_3, D_1, U)\}\ ,$$

i.e., retrieve all names who work in department D_1. Here, the level of D_1 must be less than or equal to the level of the querying user. In general an open query is of the form:

$$\{< v_1, v_2, ..., v_n >|\ F\}\ ,$$

where $v_1, v_2, ..., v_n$ are the free variables in the formula F. The answer to an open query is the set of tuples of constants corresponding to tuples of entities that are assigned to the variables $v_1, v_2, ..., v_n$ in valuations that satisfy the formula F [Fro86].

To answer queries efficiently in this approach, relational algebraic operations may be extended appropriately to multilevel relational operations. These extended operations may then be used. One possible approach to extending relational algebraic operations to multilevel relational ones is discussed in [DLS$^+$87]. AI techniques to process queries in multilevel databases are given in [TTK88]. In some cases evaluation of queries can be made more efficient by reference to the schema. For example, if the constraint that classifies all salaries in EMP at a secret level is enforced and an unclassified user requests the salary values, this constraint could be used to answer the query without accessing the database. The work on semantic query optimization [CGM88] may be extended for multilevel query processing, which makes use of integrity constraints to process queries efficiently. These issues need to be investigated further.

Per-Level World Method

In this method each world operates independently of one another. Queries posed by a user at a certain level are evaluated against the relational structure corresponding to that level; that is, as before, both open as well as closed queries are expressed as formulas of first-order logic. However, the language in which the query is expressed is that of the structure V_i where i is the level of the querying user. The satisfiability of the query is checked against the structure V_i.

18.3.2 Database Updates

System-High World Method

Updating a database is creating a new multilevel structure V. Integrity checking then amounts to making sure that V is a model of the schema rules. In other words, it has to be ensured that the model satisfies all of the integrity constraints after the update. Techniques that only have to test those constraints that have been affected by the updates have been proposed. This is especially important for security constraints. The system-high world method causes problems when updates are introduced. These problems are discussed below.

Database updates that cause security levels of data to change could cause problems. For example, suppose the content-based constraint that classifies all names who earn more than 50K at a secret level is enforced. If an update in EMP causes the salary in the first tuple to increase from 40K to 60K, then the name n_1, which was previously classified at the unclassified level, should now be secret if the database is to be in a consistent state. The update is handled by two subjects. One deletes the unclassified name and the other inserts the secret name. However, this would mean that n_1, which was visible to an unclassified user, is now invisible.

The system-high world method does not accommodate polyinstantiation. Polyinstantiation, as stated in [DLS+87], occurs when there are two tuples with the same primary key but classified at different levels. Polyinstantiation is not possible here since each piece of data is assigned only one level according to the security constraints; that is, regardless of who enters the data, the data is classified only according to the security constraints.

Per-Level World Method

In this method updates are made independently to the different worlds; that is, if the database is updated, then a new relational structure is created corresponding to the world in which the update took place. Integrity checking amounts to checking the satisfiability of the schema rules in this world against the newly created structure.

In the per-level method, it is not necessary to incorporate security constraints. This is because the level of the data is the level of the user who created the data, and users operate only in the world at their level. Therefore, levels of data do not change dynamically after updates.

The discussion on the per-level world method has stressed that the worlds operate independently. However, the world at a particular level has all the worlds below its level accessible to it. Conceptually, one can think of copies of relational structures at all levels less than or equal to level L being available to level L. This raises the question as to how polyinstantiation can be accommodated. When a tuple at level L that is duplicated from a lower level is updated, only the newly updated tuple is accessible to the world at level L; that is, the versions of this tuple at the lower levels are no longer accessible to the world at level L. Any further modifications made to this tuple at the lower levels are also not accessible to the world at level L. Furthermore, the only version of this tuple available to worlds higher than L is the version at level L if no modifications are made to this tuple at a level higher than L.

18.4 Proof Theoretic Approach

In the system-high world method of the proof theorretic approach to formalizing multilevel databases, the schema plus the multilevel databases are regarded as proper axioms of a first-order theory T. Some slice of the real world should be a complete model of this theory. The theory is in error if (1) it is inconsistent or (2) it is consistent, but the universe of discourse is not its model. However, it is not possible to prove that the real world is a model of T. Therefore integrity checking amounts to checking the theory for consistency. This issue will be addressed again later. The proof theo-

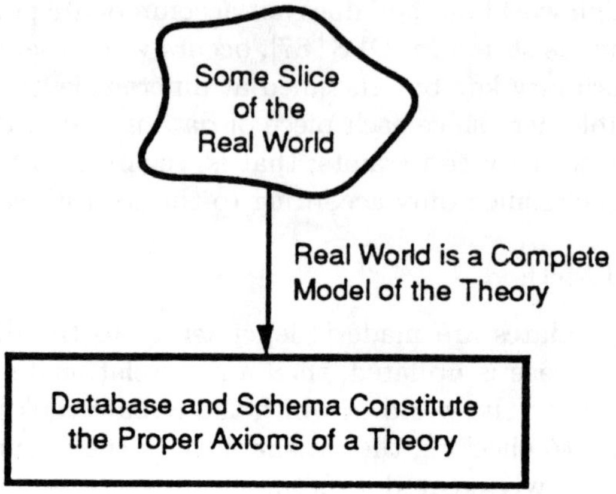

G8384-2630

FIGURE 18.4. Proof theoretic approach.

retic approach adapted from [Fro86] for multilevel databases is shown in Figure 18.4.

In the proof theoretic approach, the closed-world assumption (CWA) is to express all positive assertions and assume negative ones by default; that is, if a formula F cannot be proved, then NOT F is assumed. Furthermore, all of the integrity constraints are treated as inference rules in this approach. Therefore, if the constraint "job title is scientist or salary is not 60K" is enforced and if job title is scientist, then it is inferred that the salary is 60K.

As in the case of the model theoretic approach, polyinstantiation cannot be accommodated in the system-high world method. Furthermore, the security levels of data may also change after database updates. In the per-level world method, there are first-order theories associated with each level. Each theory has some slice of the real world as its model. As in the case of the system-high world method, all of the integrity constraints are treated as inference rules. This is a characteristic of the proof theoretic approach and not specific to any of the two methods. In the per-level method, as the theories are independent of one another, polyinstantiation can be accommodated.

The proof theoretic approach has important implications. It forms the basis for multilevel deductive databases. A discussion on multilevel knowledge bases based on this approach is given in [Thu]. Berson and Lunt's work on multilevel knowledge bases based on production systems is also closely related [BL87]. Other rule-based approaches to secure systems are discussed in [LT88,TTK88,KTT89].

The following discussion on query evaluation and database updates will concentrate only on the system-high world method. The essential points of the argument can be clearly exhibited with this case.

18.4.1 Query Evaluation

In the proof theoretic approach, a closed-world query is regarded as a closed formula F of the language of the theory T. The answer is "Yes" if F is a theorem, "No" if NOT F is a theorem, and "Don't Know" if otherwise.

Consider the following knowledge base:

$$L_2 = \text{secret} \leftarrow \text{EMP}(X_1, L_1, X_2, L_2, X_3, L_3, X_4, L_4)$$
$$\wedge\ X_3 > 60\text{K}$$
$$\text{EMP}(s_1, U, n_1, S, 70K, U, d_1, U) \leftarrow$$
$$\text{EMP}(s_2, U, n_2, U, 40K, U, d_2, U) \leftarrow .$$

The last two rules constitute the database. The first is a security constraint. It classifies names of all those who earn more than 60K at secret levels.

An example of a closed-world query posed by an unclassified user is "Is it the case that $\text{EMP}(s_1, U, n_2, U, 40K, U, d_2, U)$ is a theorem of the knowledge base?"

This query is negated to:

$$\leftarrow \text{EMP}(s_1, U, n_2, U, 40K, U, d_2, U).$$

The above denial is resolved with the last rule to obtain the empty clause. Therefore the answer to the query is "Yes."

Open queries may be expressed as follows:

$$\{< v_1, v_2, ..., v_n > \mid F\}$$

where $v_1, v_2, ..., v_n$ are the free variables in F. The answer to an open query is a set of tuples which when substituted for the free variables in F make the substitution instance of F, a theorem of the knowledge base [Fro86].

Efficient techniques devised for multilevel databases for query evaluation may also be applied to multilevel deductive databases. For example, arbitrary queries could be reduced to completely open queries that are evaluated first, and then multilevel relational algebraic operations could be applied to the result. This technique needs to be investigated further.

18.4.2 Database Updates

In the proof theoretic approach, when the database is updated, the consistency of the theory has to be checked. Note that the database may be updated explicitly or implicitly after a query is evaluated. Until recently, consistency checking followed the theoremhood view of constraints checking. This was first proposed in [NY78] and later enhanced in [Nic82], [LT84], and [Dec86]. To prove that a theory is consistent, i.e., the database satisfies its constraint set, I, where I is a set of closed formulas, every formula of I is proved to be a logical consequence of the completion of D. Techniques have also been developed to prove the theoremhood of only the integrity constraints that are affected by the update.

Recently Sadri and Kowalski [SK88] have proposed an alternative approach, the consistency method, for checking the validity of integrity constraints in deductive databases. In this method, the database is assumed to be consistent before the update. After it is updated it is checked for consistency according to a proof procedure. This proof procedure has been implemented in Prolog and could be adapted for multilevel databases also. Briefly stated, this proof procedure is as follows:

1. The database is assumed to be consistent before the update.
2. All integrity constraints are expressed as denials.
3. If the update is an insert, then the inserted clause is included as an assertion.
4. If the update is a delete, then the negation of the deleted clause is included as an assertion.
5. A proof procedure which extends Clark's [Cla78] SLDNF proof procedure is applied.
6. If the empty clause is derived, then the database is inconsistent.

It will be seen later that this proof procedure can also be used to detect inferences.

18.5 Environments and Fixed Points

In this section, the notion of an environment associated with a level will be introduced first. It will then be proved that the set of environments forms a complete lattice. Subsequently properties of environments will be stated and proved using results from Tarski's fixed-point theory of lattices [Tar55]. In particular, an important fixed-point characterization of the least environment is given where the least environment is the environment associated with the lowest level in which the entire database can be displayed without causing any security violation. Finally the declarative and procedural semantics of multilevel databases will be discussed. These semantics describe the model and proof theoretic approaches. All of the discussion in this section has been influenced by Lloyd's approach to the treatment of procedural and declarative semantics of logic programs [LT84]. Furthermore, the results obtained in [LT84] have been extended for multilevel databases here.

18.5.1 Environments

Corresponding to each level, there is an environment denoted by $E(L)$, which consists of all data classified at a level less than or equal to L. This data may be the extensional data in the database or may be derived from the extensional data by logical rules of inference. For convenience it is assumed that the levels are numbered 1, 2, 3, ... It is also assumed that the set of levels form a complete lattice, i.e., the set of levels is a partially ordered set where for every subset X of the set, lub(X) and glb(X) exist.

Result 1 The set of environments *SetE* forms a complete lattice under set inclusion. □

Proof: The proof is trivial. *SetE* is a partially ordered set where the partial order is set inclusion. □

SetE is complete as every subset X has a glb and lub. This can be shown by induction on the number of elements in X. For example, take the case when X consists of two environments $E(i)$ and $E(j)$. If $i < j$, then $E(i) \subseteq E(j)$. $E(j)$ is the lub of X and $E(i)$ is its glb. If i and j are incomparable levels, then as the set of levels forms a complete lattice, there are levels k_1 and k_2 such that $E(i) \subseteq E(k_1)$, $E(j) \subseteq E(k_1)$, $E(k_2) \subseteq E(i)$, and $E(k_2) \subseteq E(j)$. Furthermore, for any other levels p_1 and p_2 that satisfy $E(i) \subseteq E(p_1)$, $E(j) \subseteq E(p_1)$, $E(p_2) \subseteq E(i)$, and $E(p_2) \subseteq E(j)$, the following holds: $E(k_1) \subseteq E(p_1)$ and $E(p_2) \subseteq E(k_2)$. Therefore, $E(k_1) =$ lub(X) and $E(k_2) =$ glb(X).

18.5.2 Mappings

Next a continuous mapping on *SetE* will be defined. A mapping T: *SetE* $\rightarrow$ *SetE* is continuous if $T(\text{lub}(X)) = \text{lub}(T(X))$ for every directed subset X of L. (A continuous mapping has been shown to be monotonic, i.e. $T(x) \leq T(y)$ whenever $x \leq y$.)

Result 2 Define a mapping T: *SetE* $\rightarrow$ *SetE* such that $T(E(I)) = \{A : A \leftarrow A_1, A_2, ...A_n$ is a rule in the database and for each $j (1 \leq j \leq n) A_j$ is classified at level $J \leq I\}$. The mapping T is monotonic. (Note: It can be seen that $E(I) \subseteq T(E(I))$.) □

Proof: It needs to be proved that whenever $E(i) \subseteq E(j)$, then $T(E(i)) \subseteq T(E(j))$. On the contrary, assume $E(i) \subseteq E(j)$ and $T(E(i)) \not\subseteq T(E(j))$. Then there is an A such that $A \in T(E(i))$ and $A \notin T(E(j))$. If $A \in T(E(i))$, then there is a rule $A \leftarrow A_1, A_2, ..., A_n$ in the database where the levels of $A_1, A_2, ...A_n$ are all less than or equal to the level i. However, as the level j dominates the level i, if there is such a rule, then A will belong to $T(E(j))$. This is a contradiction. □

Result 3 Let T be defined as in Result 2. Then T is continuous. (Note that as every continuous mapping is monotonic, Result 3 implies Result 2.) □

Proof: It needs to be proved that for every directed subset X of *SetE*, the following holds:

$$T(\text{lub}(X)) = \text{lub}(T(X)).$$

The proof is by induction on the number of elements in X. For example, if X consists of two elements $E(i)$ and $E(j)$ and if one is a subset of the other, the result is immediate. If not, i.e., if i and j are incomparable, then:

$$\text{lub}(T(X)) = \text{lub}(T(E(i)), T(E(j))) .$$

Let the level of $\text{lub}(T(X))$ be k. Then $E(k)$ will consist of all the information in $T(E(i))$ and $T(E(j))$ and all the information that can be deduced from $T(E(i))$ and $T(E(j))$. If $E(p)$ is the lub of X, then $T(E(p))$ will consist of all the information in $E(i)$ and $E(j)$ and all the information that can be deduced from $E(i)$ and $E(j)$. Since $E(i) \subseteq T(E(i))$, and $E(j) \subseteq T(E(j))$, it can be seen that $E(k)$ is the same as $T(E(p))$. □

18.5.3 Fixed Points

Next the notions of least fixed point and greatest fixed point will be defined. An environment $E(L)$ is the least fixed point of T if $E(L)$ is a fixed point, thus, $T(E(L)) = E(L)$, and for all fixed points $E(L')$ of T the relationship $E(L) \subseteq E(L')$ is true. Similarly the notion of greatest fixed point of T can be defined. Since T has been shown to be a monotonic mapping on *SetE*, which is a complete lattice, the following results on fixed points hold.

Result 4 T has a least fixed point $\text{lfp}(T)$ and greatest fixed point $\text{gfp}(T)$. Furthermore:

$$\begin{aligned}
&\text{lfp}(T) = \text{glb}\{E(L) : T(E(L)) = E(L)\}\\
&= \text{glb}\{E(L) : T(E(L)) \subseteq E(L)\}\\
&\text{gfp}(T) = \text{lub}\{E(L) : T(E(L)) = E(L)\}\\
&= \text{lub}\{E(L) : E(L) \subseteq T(E(L))\}
\end{aligned}$$

□

Result 5 If $E(L) \leq T(E(L))$, there is a fixed point $E(L')$ of T such that $E(L) \subseteq E(L')$. Similarly if $T(E(L)) \subseteq E(L)$, then there is a fixed point $E(L')$ of T such that $E(L') \subseteq E(L)$. □

18.5.4 Least Environment

The next result obtains an important fixed point characterization of the least environment. The least environment is the environment associated with the lowest level into which the entire database may be displayed without security violation. (Note: (1) The least environment may change as the database evolves over time, and (2) it is assumed that an environment does not consist of any intensional data, i.e., the database is a complete model of the real world.)

Result 6 Least environment is lfp(T). □

Proof: The following statement (A) needs to be proved first:

(A): If an environment E(L) is a model of the database then $T(E(L)) \subseteq E(L)$.

(Note that $E(L)$ is a model of the database if the entire database can be displayed in $E(L)$.)

Proof of (A): $E(L)$ is a model of the database D if for each ground instance $A \leftarrow A_1, A_2, A_3, ..., A_n$ of each clause in D, $\{A_1, A_2, A_3, ..., A_n\} \subseteq E(L)$ implies $A \in E(L)$ if and only if $T(E(L)) \subseteq E(L)$.

The proof of Result 6 is now fairly straightforward:

Least environment = glb$\{E(L) : E(L)$ is a model of $D\}$
= glb$\{E(L) : T(E(L)) \subseteq E(L)\}$
= lfp(T).

□

18.5.5 Declarative and Procedural Semantics

Next the declarative and procedural semantics of multilevel databases will be discussed. These semantics are analogous to the model theoretic and proof theoretic formalisms, respectively. The discussion is influenced by Lloyd's work on the declarative and procedural semantics of logic programs [Llo84].

The declarative semantics may be described as follows: Let D be a multilevel database and Q a query posed by a user at level L. Let Q_s be obtained from Q by replacing the free variables of Q by the substitution s. Then s is safe and correct if Q_s is true in $E(L)$.

This definition of safe and correct substitution captures the intuitive meaning of a safe and correct answer. It provides a declarative understanding of the desired output from a database and a query.

The procedural semantics of multilevel databases provide counterparts to least environment and a safe and correct answer to a query. These counterparts are the success set and computed answer substitution. They are described as follows:

Let D be a multilevel database. The success set of D is the set A such that $D \cup \{\leftarrow A\}$ has a SLD refutation. If Q is a query and R a computation rule, an R-computed answer substitution s for $D \cup \{Q\}$ is the substitution obtained by restricting the computation $s_1, s_2, ..., s_n$ to variables of Q where $s_1, s_2, ..., s_n$ is the sequence of most general unifiers used in a SLD refutation of $P \cup \{G\}$ via R.

It can be shown that the success set of a database is in fact its least environment. Furthermore, Clark's theorems [Cla79] on the soundness and completeness of SLD resolution are applicable to multilevel databases.

18.6 Environments and Inference

Security violation via inference occurs when users acquire unauthorized information from various sets of information that they have legitimately acquired. Three different characterizations of the inference problem that are more or less equivalent have been proposed.

Morgenstern [Mor87] has established a framework to study the inference problem. Inference rules are specified in a constraint language, and the inference problem is characterized in terms of information theory. More recently Hinke's approach [Hin88] considers logical inferences on the extensional data only. (Note that the discussion in the previous section also considers only the extensional data and the inferences that can be drawn from this data.)

The approach taken in [Thu87] is to handle inferences during query processing. The author discusses inference based on environments. Here the environments consist of data that is released from the database as well as any real-world information. For example, the environment associated with the level L consists of the data released at level L plus any real-world information available at level L. An environment at level L includes all the environments at level $L' \leq L$. If a user at level L can logically deduce from any subset of $E(L)$ some data that should be classified at a level L'' that either dominates or is incomparable to L, then security violation by inference has occurred. While [Mor87] proposes to design the database in such a way that inferences that violate security cannot be made, the approach taken in [Thu87] enforces inference controls before a response is released.

Although algorithms have been given to detect certain types of inferences in the previous work on inference, there is still lot of work that remains to be done in this area. In this section yet another algorithm is given to detect inferences. It applies Sadri and Kowalski's [SK88] constraint satisfaction method to consistency checking (which was described in Section 4) to detect inferences. The essential points of the argument are as follows.

The query evaluation process is viewed as updating the environments; that is, whenever a response is released into $E(L)$, all environments $E(L')$ where $L' \geq L$ are updated. In most cases the update consists of only the insert operation. However, if it is required that an environment can contain only a certain amount of data, or if the data in the environment changes, then some of the data in the environment has to be deleted. When the environment is updated, the extended SLDNF proof procedure is applied. If the empty clause is derived, then a security violation by inference has occurred provided it is assumed that data cannot be downgraded (i.e., the constraints are such that the level of the data will never be lower than its current value). The response is then not released to the user. Note that an empty clause will be derived only if the constraints are not satisfied. Therefore security violation occurs only if the environment does not satisfy the constraints. This is stated in the next result.

Result 7 Let a response R be released into environment $E(L)$. Let the extended proof procedure be applied to $E(L')(L' \geq L)$. If the empty clause is deduced, then security violation by inference has occurred. □

Proof: First note that whenever a piece of data is released into an environment L, all the environments associated with levels $L' \geq L$ need to be checked for security violation by inference, i.e., it has to be ensured that from any subset of $E(L')$, it is not possible to deduce data at level $L'' > L'$. (However, results from the previous section show that when real-world information is not included, it is only necessary to check the levels $L+$ where $L \leq L+ \leq Lmin$ where $Lmin$ is the least environment. The description of the least environment has been given in the previous section.)

Now suppose that the response R is added to the environment. If an inconsistency occurs (i.e., if the empty clause is deduced), then one or more constraints are violated by the inclusion of R. This is only possible if the level of some data, which was classified at a level $L'' \leq L'$, is now increased to a level $L+ > L'$. Therefore if the response R is released into $E(L)$, a user at level L' will infer information at level $L+ > L'$, to which he or she is not authorized. This is a security violation. □

18.7 Handling Negative and Indefinite Information

Many proposals have been put forward to handle negative and indefinite information in deductive databases [CCF+87]. In this section, the issues involved in extending some of these proposals to handle negative and indefinite information in multilevel databases will be addressed. In particular, the following proposals will be discussed:

- Reiter's closed-world assumption.
- Clark's negation by failure.

Other interesting proposals include Minker's generalized closed-world assumption [Min82,GM86] and Frost's "theory plus incomplete relational structure" approach [Fro86]. The latter two proposals attempt to provide solutions to indefinite constraints such as "Man(x) or Woman(x)." It is currently being investigated as to how the latter two proposals may be extended to multilevel databases, and therefore they will not be discussed here.

18.7.1 Closed-World Assumption

Reiter's closed-world Assumption (CWA) [Rei78] may be stated as follows: To answer a query Q positively, it needs to be shown that:

$$DB \cup \overline{EDB} \vdash Q$$

where $\overline{EDB}$ is the complement of the extensional database.

For example, let p_1, p_2, p_3 and p_4 be members of a one-place relation PERSON, some of which may also belong to another one-place relation EMP. Let the database consist of the following assertions:

$$\text{EMP}(p_1) \leftarrow$$
$$\text{EMP}(p_2) \leftarrow.$$

That is, p_1 and p_2 are the only employees. Then the following are assertions in $\overline{EDB}$:

$$\overline{EMP}(p_3) \leftarrow$$
$$\overline{EMP}(p_4) \leftarrow.$$

If a user poses the queries EMP(X) and $\overline{EMP}(X)$, then the respective responses will be the sets $\{p_1, p_2\}$ and $\{p_3, p_4\}$.

Now, in the case of multilevel databases, the negative information should be assigned classification levels. If the per-level world method is adopted, then each world is treated separately and has its own positive and negative information. As a result, inconsistencies will not arise. For example, if the fact that p_1 is an employee is unclassified and the fact that p_2 is an employee is secret, then the unclassified world will consist of the assertions:

$$\text{EMP}(p_1) \leftarrow$$
$$\overline{EMP}(p_2) \leftarrow$$
$$\overline{EMP}(p_3) \leftarrow$$
$$\overline{EMP}(p_4) \leftarrow.$$

The secret world consists of the assertions:

$$\text{EMP}(p_1) \leftarrow$$
$$\text{EMP}(p_2) \leftarrow$$
$$\overline{EMP}(p_3) \leftarrow$$
$$\overline{EMP}(p_4) \leftarrow.$$

(Note that the assertions EMP(p_1), $\overline{EMP}(p_3)$, and $\overline{EMP}(p_4)$ in the secret world may be obtained from the unclassified world to avoid duplicate information.)

In the secret world, if, for example, p_1 is no longer an employee and this change should not be known at the unclassified world, then EMP(p_1) is changed to $\overline{EMP}(p_1)$ in the secret world only; thus EMP(p_1) will remain in the unclassified world. Positive as well as negative queries posed by a user are evaluated against the world corresponding to the level of the user. Therefore the following results obtained by Reiter on closed-world consistent databases may be applied to closed-world consistent multilevel databases.

Result 8 If the database at a level L is consistent and the query is quantifier free, then:

- $\{x : \overline{F}\}$ (CWA,L) = C - $\{x : F\}$ (CWA,L)
- $\{x : F_1 \wedge \overline{F_2}\}$ (CWA,L) = $\{x : F_1\}$ (CWA,L) - $\{x : F_2\}$ (CWA,L)

where C is the domain under consideration. (Note that $\{x : F\}$ (CWA,L) means the set of all x that satisfies the query F when evaluated under the CWA against the world at level L.) □

If the system-high world method is adopted, then Result 8 cannot be applied for multilevel databases unless certain assumptions are made. For example, consider a database DB consisting of the following positive information:

$$\text{EMP}(p_1, U) \leftarrow$$
$$\text{EMP}(p_2, S) \leftarrow.$$

That is, for a U user the only employee is p_1, whereas for an S user the employees are p_1 and p_2. The negative information will be represented by the assertions:

$$\overline{EMP}(p_2,U) \leftarrow$$
$$\overline{EMP}(p_3,U) \leftarrow$$
$$\overline{EMP}(p_4,U) \leftarrow$$

Since at this point $DB \cup \overline{EDB}$ is consistent, the Result 8 can be applied. However, if a secret user wants to delete the fact that p_1 is an employee without letting an unclassified user know about it, then $\overline{EMP}(p_1,S)$ will be inserted as negative information. Then $DB \cup \overline{EDB}$ becomes inconsistent and therefore Result 8 cannot be applied for query evaluation. For example, if a secret user wants to retrieve all those who are not employees, then applying Result 8 (i), p_1 will not be included in the answer. This is because $\{x$: EMP(x)$\}$ (CWA,S) will consist of the set $\{p_1, p_2\}$ and C = $\{p_1, p_2, p_3, p_4\}$. One possible solution to overcome this inconsistency is to enforce the rule that all negative information is classified at the lowest level. This issue needs to be investigated further.

18.7.2 Negation by Failure

The negation by failure rule formulated by Clark [Cla78] may be described as follows: "If every possible proof of P fails, then infer NOT P." For example, let the database consist of the following assertions:

$$\text{EMP}(p_1) \leftarrow$$
$$\text{EMP}(p_2) \leftarrow.$$

To prove $\overline{EMP}(p_3)$, it needs to be shown that every possible proof of $\text{EMP}(p_3)$ fails. In fact, this is the case, as the denial $\leftarrow \text{EMP}(p_3)$ cannot be resolved.

To extend the negation by failure rule to multilevel databases, levels need to be associated with data. Suppose the multilevel database consists of the following assertions:

$$\text{EMP(p1,U)} \leftarrow$$
$$\text{EMP(p2,U)} \leftarrow.$$

Now, to answer the query $\overline{EMP}(p_3,U)$ (i.e., an unclassified user wants to know whether p_3 is not an employee), the query is written as a denial:

$$\leftarrow \overline{EMP}(p_3,U).$$

Applying the negation as a failure rule, since $\overline{EMP}(p_3,U)$ is ground, it needs to be shown that all proofs of $\text{EMP}(p_3,U)$ fail. Therefore $\text{EMP}(p_3,U)$ is written as a denial:

$$\leftarrow \text{EMP}(p_3,U)$$

and an attempt is made to deduce the empty clause from this denial and the positive assertions in the database. Since $\leftarrow \text{EMP}(p_3,U)$ cannot be resolved, proof of $\text{EMP}(p_3,U)$ fails. Therefore the answer to the query is "Yes."

Next, if a secret user poses a query $\overline{EMP}(p_2,S)$, the query is written as a denial:

$$\leftarrow \overline{EMP}(p_2,S).$$

Applying negation as failure rule, it needs to be shown that all proofs of $\text{EMP}(p_2,S)$ fail. The clause is written as a denial $\leftarrow \text{EMP}(p_2,S)$ and an attempt is made to deduce the empty clause. Although there is no assertion $\text{EMP}(p_2,S) \leftarrow$ in the database, from $\text{EMP}(p_2,U)$ it can be deduced that $\text{EMP}(p_2,S)$ holds; that is, the rule $\text{EMP}(p_2,S) \leftarrow \text{EMP}(p_2,U)$ is assumed. (Note that this is a valid assumption as any data classified at a level U can be regarded as being classified at a level S.) Therefore, in this case, the empty clause is deduced. This means that there is a proof for $\text{EMP}(p_2,S)$. Thus the answer to the query is "No."

The problems mentioned in the CWA method also occur with the "negation as failure" rule method. For example, how can an S user delete the fact that p_2 is no longer an employee without letting the U users know. It also remains to be investigated as to which method is more appropriate to handle negative information in multilevel databases.

18.8 Formal Semantics of Time

Most of the discussion on multilevel databases presented so far views the database as a collection of time-varying relations. However, neither the notion of time nor temporal semantics has been included in the multilevel relational model. This is also the case with the relational model proposed by Codd [Cod70]. However, recently attempts have been made to incorporate the notion of time into relational databases. In particular, historical databases have been used for modeling the changing state of information about some part of the real world, and various types of logics such as temporal logic and intensional logic have been used in defining the formal syntax [CW83]; that is, the historical database is a model of the theory based on temporal or intensional logic.

It is currently being investigated as to whether Clifford and Warren's work [CLIFF83] on the formal semantics of time for relational databases may be extended for multilevel databases. In particular, a multilevel historical database is defined to be a model of some slice of the changing world. The constraints enforced on the changing world are the axioms of a theory based on intensional logic. An example of the use of this approach is given below.

Suppose the database consists of two historical relations S-EMP and U-EMP, as shown in Figure 18.5. It is assumed that S-EMP is a secret relation, whereas U-EMP is an unclassified relation; i.e., the per-level world method is assumed for historical databases. Now, if an S user wants to retrieve the salary of n_1, then in nonhistorical databases the value 70K will be returned. However, it could be the case that the 30K value entered in U-EMP may be more recent and may reflect the real-world more accurately. On the other hand, even if the 30K value is more recent, it may not reflect the real-world situation as the actual salary may not be disclosed at the unclassified level. Therefore, if the state or time at which, say, the tuple was entered into the database is also stored with the remaining data, then the times t_2 and t_3 may be compared before a response is returned; that is, if t_2 is less than t_3, the indefinite value "70K or 30K" may be returned. The secret user can then determine which of the two values is correct. If t_2 is greater than t_3, then the value 70K is returned. If an unclassified user poses a query to retrieve the salary of n_1, then the most recent salary for n_1 will be returned. Since t_1 is less than t_3, the salary that will be returned is 30K.

Queries such as "Has n_1's salary increased since time t_1?" may also be posed. If an unclassified user poses this query, the answer is "Yes." If a Secret user poses this query, the answer is "Yes" if t_2 is greater than t_3.

S-EMP			
SS#	Name	Salary	State
.	.	.	.
.	.	.	.
.	.	.	.
.	.	.	.
.	.	.	.
S1	n1	70k	t2
.	.	.	.
.	.	.	.
.	.	.	.
.	.	.	.
.	.	.	.
.	.	.	.
.	.	.	.
.	.	.	.

U-EMP			
SS#	Name	Salary	State
.	.	.	.
.	.	.	.
S1	n1	20K	t1
.	.	.	.
.	.	.	.
.	.	.	.
S1	n1	30k	t3
.	.	.	.
.	.	.	.
.	.	.	.
.	.	.	.

FIGURE 18.5. Two historical relations.

If t_2 is less than t_3, then it must be determined whether 20K is less than (70K or 30K). In this case the answer is still "Yes." Note that if the salary at time t_1 had been 40K instead of 20K, then the relation "40K < (70K or 30K)" evaluates to an unknown value. Therefore the answer in this case will be "Unknown."

In general, the following relationship between indefinite values holds:

$A_1 \vee A_2 \vee A_3 \vee ... \vee A_n < B_1 \vee B_2 \vee B_3 \vee ... \vee B_m (m = 1, n \geq 1)$
is
True if $A_i(1 \leq i \leq n) < B_j(1 \leq j \leq m)$
False if $A_i(1 \leq i \leq n) > B_j(1 \leq j \leq m)$
Unknown if otherwise.

It can be seen that by incorporating the notion of time into multilevel databases, answers to queries match the real world more accurately.

18.9 Other Related Topics

Other topics in multilevel databases that may require formal treatment include the theory of multilevel relational databases, consistency and completeness of security constraints and assigning security levels to data. Some of the issues involved in each of these topics are discussed below.

18.9.1 Theory of Relational Databases

The theory of relational databases has played a central role in the design of relational database management systems. The theory provides rules for designing database schemas. In particular, the notion of dependencies between attributes of a relation have been defined in the form of functional and multilevel dependencies. Different properties or "normal forms" for relation shemes have been defined. Important normal forms are the third normal form and Boyce-Codd normal forms. It has been shown that these normal forms are guaranteed to overcome many of the problems such as redundancies and anomalies that exist with database updates.

Application of this theory to multilevel databases is still in its infancy. Denning et al. [DLS$^+$87] discuss some of these concepts (such as entity integrity and referential integrity.) in their work on a multilevel relational model. A preliminary attempt to formulate a theory of multilevel databases is discussed in [Onu87]. The use of functional and multilevel dependencies to detect inferences is discussed in [SO87]. This work also provides insight into how solutions to the inference problem in traditional database systems [Bee80] may be applied to provide solutions to the inference problem in multilevel database systems (note that the inference problem in traditional database systems is the membership problem for functional and multilevel dependencies).

An important issue that needs to be addressed in multilevel database systems is database design; that is, formulating rules for efficient ways to design the database schemas. Thus a greater effort towards developing a theory of multilevel relational databases is required if the advantages of producing an efficient and cost-effective multilevel relational database system is to be realized.

18.9.2 Consistency and Completeness of Security Constraints

A set of security constraints is said to be consistent of no two constraints in the set conflict with each other. A set of security constraints is complete if every piece of data is assigned a security level by this set. In [AD87], algorithms are given to check for the consistency and completeness of a set of security constraints. Here, it is assumed that two constraints are in conflict with each other if they classify the same piece of data at the same time at different security levels. A more realistic but complex definition of consistency of constraints is given in LDV, where it is assumed that a set of constraints is consistent if it is not possible for users to acquire unauthorized information from the data/metadata classified according to this set. However, only informal algorithms have yet been given to determine whether a set of constraints is consistent according to the more complex definition of consistency.

Consistency checking, even in the case of integrity constraints, is still in the research stages. Recently theorem-proving techniques have been used to check for the consistency of a set of integrity constraints [BM86]. Similar approaches should also be investigated for security constraints.

18.9.3 Assigning Security Levels to Data

Assuming a set of constraints is consistent, the next question is how to assign security levels to data according to the constraints. Although most of the approaches to designing MLS/DBMSs use some type of security constraints, very little attention has been given as to how to assign security levels to the data.

In [DAH+87b], an informal algorithm is given to assign security levels to data. This algorithm represents the data in the database as well as the security constraints as nodes of a bipartite graph. A node is fired if certain conditions are satisfied. As a result of the firing, security levels are assigned to associated data. Since the database data is also represented by the graph, if the database is large, the graph may be unmanageable.

In [Thu88], an algorithm is described where security constraints are stored in a connection graph. When the data is updated, the algorithm examines the relevant security constraints and computes the security level of the data. In certain cases, if multiple paths in the connection graph must be followed, then parallel execution is also possible. The efficient representation of the security constraints enhances the performance of this algorithm. More work needs to be done to formalize this algorithm.

18.10 Conclusion

This paper has focused on a set of issues that needs to be explored further to design better multilevel database systems. In summary, these included:

- Logic to formalize multilevel database concepts
- Fixed points of environments
- Inference problem
- Handling negative information
- Incorporating the notion of time
- Theory of multilevel relational databases.

Some of the issues related to the theory of multilevel databases, consistency and completeness of security constraints and assigning security levels to data were also briefly discussed.

It is hoped that this paper will provide one of the directions for research in the foundations of multilevel databases in the future.

18.11 REFERENCES

[AD87] S.G. Akl and D.E. Denning. Checking classification constraints for consistency and completeness. In *Proceedings of the 1987 IEEE Symposium on Security and Privacy*, April 1987.

[Bee80] C. Beeri. On the membership problem for functional and multilevel dependencies in relational databases. *ACM Transactions on Database Systems*, 5(3), 1980.

[BL87] T.A Berson and T.F. Lunt. Multilevel security for knowledge-based systems. In *Proceedings of the 1987 IEEE Symposium on Security and Privacy*, April 1987.

[BM86] F. Bry and R. Monthes. Checking consistency of database constraints: A logical approach. In *Proceedings of the VLDB Conference*, 1986.

[CCF+87] P. Chisholm, G. Chen, D. Ferbrache, P. Thanisch, and J. Williams. Coping with indefinite and negative data in deductive databases, a survey. *Data and Knowledge Engineering Journal*, 2(4), 1987.

[CGM88] U. Chakravarthy, J. Grant, and J. Minker. Foundations of semantic query optimization. In *Foundations of Deductive Databases and Logic Programming*. Morgan Kaufmann, 1988.

[Cla78] K. Clark. Negation as failure. In *Logic and Databases*. Plenum Press, 1978.

[Cla79] K. Clark. Predicate logic as a computational formalism. *Research Report 79/55*, Department of Computing, Imperial College, London, 1979.

[Cod70] E.F. Codd. A relational model for large shared data banks. *Communications of the ACM*, 13(6), June 1970.

[CW83] J. Clifford and D. Warren. Formal semantics for time in databases. *ACM Transactions on Database Systems*, 8(2), 1983.

[DAH+87a] D.E. Denning, S.G. Akl, M. Heckman, T.F. Lunt, M. Morgenstern, P.G. Neumann, and R.R. Schell. Views for multilevel database security. *IEEE Transactions on Software Engineering*, 13(2), February 1987.

[DAH+87b] D.E. Denning, S.G. Akl, M. Heckman, M. Morgenstern, P.G. Neumann, and R.R. Schell. Views for multilevel database security. In *Proceedings of the 1986 IEEE Symposium on Security and Privacy*, April 1987.

[Dec86] H. Decker. Integrity enforcement on deductive databases. In *Proceedings of the Expert Database Systems Conference*, South Carolina, 1986.

[DJT87] P.A. Dwyer, G.D. Jelatis, and B.M. Thuraisingham. Multilevel security in database management systems. *Computers and Security*, 6(3), June 1987.

[DLS+87] D.E. Denning, T.F. Lunt, R.R. Schell, M. Heckman, and W.R. Shockley. A multilevel relational data model. In *Proceedings of the 1987 IEEE Symposium on Security and Privacy*, April 1987.

[DOST88] P. Dwyer, E. Onuegbe, P. Stachour, and B. Thuraisingham. Query processing in LDV - a secure database management system. In *Proceedings of the Fourth Aerospace Computer Security Conference*, December 1988.

[Fro86] R. Frost. *Introduction to Knowledge-Based Systems.* Collins, 1986.

[GM78] H. Gallaire and J. Minker. *Logic and Databases.* Plenum Press, 1978.

[GM86] J. Grant and J. Minker. Answering queries in indefinite database and the null value problem. *Advanced Computer Research*, 3, 1986.

[Hin88] T.H. Hinke. Inference aggregation detection in database management systems. In *Proceedings of the 1988 IEEE Symposium on Security and Privacy*, April 1988.

[KTT89] T.F. Keefe, M.B. Thuraisingham, and W.T. Tsai. Secure query processing strategies. *IEEE Computer*, 23(3), March 1989.

[KTTar] T.F. Keefe, W.T. Tsai, and M.B. Thuraisingham. SODA: A secure object-oriented database system. *Computers and Security*, forthcoming.

[Llo84] J. Lloyd. *Foundations of Logic Programming.* Springer-Verlag, 1984.

[LT84] J. Lloyd and R. Toper. Making prolog more expressive. *Logic Programming Journal*, 1(3), 1984.

[LT88] T.F. Lunt and B.M. Thuraisingham. Security for large AI systems. In *Proceedings of the AAAI-88 Workshop on Databases in Large AI Systems*, August 1988.

[Mai83] D. Maier. *Theory of Relational Databases.* Computer Science Press, 1983.

[Min82] J. Minker. On indefinite databases and closed-world assumption. In *Proceedings of the Sixth Conference on Automated Deduction.* Springer-Verlag, Lecture Notes in Computer Science, 1982.

[Min88] J. Minker. *Foundations of Deductive Databases and Logic Programming.* Morgan Kaufmann, 1988.

[Mon73] R. Montague. The proper treatment of quantification in ordinary English. In *Approaches to Natural Languages.* Dordrecht, Germany, 1973.

[Mor87] M. Morgenstern. Security and inference in multilevel database and knowledge-base systems. In *Proceedings of the ACM International Conference on Management of Data (SIGMOD-87)*, May 1987.

[Nic82] J. Nicolas. Logic for improved integrity checking in relational databases. *Acta Informatica*, 18(3), 1982.

[NY78] J. Nicolas and K. Yazdania. Integrity checking in deductive databases. In *Logic and Databases.* Plenum Press, 1978.

[Onu87] E. Onuegbe. Polyinstantiation, functional dependencies and multivalued dependencies. *Technical report*, Honeywell Internal Report, 1987.

[Rei78] R. Reiter. On closed-world databases. In *Logic and Databases.* Plenum Press, 1978.

[SK88] F. Sadri and R. Kowalski. Theorem-proving approach to database integrity. In *Foundations of Deductive Databases and Logic Programming.* Morgan Kaufmann, 1988.

[SO87] T. Su and G. Ozsoyoglu. Data dependencies and inference control in multilevel relational database systems. In *Proceedings of the 1987 IEEE Symposium on Security and Privacy*, April 1987.

[ST] P. Stachour and M.B. Thuraisingham. Design of LDV: A multilevel secure relational database management system. *IEEE Transactions on Knowledge and Data Engineering*, forthcoming.

[Tar55] A. Tarski. A lattice theoretical fixpoint theorem and its application. *Pacific Journal of Math*, 5(3), 1955.

[Thu] M.B. Thuraisingham. Toward the design of a secure database/knowledge base management system, forthcoming.

[Thu87] M.B. Thuraisingham. Security checking in relational database management systems augmented with inference engines. *Computers and Security*, 6(6), 1987.

[Thu88] M.B. Thuraisingham. An algorithm for assigning security levels to data. *Technical report*, Honeywell Technical Note, October 1988.

[Thuar] M.B. Thuraisingham. Security in object-oriented database management systems. *Journal of Object-Oriented Programming*, forthcoming.

[TTK88] M.B. Thuraisingham, W.T. Tsai, and T. Keefe. Secure query processing using AI techniques. In *Hawaii International Conference on Systems Sciences*, January 1988.

[Ull88] J.D. Ullman. *Principles of Database and Knowledge-Base Systems*, Volume 1. Computer Science Press, Rockville, Maryland, 1988.

19

An Application Perspective on DBMS Security Policies

Rae K. Burns[1]

19.1 Introduction

Any multilevel-secure (MLS) database management system (DBMS) requires a security policy that is sufficiently flexible to support the security requirements of a range of database applications. In general, the currently proposed DBMS security policies do not provide the types of features that are required by typical database applications. This paper discusses four major problems with current DBMS security policies:

1. Automatic polyinstantiation
2. Simplistic Bell-LaPadula interpretation
3. View-based controls and constraints
4. Lack of transaction authorization controls.

The problems in each of these areas lead to DBMS security policies that are inadequate to support the development of complex multilevel database applications.

19.2 Problems with Automatic Polyinstantiation

Polyinstantiation is a term introduced by the SeaView project [LDN$^+$88] to describe the effects of multiple instances of data, differentiated only by the access class of the data. The primary objective of automatic polyinstantiation is to avoid channels of information flow from a "high" user process to a "low" user process. For instance, with element-level labeling, when a high user updates a low data item, the low data is left unmodified, and the data element is polyinstantiated at high. In other words, two instantiations of the data element would exist within the database, one visible only to a high user, and the other visible to both high and low users. Uncontrolled use

[1]MITRE Corporation

of polyinstantiation potentially leads to a proliferation of data marked at different access classes; the application would need to determine which instantiation of a data element should be considered the "real" data element at any particular access class.

19.2.1 Polyinstantiation and Entity Integrity

Even with tuple level labelling there are serious problems if data is automatically polyinstantiated. Specifically, there is no way to enforce entity or referential integrity.

Entity integrity is an essential component of any database application. An application entity is represented within a relational database by a unique primary key within a base relation. For instance, each employee is represented within a payroll application by a unique social security number. If there were two base employee tuples with the same social security number, this would be a violation of entity integrity. However, if an employee tuple were polyinstantiated, there would be, in effect, two representations of the same application entity. The application semantics of multiple representations of the same entity, with instantiations at different access classes, would need to be clearly understood by the application developers. What does it mean to have a SECRET instantiation of an employee as well as a TOP SECRET instantiation? Which instantiation contains the correct information about the employee? If a TOP SECRET instantiation already exists and a data entry clerk attempts to insert a SECRET instantiation, is it appropriate to create the SECRET version, or is it an error on the clerk's part to be entering that employee's data at SECRET instead of TOP SECRET?

In general, the purpose of entity integrity within a DBMS is to provide a mechanism to assure that each application entity is unique within the database. If the application has a need to polyinstantiate information intentionally, then the appropriate semantics can be built into the application. For instance, if the information about an employee that is available to a SECRET user is intended to be different than that available to a TOP SECRET user, then the application can directly incorporate the semantics of the differences within the database design. While automatic polyinstantiation derives from a requirement to control the flow of information from high processes to low ones, intentional polyinstantiation directly involves the application semantics.

19.2.2 Polyinstantiation and Referential Integrity

Automatic polyinstantiation adversely impacts the enforcement of referential integrity as well. The purpose of referential integrity is to assure that all references to application entities actually refer to existing entities. For example, within a payroll database, there might be an assignments relation that assigned an employee part-time to several different projects. Referential integrity requires that for each employee represented in the assignments relation, there is a corresponding tuple within the base employee relation. In other words, it makes no sense within the application for a person to be assigned to a project if that person is not actually an employee of the company.

There are two fundamental conflicts between polyinstantiation and the enforcement of referential integrity. The first problem has been termed referential ambiguity [Gajme]. If a tuple has been polyinstantiated, any references to the entity represented by that tuple will be ambiguous since it cannot be determined which instantiation of the tuple is the object of reference. If an employee tuple were polyinstantiated, then a social security number used within the assignments relation would logically refer to more than one instantiation.

The second conflict is evident when tuples are deleted from the database. Referential integrity enforcement requires that the DBMS examine references to a tuple whenever the tuple is to be deleted from the database. In general, there are several alternatives that the DBMS may enforce for delete operations: delete all related tuples, set the foreign key attribute values in related tuples to null, or reject the delete operation if there are any existing references. For example, if an employee has terminated and is to be deleted from the database, then conceptually, all of the employee's assignments must also be deleted. However, assume that an employee (whose base tuple might be unclassified) is assigned to a TOP SECRET project in the assignments relation. An UNCLASSIFIED user, unaware of the TOP SECRET assignment, could delete the employee tuple. The result would be a "dangling reference" in the assignments relation, a reference to a non-existent foreign key tuple.

An alternative to the dangling reference involves re-instantiation of the employee tuple at TOP SECRET. If the employee tuple is re-instantiated, the referential integrity of the high reference in the assignments relation is maintained, while the unclassified user remains unaware of the existence of the TOP SECRET project. To enforce this form of polyinstantiation, the DBMS would need to be aware of (i.e., have access to) database information that is more highly classified than the access class of the user's process. In other words, to support referential integrity, there must be some portion of the DBMS that is trusted to examine references and enforce referential integrity. The Schaefer/Hinke [HS75] and SeaView approaches [LSS+88] that use a totally untrusted DBMS cannot successfully enforce referential integrity in a multilevel database.

19.2.3 Polyinstantiation verses Application Consistency

From the examples described above, it can be seen that the concept of automatic polyinstantiation is in direct conflict with those features of a relational DBMS that provide for the logical consistency of a database application. Since the basic purpose of polyinstantiation is to limit the possibility of information flow from a high user process to a low process, the potential information flows should be thoroughly understood.

For the enforcement of entity integrity, the fundamental information flow is a rejection of an insert operation for a tuple whose primary key value is already contained in an existing tuple. Similarly, the enforcement of referential integrity may result the rejection of a delete operation. Any rejection of these operations is both an inference channel and a covert signalling channel. If an insert or delete operation is rejected, a low user can infer that the key attributes refer to an application entity for which that user is not cleared. This is equivalent to, in the paper world, knowing that project X is classified, but not knowing any details about project X. The covert signalling channel would provide a means for a Trojan horse program to signal information to a low process by modulating the existence of a particular high tuple.

Both of these channels can be easily audited and the use of the specific database operations controlled by the DBMS. The risks of these channels being exploited by malicious users or software must be weighed against the relative ineffectiveness of an MLS DBMS that cannot support entity and referential integrity.

19.2.4 Problems with Simplistic Mandatory Policies

One of the major problems with a simple mandatory policy, based directly on the Bell-LaPadula model [BL76], is that it does not take into account the interrelationships among the data elements within a database. In particular, a policy that inserts tuples only at the level of the subject is too simplistic to meet a typical application's needs.

For example, assume a database that records tracking information about ships, some of which are military and others commercial. If all information about a particular ship were considered SECRET, it would be inappropriate for the tracking information recorded by some commercial source to be included in the database as unclassified. The information would need to be classified SECRET as soon as it was determined that it referred to a SECRET ship. Similarly, if "all flights to Iran" were SECRET, it would be a security violation if an unclassified user process inserted an unclassified tuple representing a flight to Iran. In both these cases, the information would need to be upgraded to reflect its classification in the context of the database application. Note also that a rejection of the insert operation in either of these cases would result in the inference that some piece of information was more highly classified than the user's session.

Since a 'write-up' is not a security violation in the Bell- LaPadula policy, the problem for a DBMS security policy is to provide a secure mechanism for specifying classification constraints [LDN+88] which automate the classification process when information is inserted or updated. The SeaView project has proposed the use of classification constraints that resemble database integrity constraints in that they constrain the access class attributes based on the data values of other attributes within the database. While these constraints appear on the surface to address the automatic classification problem, they have several problems, discussed below, that are inherent in the use of database query language constructs (such as, views) for mandatory security.

19.3 Problems with View-Based Controls and Constraints

The single major problem with view-based mandatory access controls has always been the assurance problem: verifying the software that performs the view interpretation and processing is well beyond the state-of-the-art in verification. While the use of labeled views for mandatory access control (instead of labeled elements or tuples) has generally been considered infeasible, the use of view constructs for classification constraints has appeared more tractable. However, in order to have assurances that data is correctly classified, the automatic classification must be performed by trusted software. But the software required to perform the automatic classification for any given database update would of necessity be extremely complex. It would first need to determine which constraints were involved, and then derive the classification based on an analysis of those constraints.

In addition, the use of a query language like SQL to specify classification constraints quickly becomes complicated and convoluted. For example, to specify the classification constraint that "all information about a SECRET ship is SECRET" requires a separate classification constraint for each relation that contains information about particular ships. To specify that locations "alpha", "beta", and "gamma" are SECRET, while locations "X", "Y" and "Z" are TOP SECRET, requires query language expressions that contain each distinct value for the location attribute. The job of the database security administrator quickly becomes unmanageable as the number of interrelated classification constraints increases. The entire security semantics of the database application must be captured as expressions within the relational query language!

What is needed is a simpler means of expressing the classification constraints for an application, one that takes advantage of the relational database itself to provide an algorithmic classification process.

19.4 Requirement for Transaction Authorizations

One final problem with proposed DBMS security policies is that they do not address a fundamental requirement of a database environment - transaction authorization. The concept of transaction authorizations is found in most database applications, where individuals act in certain roles, performing only specific tasks, or subtasks, and are prohibited from performing other functions involving the same database information [CW87,Mur87]. This goes beyond simple access controls on programs and data; a user is authorized to perform a certain function on a specific set of data items. The transaction authorization controls (TAC) provide mechanisms for the enforcement of least privilege and separation of duty. Both of these concepts are critical to database security since they reduce significant security exposures (such as, inference and tampering).

Most commercial DBMS products provide "high-level" transaction authorization controls in the form of menu packages or program authorizations. The level of assurance for these controls is not sufficiently high for multilevel applications. They generally execute within the user's process and depend on security parameters and data that are not well protected. In order to enforce least privilege and separation of duty adequately within a multilevel secure DBMS, the transaction authorization controls must be included within the DBMS security policy and enforced by trusted software.

19.5 Summary

If a DBMS security policy is to support multilevel applications adequately it must address the problems detailed in this paper:

1. It must support entity and referential integrity.
2. It must provide features for automatic classification of data, based on the application's security requirements.
3. Query language structures, such as constraints or views, should not be used for mandatory access controls or automatic classification.
4. Transaction authorization controls must be included within the DBMS security policy.

In order to adequately address these problems, a DBMS security policy will need to reflect the security requirements of complete database applications more accurately. The security mechanism provided by the DBMS will need to be as simple as possible, both to implement and to administer, while providing sufficient application flexibility.

19.6 References

[BL76] D.E. Bell and L.J. LaPadula. Secure computer systems: Unified exposition and Multics interpretation. *Technical Report ESD-TR-75-306*, The MITRE Corporation, Bedford, Massachusetts, March 1976.

[CW87] D.D. Clark and D.R. Wilson. A comparison of commercial and military computer security policies. In *Proceedings of the 1987 IEEE Symposium on Security and Privacy*, 1987.

[Gajme] G.E. Gajnak. Some results from the entity relationship multilevel secure DBMS project. In *Research Directions in Database Security* (T. F. Lunt, ed.), this volume.

[HS75] T.H. Hinke and M. Schaefer. Secure data management system. *Technical Report RADC-TR-75-266*, System Development Corporation, November 1975.

[LDN+88] T.F. Lunt, D.E. Denning, P.G. Neumann, R.R. Schell, M. Heckman, and W.R. Shockley. Final report vol. 1: Security policy and policy interpretation for a class A1 multilevel secure relational database system. *Technical report*, Computer Science Laboratory, SRI International, Menlo Park, California, 1988.

[LSS+88] T.F. Lunt, R.R. Schell, W.R. Shockley, M. Heckman, and D. Warren. A near-term design for the SeaView multilevel database system. In *Proceedings of the 1988 IEEE Symposium on Security and Privacy*, April 1988.

[Mur87] W.H. Murray. Data integrity in a business data processing system. In *Report of the Invitational Workshop on Integrity Policy in Computer Information Systems (Appendix 6)*, October 1987.

will need to be as simple as possible both to implement and to understand while providing sufficient flexibility.

References

20

New Approaches to Database Security: Report on Discussion

Catherine Meadows[1]

20.1 Introduction

Although multi-level secure operating systems have been a reality for several years, their use has yet to become widespread. This is due, in part, to the lack of secure software available for such systems, in particular to the lack of secure software for data-intensive applications, for which multi-level secure databases are a necessity.

Database security is difficult for two reasons. The first of these is what we might call a "mechanical" reason; the data items that must be protected are relatively small, thus providing a challenge to the system, which must manage many small items securely, and often must handle data at different levels within one transaction. This is true even when data is classified at a relatively coarse level of granularity, such as at the relational level, since, although stored data may be labelled as large chunks, data may still be entered or read in small pieces. Moreover, a user nay need to obtain data that is the result of joins taken over relations at different security levels; thus the ability to perform multilevel transactions is desirable even with very coarse classification granularity. However, although problems of this sort are more difficult than the problems posed by the design of a secure operating system, they are similar in nature. Both the database management system and the operating system must manage items while maintaining integrity of security labels, granting access only to authorized users, and preventing or reducing the bandwidth of covert channels.

The other class of problems that arises is one which we might refer to as "semantic." Under this heading we include inference and aggregation problems, which arise from the fact that the data items involved are closely related semantically. Thus a datum must be protected not only on the basis of the label assigned to it, but on the basis of the labels assigned to the data which can be inferred from it. In other words, security labels can not be assigned arbitrarily. We also include under this heading the sort of problems that arise from the fact that the nature in which a particular

[1]Center for Secure Information Technology, Naval Research Laboratory

datum is intended to be used may mean that the operations permitted or proscribed will have to be more specialized than the usual "read", "write", and "execute". Recent work that attempts to deal with this last problem, for example [CW87,Vin88], although it does not explicitly address the problem of database security, was conceived with data-intensive applications in mind.

Thus database security not only inherits many problems from operating system security, but raises new problems of its own. Since new problems require new approaches, a discussion of the possible new approaches seemed to be in order.

20.2 Report on Discussion

The discussion started out with an attempt to list and characterize the various new approaches to database security. This attempt quickly led to problems, since it was often hard to distinguish between a new approach and an old approach that had never been adequately tested. It was then decided simply to list approaches and the problems they were meant to solve. This also proved unsatisfactory, since it created the impression that the approaches were motivating the problems, instead of the other way around. Thus the rest of the session was devoted to compilation and discussion of open problems in database security. Interestingly enough, there was some overlap between the list of approaches and the list of problems, indicating, perhaps, that many appraoches that offer solutions to old problems can pose new problems of their own, or perhaps that some problems may already carry within them the seeds of their solutions.

Although aggregation and inference problems were a subject of much debate during the rest of the workshop, no explicit mention was made of them in this discussion. However, many of the problems cited arise because of aggregation and inference problems; we made note of that whenever this occurs.

The problems discussed fell, roughly, into four categories. We consider each of these categories separately below.

20.2.1 Open Problems in Computer Security

This category consisted of problems that are considered to be open problems for general operating systems as well as databases. In other words, these are problems that have not yet been solved for operating systems, and remain problems for secure database systems. Under this heading we include:

Changes to Secure Database Systems

- How can we modify or update a secure database system while assuring that it remains secure? How can we avoid the necessity for a complete re-evaluation every time a database system is modified?

User Interfaces for Secure Systems

- How can we make secure systems more user-friendly? Is it possible for user interfaces to support trusted security labels?

Denial of Service

- How can we guard against denial of service caused by hostile programmers or users?

Auditing of Secure Systems

- How do we analyze data in audit logs? How do we guard against covert channels when the auditing system is used?

Secure Applications

- As noted at the beginning of this report, the development of many secure applications depends on a secure DBMS. Thus the development of a secure DBMS would go a long way to solving this problem. On the other hand, much remains to be done even after secure database systems are developed.

20.2.2 Old Problems for Operating Systems but New Problems for Database Systems

The next class of problems we can characterize as old problems that are solved or at least partially solved for secure operating systems but become harder for secure database systems. Among these we include:

Integrity across Security Levels

- How can we maintain integrity constraints defined across security levels without introducing covert channels? We include this problem under the heading of old problems that become harder for secure database systems because of its similarity to the problem of managing shared resources in operating systems. Constraints on shared resources in operating systems can open up covert channels in operating systems in the same way that constraints on data defined over security levels open up covert channels in database systems. The solution to the problem for database systems may be the same as the solution for operating systems: partition a constraint that crosses security levels into two or more constraints that do not cross security levels so that data that satisfy the multiple constraints also satisy the original constraint.

Determining the Level of Assurance Necessary for a Secure Database System

- Due to the greater complexity of database systems, it may not be possible to provide the same level and kind of assurance for a secure DBMS as we can for a secure operating system. What kind of compromises is it necessary to make? Is it possible to provide new techniques for assurance?

Multilevel database recovery

- How can we recover a multilevel database after a crash without violating security?

Containing covert channels

- This problem is similar to the problem for operating systems but becomes harder because of the greater interdependency of data at different security levels.

Strategies for Access Denial

- Both secure operating systems and database systems require strategies for access denial. However, again because of the greater interdependency of data in a database, the strategies may be more complicated.

Discretionary access policies, mechanisms, languages

- Under this heading we can put two open problems. One of these arises from the fact that the smaller granularity of data in a DBMS means that maintaining integrity of discretionary access labels becomes very difficult. How can we assure integrity, and what is the maximum level of assurance we can provide? The second problem arises from the fact that the various uses to which data can be put may mean that we need more precisely defined discretionary access than the standard "read", "write", and "execute". How can we define a meaningful discretionary access policy for a given application, and how can we enforce it?

Assurance Tools

- The special problems that secure database systems pose will mean that we will need specialized tools to guarantee assurance. For example, the complexity of classifying data means that it would be helpful to have a tool for guaranteeing the completeness and consistency of classification, as in [AD87]. Tools for detecting inference channels would also be helpful [Hin88,Mor88,SO87,Thu87].

Developmental Tools that Support Security

- Tools exist that assist in the development of databases, but they do not support security well. How can we improve them?

Analysis of Problems and Solutions

- What are the threats to multilevel secure database systems? How can we rate them in terms of importance? How can we analyze and rate the solutions that have been proposed?

20.2.3 Database-Specific Problems

The third group consisted of problems that are more or less unique to database systems. Under this heading we include:

Development of classification tools

- The greater interdependency of data in a database system may mean that it may not be possible to classify data and certify that the classification scheme is correct, complete, and consistent completely by hand. Thus it may be necessary to develop software tools both to assist in the classification of data and to guarantee the correctness of the classification scheme.

Adaptive Security Policies

- As a database and the uses to which it is put change over time, it may be necessary to change the security policy to which it conforms. How can we do this in a secure, consistent, and timely way?

Test Cases

- The security requirements of a secure database system can vary greatly with the application to which it is put. Thus it is necessary to have examples of real world applications in order to determine how well our ideas work and whether our systems provide solutions to real problems.

Multilevel Transactions

- In a secure database system, it is often necessary to perform transactions that involve data classfied at different security levels. How can we ensure that this is done is a secure way?

20.2.4 Challenge Posed by Advances in Database Technology

Under this heading we put all problems that involve ensuring that new database technologies can be secure. Interestingly enough, it was from this class of problems that most of the examples of overlap between problems and solutions came. This was apparently because many of the database technologies that pose problems to secure system designers can also be used to solve open problems in computer security. For this reason, in the discussion of the challenges posed by these technologies, we will also include a discussion of the sorts of problems that they can be used to solve.

Distributed Secure Database Systems

- The difficulty of specifying and proving correctness of concurrent systems is well known; therefore it is to be expected that the development of a secure distributed database system would pose a challenge. However, it has been pointed out that, in many ways, a multilevel secure database system behaves like a virtual distributed database system, with the different security levels forming the different components of the database. Thus it may be possible that the techniques already developed for guaranteeing and proving correctness of distributed database systems can be adapted to database security.

Secure Object-Oriented Database Systems

- The object-oriented data model was developed to assist the user in specifying and management of complex data types. The flexibility and complexity of object-oriented database systems means that the development of a general secure object-oriented database system may be very difficult. But the very fact that the object-oriented approach was designed with flexibility and support for complexity in mind may mean that it can be used in designing systems that must meet complicated and frequently changed discretionary access requirements. This approach has already been suggested by [Vin88]. Also, in Chapter 17 of this book, it is shown how the notion of composite object may be used to support the container model of computer security as described in [LHM84].

Knowledge Base Security

- The complexity and unpredictibility of knowledge bases means that the development of multi-level secure knowledge bases could be very difficult. However, the ease with which knowledge bases can be used to model various kinds of relations between data means that they may be helpful in modeling and detecting inference channels. Under this heading we put the work done in modeling inference channels in knowledge bases [Thu87] and the classification expert system [LB87].

Security Models for Different Data Models

- Most work in database security has restricted itself to the databases constructed according the relational data model, both because of its popularity and because of the well-developed theory associated with it. However, in some cases it may be desirable to develop secure database systems constructed according to other models. As an example, we have George Gajnak's work on the entity-relationship model in this proceedings, Chapter 16 of this book, in which use is made of the explicit representation of relationships between data items provided by this model to solve the problem of referential ambiguity when polyinstantiation is allowed.

Parallel Database Systems

- Recently parallel database systems have attracted interest as a means for providing support for efficient searches of large databases. However, little has been done to develop secure versions of such database systems. It should be noted however, that parallel machines may also provide support for database system security by providing a natural means for separating processes by security levels.

Secure DBMS Chips

- How do we build a secure database system using chips with database functions built in? What challenges does such technology raise, and what problems can it solve?

20.3 Conclusion

As we have seen the open problems in secure database system design are many and daunting. Moreover, although many problems arise from the specific nature of database systems, others are old problems inherited from secure operating system design that were either never adequately solved in the first place or have become more difficult for secure database systems. Still other problems are posed by the emergence of new database system technologies. However, these technologies, although they present challenges, can also be used to help solve open problems in database system security.

20.4 References

[AD87] S.G. Akl and D.E. Denning. Checking classification constraints for consistency and completeness. In *Proceedings of the 1987 IEEE Symposium on Security and Privacy*, April 1987.

[BL87] T.A Berson and T.F. Lunt. Multilevel security for knowledge-based systems. In *Proceedings of the 1987 IEEE Symposium on Security and Privacy*, April 1987.

[CW87] D.D. Clark and D.R. Wilson. A comparison of commercial and military computer security policies. In *Proceedings of the 1987 IEEE Symposium on Security and Privacy*, 1987.

[Hin88] T.H. Hinke. Inference aggregation detection in database management systems. In *Proceedings of the 1988 IEEE Symposium on Security and Privacy*, April 1988.

[LB87] T.F. Lunt and T.A. Berson. An expert system to classify and sanitize text. In *Proceedings of the Third Aerospace Computer Security Conference*, December 1987.

[LHM84] C.E. Landwehr, C.L. Heitmeyer, and J. McLean. A security model for military message systems. *ACM Transactions on Computer Systems*, 2(3), August 1984.

[Mor88] M. Morgenstern. Controlling logical inference in multilevel database systems. In *Proceedings of the 1988 IEEE Symposium on Security and Privacy*, April 1988.

[SO87] T. Su and G. Ozsoyoglu. Data dependencies and inference control in multilevel relational database systems. In *Proceedings of the 1987 IEEE Symposium on Security and Privacy*, April 1987.

[Thu87] M.B. Thuraisingham. Security checking in relational database management systems augmented with inference engines. *Computers and Security*, 6(6), 1987.

[Vin88] S.T. Vinter. Extended discretionary access controls. In *Proceedings of the 1988 IEEE Symposium on Security and Privacy*, April 1988.

21

Metadata and View Classification

LouAnna Notargiacomo [1]

21.1 Introduction

The discussion during the metadata and view session centered on the proper classification rules to be applied to each metadata level and the relationship of the user's operating level and the metadata level on the base data level.

The main issues discussed during this session were: the handling of metadata that describe a multilevel database; the proper classification rules governing metadata; the different approaches to protection of metadata; different approaches to end user access to metadata; and the affect of the user's session level on query and result labels.

21.2 Justification for Metadata Protection

There are various reasons why a metadata database should be protected as sensitive data. First, the metadata for a multilevel database contain data that may by themselves represent sensitive information, separate from any relationship with the underlying database. This information includes attribute descriptions and domains, the relationships between attributes, and the location of database partitions. For example, the field length of an attribute may divulge a capability to collect information with a specific precision. This fact in many contexts allows the inference of a data gathering capability that is highly sensitive.

The second reason for classification of metadata is as a method of controlling access to the underlying data. This may be necessary in situations where these metadata are used as access control input. For example, in systems where access views are used as mandatory access control mechanisms (e.g., sanitization views), the DML view statement would require appropriate protection.

Finally, in some cases, the existence of data and the relationships among data are by themselves sensitive.

---

[1]MITRE Corporation

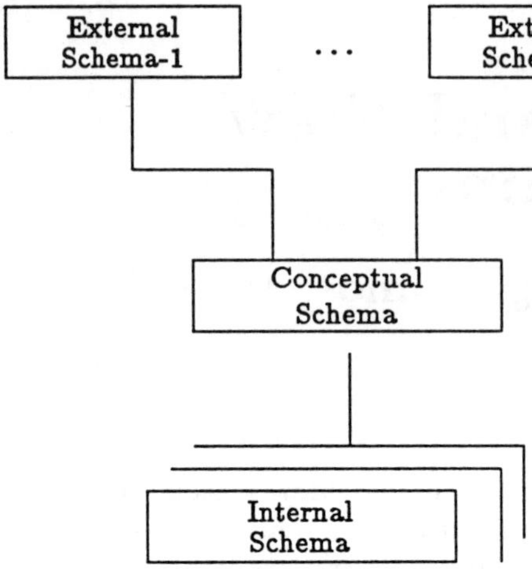

FIGURE 21.1. Database schema architecture.

21.3 Metadata Classification Approaches

The basic ANSI SPARC database model is an appropriate method for describing the internal structure and relationship between metadata layers. For a single database there are three layers: external, conceptual, and internal (shown in Figure 21.1).

The Internal Schema layer defines the mapping of the overall conceptual description of the database to the actual data storage structures. The Conceptual Schema layer defines an entire multilevel database as it occurs logically in the real world. The External Schema layer represents multiple variations to the overall database that are designed to satisfy a particular end user's needs. A relational database view is an example of an External Schema.

For each schema layer, common definitions and guidelines for the classification of metadata are presented.

21.3.1 Internal Schema

Most MLS DBMS designs map the actual data onto single level storage segments that may be protected by the underlying MLS operating system. The metadata at this lowest level are marked at the same level as the data they describe. The data granularity at this level might be at the element, tuple, or relation level.

21.3.2 Conceptual Schema

At the conceptual level, relations are defined as they occur in the actual application, and are therefore by definition multilevel. In typical MLS DBMS designs to date, a subject process operating on behalf of the end user at the user's access level is initiated for each user session. In order to allow all such processes access to required metadata at the Conceptual level, these data are labeled at the greatest lower bound of any base data that the metadata describe.

For example, for a DBMS with tuple level access control, a relation could be defined as containing tuples within the range level(1) $\leq$ level(2), where level(2) dominates level (1). The definition of the relation at the conceptual level would be labeled at level(1).

21.3.3 External Schema

The relational DBMS view capability allows users to create database subsets by assigning a name to a retrieval request. Subsequent query commands and view definitions can then reference the view, and as a result, the DML and view commands are concatenated prior to execution.

For clarity, the following terminology will be used: view schema, view definition, and view data. The view schema is the external representation of the view and is defined as a relation name followed by a set of attribute names contained in the view. In addition, the view schema could contain attribute length and type information, and end user access control information (e.g., the DML permissions attached to a view for the end user requesting this information). The view definition is the DML command that defines the operations to be performed against the database to form the view. The view data is the base data returned from or affected by the execution of a query command.

Two approaches are currently being used to determine the proper classification of view definitions, (1) based only on the level of the data that may be retrieved through the view, and (2) based also on the data contained in the view statement itself. In the first approach, the view would be labeled at the least upper bound of all Conceptual level relations referenced in the view definition. The second approach factors in the sensitivity level of data contained in the view definition, for example, SELECT parameter variables and constants. Since these data are in effect JOINed with data retrieved from the underlying database, no data retrieved through the view could be labeled at a level below the view definition data. Using this approach, the access view data would be labeled at the least upper bound of the data contained in the view definition statement and all referenced Conceptual level relations.

21.4 Metadata Protection Schemes

There are two methods for the protection of metadata; (1) to treat the metadata database as any other multilevel database, and therefore, have available the full DBMS functionality, or (2) to partition the metadata into operating system storage segments, using the MLS operating system to protect them, and therefore implementing special purpose code for access.

It was the consensus of the group that the best protection method for the metadata database is to use the first method, treating it as any other database and therefore, use the MLS DBMS system to protect and access the metadata. It should also be recognized that with this approach, the metadata that describe the metadata database (the meta-metadata) would then be protected by the second method since continuing to use the first method would result in an infinite loop.

21.5 User Access to Metadata

Two type of users require access to the metadata database, the Database Administrator (DBA) or Database Security Officer (DBSO), and the end users. It is clear that the DBA/DBSO require complete access to the metadata database in order to define and maintain the database. In addition, end users require some access to the metadata in order to obtain the information they need to query the database. Most DoD environments require some metadata browse capability.

Two policy approaches have been proposed for this access: to allow users to browse through all external schema that defines any data the user has access to as defined by the mandatory access rules, or to attach discretionary access privileges or restrictions on the external schema data, as on any other data.

The consensus of the workshop attendees was that the first approach violated the rules of least privilege and that the second approach should be used.

21.6 Affect of User Session Level on Data Classification

The state of the art in MLS operating system development does not allow a user application to operate within a range (to operate as a trusted subject), but only to operate at a single-level per session. With this type of environment in mind, all end user interaction with an MLS DBMS is through single level subject applications. Continuing with this assumption, it is unsafe to label data returned to the user at anything but his logon level since the application cannot be trusted to maintain the label, although some MLS DBMS systems are being designed to return untrusted, advisory labels at a lower granularity (tuple or element).

Another factor to consider is the flow of information in query processing from the user's query statement into the data result. Since there are data embedded in the query statement (constants, relation and attribute names), there is a flow from the user's query into the end result (either a database insert or modification, or data retrieved from the database). If the user is operating at a single level, the query should be treated as a labeled object and be marked at the user's level. Therefore, the result should never be marked lower than the query level except for untrusted, advisory labels.

It should be noted that a relational view is equivalent to a query statement, and therefore, there is a flow of data from the view into the data result that should be reflected in the data label (the data should never be labeled below the level of a view used in the database operation).

Currently research is proceeding into the development of multilevel user environments that would allow a user to operate over a range. The development of multilevel database interface packages should appear in the near future. With this in mind, the implication of multilevel subjects requires that queries either be labeled at the high of the user's range, or that the command syntax be modified explicitly to allow the user to specify the level of the query.

If the query is labeled at the high of the range, all results would then be labeled at the high of the range so that the advantages of allowing the user to operate in a range would be lost. If the user explicitly labels the query (where the label represents the level of the data in the query) then the data results would always dominate the level of the query.

All reasons for query labeling apply equally to views. Therefore, all returned or input data should be labeled at the HWM of all base data touched during command execution, the level of the user command, and the level of all referenced views.

22

Database Security Research at NCSC

John R. Campbell[1]

22.1 Introduction

I have been requested to enumerate what we are doing in database security, what we are interested in doing in the future, and to suggest items that we would like discussed at this meeting.

The Secure Research and Development Branch, Office of Research and Development, National Computer Security Center, is interested in encouraging and supporting a balanced program of database computer security research and development. Highly secure multilevel systems need to be built and research done to answer basic questions regarding this development. Much is known about securing database systems at lower levels of security. This information, plus the answers to additional security questions, must be placed in commercial systems so that users have the additional security they are demanding.

22.2 Sponsored Research Projects

I visited a vendor's site in California that has 2000 software developers. Another site has 120 people working on one database product. How does our tiny group and light funding influence a marketplace that is so large and so important?

The answer is any way we can. We currently have three projects that are either being developed in-house or are being done in partnership with database vendors.

The first project involves developing commercial database machine prototypes that we think would be rateable at the C2 and B1 levels. The isolation of a database machine from host operating systems helps secure the machine. The purpose of the project is to do the necessary research and development to get the additional security out to the users as soon as possible. The machine selected, the Teradata DBC/ 1012, is a modular,

[1]National Security Agency

high performance, MIMD or network computer that runs in a fault tolerant mode. The building blocks of the modules are 80286 chips. The project so far has raised interesting questions on audit, object reuse, and superuser access.

The second project involves developing a secure commercial host database system prototype that should be rateable at the C2 and B1 levels. The commercial system selected will be relational, widely used, and built by a vendor that has a database security track record. This project also will develop secure prototypes as quickly as possible. Interesting questions likely to be raised by this project include the interface problem between Trusted Computer Bases (TCBs) in the Operating Systems (OSs) and Database Management Systems (DBMSs).

The third project, which is an in-house project, involves building an "A1-like" DBMS on an OS that we believe very secure. Interrelationships between the security policies and trusted components of DBMSs and OSs need to be examined. A secure, proof-of-concept secure, DBMS prototype for this OS exists, and this model will be studied carefully.

Rome Air Development Center (RADC) is managing the Secure Data Views Project, a multilevel secure "A1" DBMS. A security policy, policy model, and formal specifications have been completed. This policy proposes defining multilevel relations as views rather than underlying single-level base relations.

RADC also has managed the Logical Coprocessing Kernel (LOCK) Data Views Project, an "A1" DBMS, which depends on LOCK mechanisms for much of its security.

RADC sponsored the development of an Entity Relationship Model which examined the difficulty of building security into a DBMS based on something other that the relational model. This model, upon which data dictionaries currently are based, proved significantly easier to install security. The model is more flexible and can provide more intelligent responses to user queries.

The Naval Research Lab (NRL) is working on a specialized database system, the Secure Military Message System. NRL is investigating techniques for constructing systems that are both useful and that provide significant assurance that their security requirements are met.

Lastly, the Navy sponsored a kernelized DBMS Project, where important parameters such as performance versus granularity were first examined and then solutions to the problem were proposed and tested.

On top of all of this activity, we sponsor Independent Research and Development (IR & D) programs that we feel have potential payoffs, we act as consultants, and we teach database security classes.

22.3 The Future

In the future, we will be interested in the following systems, a few of which—like Ada and Integrity—already are being worked on, but all of which need much more work:

1. Distributed Database Management Systems. Our top priority is securing Distributed DBMSs. Distributed DBMSs currently exist. Network problems and problems unique to Distributed DBMSs have to be examined in addition to the OS DBMSs we now have. This is a very large and important area.

2. Development of Standards. We need to talk a standard language even though our backgrounds are different–DoD, banking, etc.– and we come from different disciplines–DoD security, mathematics, computer science, applications areas, and the like. Standard interfaces between OS and DBMS, and between DBMS and network would be most laborsaving. Can these interfaces be defined so that an underlying system does not have to be recertified repeatedly when each new application is introduced?

3. Database System Verification. Our tools for stand-alone operating systems are meager. Where are the tools for Distributed DBMS verification?

4. Smart Database Management Systems. Systems with integrated expert and database components or systems that store rules and system-generated knowledge, do exist. How do we safeguard these systems?

5. Very Large and Multimedia Systems. Security solutions that minimumly degrade system performance are needed because the databases of the future will be very large. Also, how do we safeguard systems that have pictures, text, and so forth?

6. Integrity. We must be able to maintain the integrity of a Distributed Smart DBMS. This includes determining whether data has been modified through unauthorized means. How does forward error correction affect security labels? Users of database systems often list the requirement for data integrity ahead of access control protection.

7. Ada. What are the problems with securing a system written in the sizeable system that is Ada?

8. Intelligent Front Ends. What are the problems of securing systems with intelligent front ends, for example, a natural language front end? Do we need a trusted path? Can there be denial of service? Can data be changed?

9. Very Dense Chip Sets. Very dense chip sets that integrate some DBMS functions into the OS are being developed, at least to some extent. What do these developments mean to database security?

10. Parallel, Fault Tolerant, and/or Correcting Systems and Array Processors. What is the effect of these new computer architectures on database security? Also, what is the effect, on database security, of array processors coupled into other systems?

11. Expert and other AI Systems. With expert or other AI systems, can you reliably classify data? Can you audit logs in real time to detect suspicious activities? What audit-reduction tools do we need?

22.4 Discussion Topics

We have many interests, and all of our questions need to be answered. Three items that we would like discussed here are: (1) The required levels of assurance for different parts of the overall database system; (2) Audit requirements; and (3) Distributed DBMSs.

1. Teresa Lunt recently presented, at the March Secure Database Subgroup Meeting, the Secure Data Views architectural solution to database security. The two TCB layers consist of a lower level, which is an "A1" security kernel enforcing Mandatory Access Control (MAC) AND Discretionary Access Control (DAC) on storage objects, and a higher level, which is an extended TCB enforcing DAC and other policies, such as consistency, on abstract objects. What level of assurance does this second level require? Is the C2 level sufficient? Is using the same level of assurance on the higher level as that of MVS with ACF2 sufficient to call the overall system an "A1" system?

2. Database systems produce much journaling information, such as before and after images, which is stored for system recovery purposes; however, the type and quantity of information suggests that security of audit journals should be a separate function from the backup journals. For example, backup journals may not associate user with protected objects. Is this the general feeling?

3. What is the best way to secure Distributed Systems? How does the Trusted Network Interpretations impact this work?

23

Position Paper on DBMS Security

Joseph Giordano[1]

23.1 Introduction

Database systems are an integral component of current and future Command, Control, Communications and Intelligence (C3I) information systems. It is predicted that today's military commander or decision-maker will rely upon data and information stored in electronic databases for battle management functions. In the truest sense of the word, database technology has advanced to the point where it is being infused into operationally-oriented system environments. As more and more data is stored in databases the problem of protecting data and information arises. The recent West German hacker scandal is proof that our nation's computer systems are inadequately protected against hostile and malicious attacks.

Since 1974, the Rome Air Development Center (RADC) has been very active in sponsoring research programs aimed at designing and prototyping a family of trusted database management systems (DBMS). The research program sponsored by RADC can be logically partitioned into four major areas of emphasis: architecures/mechanisms, auditing and tools, automated/expert database design tools, and data integrity.

Past and current RADC programs in the architecures/mechanisms area, developed in conjunction with the National Computer Security Center, Strategic Defense Initiative Organization, and Electronic Systems Division, include Hinke-Schaefer, SeaView, LOCK data views, the secure entity-relationship model, integrity lock, and secure distributed DBMS. The yeoman efforts of the researchers on the aforementioned projects, in addition to the excellent work being done by TRW on Sybase and Mitre on the kernelized DBMS, have resulted in enormous contributions toward understanding how one could go about designing, developing, and verifying a trusted DBMS.

To date, very little work has been done in the area of auditing for secure DBMS's. It is of critical importance that the DoD laboratories involved in database security research and development begin laying the ground-

[1]U. S. Air Force, Rome Air Development Center

work for a research program in this area. Some relevant issues requiring investigation include what auditing means in the context of a DBMS, how application-specific requirements and granularity of labeling affect audit mechanisms, and how advanced technology such as workstations and expert systems can be exploited in building useful and robust DBMS auditing subsystems.

Another area of extreme importance is providing automated and expert support in the design, analysis, and maintenance of multilevel database structures. An operational user can be given the most rigorously verified trusted DBMS architecure, but, if the database is designed with inherent security flaws, then all could be for nothing. A recent personal experience with "real-world" database designs made me realize how easily a well-meaning database designer could mistakenly build a security-flawed structure containing a glaring inference or aggregation channel. Automated support must be provided to database designers which allows them to build multilevel databases, analyze database structures based on knowledge of both the database itself and the surrounding application domain, and maintain the security of the database as new requirments are either added or deleted to or from the system.

The final area of emphasis is that of data integrity. Data integrity means many things to many people. In the C3I and battle management world, data integrity is critical since polluted or maliciously modified data can have catastrophic effects on the outcome of the mission or battle. Plainly, more research is needed in defining data integrity for secure DBMS's. Prototypes and experiments must be developed to examine and document the usefulness of well-known integrity mechanisms such as the Biba model, as well as the not so well-known mechanisms of polyinstantiation, referential, and semantic integrity.

In addition to the research areas outlined above, two emerging technologies come to mind which have direct applicability to the military database environment. Each warrants consideration in the context of multilevel security. First, is the rapidly advancing technology area of object-oriented DBMS. Object-oriented DBMS's, such as the Microelectronics and Computer Technology Corporation's (MCC) experimental Orion system, are touted as being capable of meeting the multimedia database and information system needs of the military. If object-oriented DBMS's prove efficacious, the database security community must mobilize and examine the security implications of this promising technology. The second area of opportunity is knowledge-base management systems (KBMS). Numerous knowledge-based applications, including the Navy Force Requirements Expert System (FRESH), the AirLand Battle Management system, and various knowledge-based intelligence applications, are quickly moving into the quasi-operational and advanced experimental phase. If knowledge-based systems are to be used in operational environments, then the security and integrity aspects of such systems must be researched and developed. It is doubtful if such systems, which will handle critical and sensitive data and knowledge, can be fielded unless adequate attention is given to security considerations early in the system development life cycle.

23.2 Conclusions

In conclusion, much progress has been made in database security; however, much needs to be done. I categorically stand behind the fact that protoypes, experiments, worked examples, and demonstrations must be developed. Also, controversial issues such as balanced assurance must be debated openly, vigorously, and impartially. With regard to the Trusted Database Interpretation, I believe that the herculean efforts of that committee should be commended, but the TDI should not preclude the genesis of new and unique approaches to database security. Finally, I commend the efforts of Ms. Teresa Lunt of SRI and Mr. Marvin Schaefer of Trusted Information Systems for putting this workshop together. It is the leadership and entrepreneurship of individuals like Teresa, Marv, and the numerous others whom I have had the pleasure of working with, that will mean success for the technology area of database security.

[illegible] systems, which will [illegible] knowledge [illegible] unless adequate [illegible] considered early in the system development [illegible].

[illegible] Conclusion

[illegible]

Index

A
A1 Secure Database Management System, 33-39
Access class attribute, 121
Access class data type, 22-24
Access class domain, 29
Access classes, 13, 16, 17-18, 22, 44
  operations on, 23-24
Access control list (ACL), 45, 168
Access views, 45, 92
ACL (access control list), 45, 168
Advanced Secure DBMS (ASD), 33, 38-39
Advisor paradigm, 140
Advisory labels, 1-2
Aggregation, inference and, 143-158
Aggregation problem, 2, 98-100, 143
Air Force Summer Study, 1
Akl, S.G., 93, 94, 98, 102, 137, 140, 199, 221, 222, 223, 224, 239, 242
Ambiguity, referential, 184-189, 229
AOG Systems Corporation and Gemini Systems Inc., 1, 10, 190
Application consistency versus polyinstantiation, 230
Architectural parameters, 47, 49
ASD (Advanced Secure DBMS), 33, 38-39
Assurance, 5-7
  balanced, 5-6, 167-170
Astrahan, M.M., 5, 10
Attribute class types, 26
Attribute classification, 121
Attribute-dependent security semantics, 130
Attribute groups, 25-26
Attribute name-value pair, 137
Attribute ranges, 25
Attribute-value association, 130
Attribute value dependency, 119
Authorization, denial of, 3
Automatic classification, 4, 166
Automatic polyinstantiation, 227-231
Automatic reclassification, 8
Automatic upgrade, 120

B
B2 design philosophy, 83-84
Balanced assurance, 5-6, 167-170
Ballou, N., 192, 197
Banerjee, J., 192, 197
Base relations, 44
Beeri, C., 221, 223
Bell, D.E., 35, 39, 190, 230, 235
Berson, T.A., 4, 10, 15, 30, 31, 132, 133, 139, 141, 166, 208, 223, 241, 242
Biba, K.J., 35, 39, 190
Bobrow, D.G., 192, 198
Boebert,W.E., 69, 80
Boyer, R.S., 92, 95
Bry, F., 222, 223

C

Cardinality aggregation, 98
CCR (container clearance required), 194-195
Chakravarthy, U., 206, 223
Chen, G., 215, 223
Chen, P.P., 174, 175, 190
Chisholm, P., 215, 223
Chou, H.-T., 192, 197
Clark, D.D., 232, 235, 236, 242
Clark, K., 200, 210, 214, 218, 223
Classi system, 4, 5
Classification, automatic, 4, 166
Classification constraints, 26-27, 93
Classification domains, 2
Classification semantics, 4-5
Classification tool, 157
Classification views, 92-93
Classifying, downgrading and, 15-133
Classifying metadata, 8-9
Classifying outputs, 126
Clifford, J., 219, 223
Clocksin, W.F., 190
Closed-world assumption (CWA), 203, 216-217
Codd, E.F., 42, 61, 219, 223
Cohen, M.S., 139, 140, 141
Committee on Multilevel Data Management Security Air Force Summer Study, 1, 10, 41, 42, 57, 61, 173, 190, 192, 197
Comparator operators, 22
Computer security, 236-239
Constraint network analysis, 151
Constraints, 26-27
Container clearance required (CCR), 194-195
Content-dependent classification, 67
Content dimension, 129
Context-dependent classification, 67
Cornwell, M., 195, 197
Covert channels, 139
Crow, J.S., 14, 30
CWA (closed-world assumption), 203, 216-217

D

DAC, *see* Discretionary access control
Data classification
  semantics of, 135-140
  user session level and, 247
Data classification problem, 102
Data integrity, 254
Data labeling strategy, 49
Data manipulation language (DML), 45, 174
Data model, relational, 18
Data model semantics, 175-180
Data movement, controlled, 74-75
Data replication strategy, 49
Database Administrator (DBA), 43
Database inference, 44, 146
Database management system, *see* DBMS *entries*
Database Owner (DBO), 82
Database security
  multilevel, 1
  new approaches to, 235-242
  position paper on, 253-255
  research at NCSC, 249-252
Database-specific problems, 239-240
Database systems, parallel, 241
Date, C.J., 44, 61
DBA (Database Administrator), 43
DBMS (database management system), 33, 64
  multilevel (MLS/DBMS), 41, 199-233
  secure distributed (SD-DBMS), 41-61, 240
DBMS security policies, 227-233
DO (Database Owner), 82
DDT (Domain Definition Table), 65-66

Decker, H., 210, 224
Dempsey, J.P., 52, 62
Denial of authorization, 3
Denning, D.E., 5, 10, 13, 14, 15, 18, 19, 28, 30, 31, 32, 45, 46, 51, 58, 59, 61, 62, 72, 79, 93, 94, 98, 10, 102, 128, 133, 137, 140, 141, 149, 156, 158, 173, 180, 190, 199, 201, 206, 207, 221, 222, 223, 224, 227, 231, 233, 239, 242
Department of Defense, 64, 80
Dependency principle, 183
Derived relations, 45
Derived tuples, 45
Description dimension, 129
Design-time analysis, 152-153
Determinacy principle, 7, 183-184
Dillaway, B.B., 128, 133
Discovered misclassification, 166
Discretionary access control (DAC), 44-45
  enforcement, 57-59
  role-based, 119
Discretionary Overlay Matrix (DOM), 66
Discretionary security, 3-4, 16, 21, 82
Distributed secure database systems, 41-61, 240
DML (data manipulation language), 45, 174
DOM (Discretionary Overlay Matrix), 66
Domain Definition Table (DDT), 65-66
Domains, 44
Dominance relation, 15
Downgrading, classifying and, 125-133
Downing, A., 28, 3
Downs, D., 58, 62
Dwyer, P., 10, 103, 128, 133, 199, 224
Dwyer, P.A., 1, 10, 69, 70, 72, 73, 79, 202, 224

E

Effective Access Matrix (EAM), 65
Enhanced Hierarchical Development Methodology (EHDM) system, 14
Entity association, 120
Entity integrity, 18
  polyinstantiation and, 228
Entity/Relationship, *see* E/R *entries*
Environments, 210-214
  inference and, 14-215
EPL (Evaluated Product List), 170
E/R (entity-relationship) project, 1
E/R data model, 173-190
E/R diagram, 110-112
E/R items, 175-179
Evaluated Products List (EPL), 170
Evolution of views, 91-94
Exception Control, 78
Existence dimension, 129-130

F

Feiertag, R.J., 92, 95
Ferbrache, D., 215, 223
File management, 78
Fixed points, 212
Floyd, J., 200, 210, 211, 213, 224
Foreign key dependency, 119
Formal semantics of time, 219-220
Formal top-level specification (FTLS), 27, 76
Frost, R., 200, 201, 203, 205, 206, 207, 209, 216, 224
FTL (formal top-level specification), 27, 76

G

Gajnak, G.E., 229, 233
Gallaire, H., 20, 224
Garvey, C., 1, 10, 35, 39, 144, 158

Garza, J.F., 192, 197
GEMO, 27-28
Generalized Typed Entity/ Relationship Model (GTERM), 175-181
Goguen, J.A., 92, 95
Grant, J., 206, 216, 223, 224
Granularity principle, 182-183
Graubart, R.D., 1, 10, 51, 58, 62
Gray, J.W., 55, 57, 62
Greenberg , I., 28 , 31
GTERM (Generalized Typed Entity/Relationship Model), 175, 181
Gypsy Verification Environment Methodology, 37

H

Haigh J.T., 128, 133
Harris, M.D., 190
Harrison, M.A., 170 , 171
Heckman, M., 1, 5, 10, 11, 13, 14, 17, 18, 19, 28, 31, 45, 46, 59, 62, 72, 79, 98, 100, 102, 103, 128, 133, 137, 140, 141, 156, 158 173, 180, 190, 199, 201, 206, 207, 221, 222, 223, 224, 227, 229, 231, 233
Heitmeyer, C.L., 1, 10, 191, 195, 197, 198, 240, 242
Hierarchical sensitivity level, 15
Hinke, T.H., 1, 10, 39, 40, 52, 62, 98, 102, 144, 145, 146, 147, 18, 214, 224, 229, 233, 239, 242
Homework problem, 4, 105-107, 135
  report on, 109-123
Honeywell, 63, 64, 65, 66, 67, 68, 70, 76, 79, 80

I

Inference, environments and, 214-215
Inference aggregation, 98
Inference control, 67
Inference problem, 14-15, 97-98, 143-158
Information Resource Dictionary System (IRDS), 174-175
Initial overclassification, 163-164
Initial underclassification, 164-165
Integrity constraints, 26
Intensional logic, 203
IRDS (Information Resource Dictionary System), 174-175

J

Jefferson, S.T., 14, 30
Jelatis, G.D., 202, 224
Jensen, C., 57, 62
Jenson, N., 39, 40

K

Kain, R.Y., 69, 80
KBMS (knowledge-base management systems), 254-255
Keefe, T.F., 147, 158, 199, 206, 209, 224, 226
Key dominance constraint, 119
Keys, 24-25
Kim, H.-J., 192, 197
Kim, W., 192, 197
Knowledge-base management systems (KBMS), 254-255
Knowledge base security, 240-241
Kohonen, T., 132, 133
Kowalski, R., 147, 158, 210, 214, 225

L

Labels, trusted and advisory, 1-2
LAN (local area network), 43
Landwehr, C.E.,11, 10, 191, 198, 240, 242
LaPadula, L.J., 35, 39, 190, 230, 235

Lattice operations, 22
Layered TCB, 6-7
LDV (LOCK Data Views), 1, 2, 63-79
Least environment, 213
Lee, R., 14, 30
Lehner, P.E., 139, 140, 141
Levitt, K., 92, 95
Local area network (LAN), 43
Lochovsky, F.H., 193, 198
LOCK (Logical Coprocessor Kernel), 63
LOCK Data Views, *see* LDV *entries*
LOCK pipeline organization, 74-75
LOCK security policy overview, 64-68
Logical Coprocessor Kernel, *see* LOCK *entries*
Logical deduction, 143
Logical inference problems, 148-152
Lunt, T.F., 1, 4, 5, 11, 13, 14, 15, 17, 18, 19, 27, 28, 30, 31, 32, 45, 46, 59, 62, 72, 79, 93, 94, 98, 100, 102, 103, 128, 132, 133, 137, 139, 140, 141,156, 158, 166, 173, 180, 190, 199, 201, 206, 207, 208, 209, 221, 223, 224, 225, 227, 229, 231, 233, 241, 242

M

MAC, see Mandatory access control
Maier, D., 200 , 225
Mandatory access control (MAC), 43, 45-46
  view-based, 231-232
Mandatory policy, simplistic, 230-231
Mandatory security, 16, 81
Mappings, 211-212
McHugh, J., 132, 133
McLean, J., 1, 10, 191, 198, 240, 242
Melliar-Smith, P.M., 14, 30
Mellish, C.S., 190
MERGE operation, 73
Meseguer, J., 92, 95
Metadata, 9, 154
  classifying, 8-9
  user access to, 246
Metadata classification approaches, 244-246
Metadata protection, 243
Metadata protection schemes, 246
Minker, J., 200, 206, 216, 223-225
Misclassification, discovered, 166
MLS (multilevel security), 15-17, 125
MLS/DBMS (multilevel database management system), 41, 199-200
Model theoretic approach, 202-207
Montague, R., 203, 225
Monthes, R., 222, 223
Morgenstern, M., 2, 11, 14, 32, 93, 94, 98, 102, 103, 128, 133, 137, 140, 147, 149, 150, 158, 199, 214, 222, 223, 224, 225, 239, 242
MSQL (multilevel SQL), 14, 21-27
MSQL Preprocessor, 28-29
Mullin, T.M., 139, 140, 141
Multi-attribute associations, 130
Multilevel database management system (MLS/DBMS), 199-223
Multilevel database security, 1
Multilevel databases, 201
  foundations of, 199-223
  principles of, 182-184
Multilevel entity integrity, 18
Multilevel referential integrity, 18-19
Multilevel relational structures, 202
Multilevel relations, 17-21, 201
  creating, 24-27
Multilevel secure database management system, 41

Multilevel security (MLS), 15-17, 125
Multilevel security characteristics, 180-181
Multilevel SQL, see MSQL entries
Multilevel subjects, 44
Murray, W.H., 232, 233

N
Name-dependent classification, 67
Narrow classification, 29
National Computer Security Center, 3, 5, 10, 13, 17, 30, 33, 39, 41, 42, 61, 64, 79, 125, 133, 167, 168, 170; *see also* NCSC *entries*
Naval Research Lab (NRL), 250
NCSC (National Computer Security Center), 249
Negation by failure rule, 218-219
Network Trusted Computing Base (NTCB) partitions, 167
Neumann, P.G., 13, 14, 18, 19, 28, 31, 92, 93, 94, 95, 98, 102, 137, 140, 141, 156, 158, 173, 190, 199, 222, 223, 224, 227, 231, 233
Nicolas, J., 210, 225
NRL (Naval Research Lab), 250
NTCB (Network Trusted Computing Base) partitions, 167

O
Object-oriented data model, 191-197
O'Connor, J.P., 55, 57, 62
Onuegbe, E., 1, 10, 69, 70, 72, 73, 79, 128, 133, 199, 221, 224, 225
Optimization, 77
Ordinary subjects, 76
Overclassification, initial, 163-164
Ozsoyoglu, G., 221, 225, 239, 242

P
Parallel database systems, 241
Partial inferences, 149
Partial replication, 56
Partially ordered set (POSET), 65
Partitioning approach, 71
Per-level world method, 206, 207
Phone book problem, 99, 155
Pipeline implications, 78-79
Pipelines, 69-79
Polyinstantiated tuples, 19-20
Polyinstantiation, 8, 14, 19-20
  application consistency versus, 230
  automatic, 227-231
  dealing with, 24
  entity integrity and, 228
  referential integrity and, 223-229
Polyinstantiation integrity, 20
Popek, G.J., 58, 62
POSET (partially ordered set), 65
Primary objects, 81
Procedures, 86
Proof theoretic approach, 207-210

Q
Quantity aggregation, 131
Queries, 8
Query processing strategy, 49

R
RADC (Rome Air Development Center), 1, 92, 250, 253
Reclassification, automatic, 8
Reference monitor, 16
Referential ambiguity, 184-189, 229
Referential integrity, 8, 18, 189
  polyinstantiation and, 228-229
Reiter, R., 200, 216 225
Relational data model, 18
Relational database, theory of, 221
Relational structures, 201-202
Relationship dominance, 121
Response pipeline design 69, 73

Response pipeline organization, 75-78
Robinson, L., 92, 95
Role-based DAC, 119
Rome Air Development Center (RADC), 1, 92, 250, 253
Rougeau, P.A., 128, 133
Rowe, L.A., 191, 198
Run-time analysis, 152-153
Rushby, J.M., 14, 30
Ruzzo, W.L., 170, 171

S

SA (System Administrator), 82
Sadri, F., 147, 158, 210, 214, 225
Safety Test, 150
Sanitization, 163
Schaefer, M., 1, 6, 10, 11, 229, 233
Schell, R.R., 1, 5, 6, 10, 11, 13, 14, 17, 18, 19, 28, 29, 31, 32, 45, 46, 59, 62, 7, 79, 93, 94, 98, 100, 102, 103, 128, 133, 137, 140, 141, 156, 158, 167, 171, 173, 180, 190, 199, 201, 206, 207, 221, 222, 223, 224, 227, 229, 231, 233
Schwartz, R.L., 14, 30
SD-DBMS (secure distributed database management system), 41-61, 240
SeaView, 1, 13-30, 93, 173
SeaView approach, 2
SeaView design, 27-29
SeaView verification, 27
Secondary objects, 82
Secure distributed database management system (SD-DBMS), 41-61, 240
Secure Military Message System (SMMS), 191-197
Secure object-oriented database systems, 240
Security
  computer, 236-239
  database, see Database security
  discretionary, 3-4, 16, 21, 82
  knowledge base, 240-241
  mandatory, 16, 81
  multilevel (MLS), 15-17
Security attributes, 55
Security classification, 15
Security constraints, 202
  consistence and completeness of, 221-222
Security-critical subjects, 76
Security levels, 16
  assigning, 222
Security markings, 13
Security semantics, 4, 129-130
  types of, 130-131
Selinger, P.G., 72, 80
Semantic level approach, 126-127
Semantic relationship graph, 145
Semantics
  classification, 4-5
  of data classification, 135-140
  data model, 175-180
  security, *see* Security semantics
Sensitivity Level, hierarchical, 15
Shockley, W.R., 1, 5, 6, 10, 11, 13, 14, 17, 18, 19, 28, 31, 45, 46, 59, 62, 72, 79, 93, 94, 98, 100, 102, 103, 128, 133, 137, 141, 156, 158, 167, 171, 173, 180, 190, 199, 201, 206, 207, 221, 224, 227, 229, 231, 233
Shostak, R.E., 14, 30
Simple-security properties, 65, 66
Single-level subjects, 44
SMMS (Secure Military Message System), 191-197
SOI (sphere of influence), 107, 121-122, 149-150
Solomon, J.O., 52, 62
Sphere of influence (SOI), 107, 121-122, 149-150
SQL (structured query language), 14, 64
  multilevel (MSQL), 14, 21-27

SSO (System Security Officer), 43, 82
Stachour, P., 1, 10, 69, 70, 72, 73, 79, 100, 103, 199, 224, 225
Star properties, 65, 66
Stefik, M., 192 , 198
Stonebraker, M., 57, 62, 191, 198
Storage covert channels, 139
Structured data, 128
Structured query language, *see* SQL
Sturms, E.D., 128, 133
Su, T., 221, 225, 239, 242
Subject categorization, 76-77
Subjects, 44
Sybase, 3
Sybase secure SQL server, 81-89
Sysaudits, 88
System Administrator (SA), 82
System Auditor, 44
System-high world method, 205-207
System Operator, 44
System Security Officer (SSO), 43, 82

T

TAC (transaction authorization controls), 232
Tarski, A., 210, 226
TCB (trusted computing base), 16-17
  layered, 6-7
TCB subsets concept, 167
TB subsetting, 6
TDI (Trusted DBMS Interpretation), 33
Technical data repository, 100
Telega, P.A., 69, 80
Telephone book problem, 99, 155
Temporal associations, 131, 138
Textual data, 131-132
Thanisch, P., 215, 223
Thuraisingham, B.M., 1, 10, 69, 70, 72, 73, 79, 100, 103, 128, 133, 147, 158, 159, 199, 202, 206, 208, 209, 214, 222, 224, 225, 226, 239, 241, 242
Time, formal semantics of, 219-220
TNI (Trusted Network Interpretation), 167
Toper, R., 210, 211, 224
Transaction authorization controls (TAC), 232
Trusted code, 36
Trusted computing base, see TCB entries
Trusted DBMS Interpretation (TDI), 33
Trusted labels, 1-2
Trusted Network Interpretation (TNI), 167
Trusted operations, 87-88
Trusted Select Approach, 53-54
Trusted subjects, 76
Tsai, W.T., 147, 158, 199, 206, 209, 224, 226
Tuple class, 17
Tuple descriptor, 73
Tuple set dependency, 120
Tuples, 35
  base, 44
  derived, 45
  polyinstantiated, 19-20

U

UDL (Universal Data Language), 110
Ullman, J.D., 10, 171, 200, 226
Underclassification, initial, 164-165
Unisys, 49, 50, 51, 55, 59, 62
Universal Data Language (UDL), 110
Universe of discourse, l54
Untrusted code, 36
User access to metadata, 246
User identifier attribute, 121
User programs, 47
User session level, data classification and, 247
User-Trusted Interface 88

V

Value constraints, 20-21

Value-dependent security semantics, 130, 136
View-based mandatory access controls, 231-232
View definitions, 8-9, 94
Vinter, S.T., 193, 198, 236, 240, 242
von Henke, F.W., 14, 30

W

Waltz, D.L., 131, 132, 133
Warren, D., 1, 11, 13, 14, 17, 28, 31, 100, 103, 219, 223, 229, 233
Westby-Gibson, D.T., 57, 62
Whitehurst, R.A., 14, 27, 30, 32
Williams, J., 215, 223
Wilson, D.R., 232, 235, 236, 242
Wilson, J., 35, 39, 40
Woelk, D., 192, 197
Wong, E., 57, 62
Woo, C.C., 193, 198
Workshop summary, 1-9
Wu, A., 144, 158

Y

Yazdanian, K., 210-225
Young, W.D., 69, 80